This book offers a critique of recent developments in the study of organizational structure in the USA. There has been a profusion of new paradigms offered in the USA and this has fragmented the field. Many of these paradigms share an anti-management quality, painting managers in an increasingly negative light. This book examines five major, contemporary US organizational theories: population-ecology, institutional, resource dependence, agency and transaction cost economics. Each of these theories and their attendant research is critically examined and severe problems are identified in either theoretical coherence or empirical validity. Lex Donaldson argues that it is possible to reintegrate the field by taking structural contingency theory as the core theory and adding on to it selective propositions from the newer paradigms. He also offers suggestions for needed reforms in the US ~   ·al and institutional system.

Cambridge Studies in Management 25

American anti-management theories of organization

Cambridge Studies in Management

Editors
WILLIAM BROWN, *University of Cambridge*
JOHN CHILD, *University of Cambridge*
ANTHONY HOPWOOD, *London School of Economics*
and PAUL WILLMAN, *London Business School*

Cambridge Studies in Management focuses on the human and organizational aspects of management. It covers the areas of organization theory and behaviour, strategy and business policy, the organizational and social aspects of accounting, personnel and human resource management, industrial relations and industrial sociology.

The series aims for high standards of scholarship and seeks to publish the best among original theoretical and empirical research; innovative contributions to advancing understanding in the area; and books which synthesize and/or review the best of current research, and aim to make the work published in specialist journals more widely accessible.

The books are intended for an international audience among specialists in universities and business schools, for undergraduate, graduate and MBA students, and also for a wider readership among business practitioners and trade unionists.

For a list of titles in this series, see end of book.

American anti-management theories of organization

A critique of paradigm proliferation

Lex Donaldson

Australian Graduate School of Management,
University of New South Wales

CAMBRIDGE
UNIVERSITY PRESS

Published by the Press Syndicate of the University of Cambridge
The Pitt Building, Trumpington Street, Cambridge CB2 1RP
40 West 20th Street, New York, NY 10011–4211, USA
10 Stamford Road, Oakleigh, Melbourne 3166, Australia

First published 1995

Printed in Great Britain at the University Press, Cambridge

A catalogue record for this book is available from the British Library

Library of Congress cataloguing in publication data
Donaldson, Lex.
American anti-management theories of organization: a critique of
paradigm proliferation / Lex Donaldson.
    p.   cm. – (Cambridge Studies in Management: 25)
Includes bibliographical references and index.
ISBN 0 521 47359 4 – ISBN 0 521 47917 7 (pbk)
1. Organizational sociology.   2. Contingency theory (Management).
3. Management – United States.   I. Title.   II. Series.
HM131.D638   1995
302.3′5–dc20   94-19499   CIP

ISBN 0 521 47359 4 hardback
ISBN 0 521 47917 7 paperback

In memoriam
Ronald Donaldson
(1914–1988)

Contents

Figures and tables

Figures

Tables

Preface

I am an organizational analyst who works in a management school. My concern is that much academic organizational analysis at present is neither valid nor suitable for management schools. My overall mission is to advance an organization theory that draws upon more traditional academic disciplines (sociology, psychology, economics, etc.), but is not subservient to them and is sovereign in its own territory. This would foster the construction of an organization theory that studies organizations in their own right, addresses managerial concerns and can hold a useful dialogue with management.

The present volume is part of a larger programme in which I argue for the continuing cogency and empirical validity of structural contingency theory, and against more recent fashions. This book follows on from an earlier volume in 1985 in which I replied on behalf of structural-functionalism and structural contingency theory to criticisms from 'radical', 'critical' and 'Marxian' organizational theory and organizational sociology. This involved dealing with their often philosophical and sociological arguments about supposed problems with systems theory and their attempts to replace it with interpretative, subjective analyses of 'action' or with conflict theory. Inevitably that volume had more of a British flavour, since many of the leading 'radicals' came from a British background: Burrell, Clegg, Davies, Dunkerley, Morgan and Silverman – although US 'radicals' were also discussed: Benson, Goldman, Heydebrand, Stephen Turner and Van Houten.

In contrast, this book focuses on the United States. It is a critique of contemporary developments in organization studies in the USA. There has been a proliferation of new paradigms in that country that has fragmented the field. Many of these new paradigms have an anti-management quality. Moreover, they are long on assertion and short on empirical evidence. I critically examine four major US organization theories herein: population-ecology, institutional and resource dependence theories, together with organizational economics (agency and transaction cost theories). In my view a sounder approach to the study of organizational structure is contained in structural contingency theory. This is an older approach but one that enjoys a greater degree of theoretical coherence and empirical validity than the newer theories. Thus we would be better served by persevering with this approach rather than pursuing fads. The contents of this book are all original and have not appeared elsewhere.

The present volume has had a long gestation. I attended the 1980 Annual Academy of Management Meeting in Detroit and then almost every Annual Academy Meeting from 1984 onwards. In those meetings I have watched a change from US executives being treated with deference, to their being assailed for their failure to produce competitiveness. Similarly, the academic theories presented there have shifted from models of positive adaptations by organizations and their managers, to agency theories of managers as cheats and devious idlers. The time has come to challenge this new anti-management stance and the several, discordant paradigms that underlie it. Our intent is that the field return to the building of a cumulative science of organizations that makes a more positive contribution to management.

Acknowledgments

I should like to thank the two successive Deans of the Australian Graduate School of Management, Jeremy Davis and Frederick Hilmer, for two sabbatical leaves in the United States to work on this book.

In 1987/8, I was a visitor in the College of Business Administration at the University of Iowa. There my hosts were Frank Schmidt and Jim Price, both of whom are steadfastly pursuing the long-term goal of producing an empirically valid general science of organizations. The doctoral seminar in organization theory at Iowa provided me with positive feedback on my endeavours, particularly Clyde Caulfield who worked with me on meta-analyses and Jim Davis, now at Notre Dame, Indiana, who continues to collaborate with me on corporate governance research. I also engaged in friendly sparring with Don McCloskey and his colleagues in the Project for Rhetoric in Inquiry. This helped me to recognize the rhetoric in contemporary US organization theory.

More recently, in 1991/2, I was a Visiting Scholar in the Stanford Center for Organizations Research (SCOR). There my understanding host was Dick Scott. John Meyer and Dick Scott both read a draft of my critique of institutional theory and their comments led to substantial additions and revisions. I also participated in the Scandinavian Consortium for Organizations Research seminar, genially chaired by Jim March. Again I received comments on an overview of this book from Jim and the colleagues therein. Jeffrey Pfeffer kindly commented upon a draft of my critique of resource dependence theory, which improved it.

While at Stanford my friendship continued with Joanne Martin which had started during her sabbatical in Sydney. She has been my guide to organizational culture – both theoretically and in the particular case of Stanford University. I also enjoyed friendly colleagueship with Bob Sutton. During my time at SCOR I was in the company of a number of other Visiting Scholars, including Hal Colebatch and Mary Zey; the latter was my intellectual companion throughout. Kay Schoonhoven was a knowledgeable and friendly colleague. All of us who were Visiting Scholars were looked after by the courtesy of the SCOR secretary, Lisa Hellrich.

I would also like to record my debt to Graham Astley who long encouraged me in this project. He also read an earlier version of this book and his detailed comments led to substantial changes. Sadly Graham did not live to see its completion. His untimely death robbed us all of a good colleague – and a real professional. Graham was never afraid to provoke a debate and I hope that he would have approved of this final version.

I have also had the good fortune to enjoy an on-going discussion of agency theory here at the Australian Graduate School of Management with Gerald Garvey, whose wit and wisdom have been a source of enlightenment.

While I was at Stanford, Marilynn Dwight did a very good job typing part of the manuscript. I would also like to record my deep thanks to the secretarial staff of the Australian Graduate School of Management, especially Pauline Keyvar and Era Koirala, whose excellent work has allowed completion of this manuscript since my return to Sydney. Thanks also to my wife, June Ohlson, who has given me constant emotional support and accompanied me on my sojourns in the United States. Latterly, June has given me invaluable help to get the manuscript into a proper state, including feedback on how to make the work more 'reader friendly'. The reader can thank June for the more lucid parts and any remaining lack of clarity is my responsibility.

Finally, I would like to acknowledge the help given by the staff at Cambridge University Press throughout the publication process, and in particular the contributions of Patrick McCartan (commissioning editor), Chris Doubleday (copy-editor) and Jayne Matthews (production controller).

1 Anti-management paradigms in organization theory

An overview of the problems

Presently in the United States there is concern that the country's economic performance is slipping, especially relative to international competitors such as Japan. This is in a way surprising since US organizations have had the benefit of being able to draw on a large body of organizational theory and research generated in US universities. However, US academic work on the topic of organization structure has become afflicted of late by an outbreak of irrationality. The topic area is now subject to several very different theoretical views which fragment the field and these are accompanied by a lack of cumulation in research. As a result there is now no unified, coherent view of organizations which can be offered to students or to managers to guide their endeavours. Moreover, organizations themselves are frequently depicted in contemporary US organization theory as irrational, and in a manner which is quite cynical. Similarly, managers are widely depicted in contemporary US academic writings in a negative light, as resisting change, as playing politics or as self-aggrandizers. Thus, instead of being able to help US organizations in their current plight, the US academic organization theory scene is in disarray and is more likely to repel managers than to aid them.

This book offers a critical discussion of recent trends in US academic work on organizations. It argues that many of the recent developments are unhelpful to managerial practitioners and are of dubious value in university management schools. Moreover, it shows that much of the academic work in the United States is scientifically wanting, lacking in theoretical coherence and often at odds with evidence from empirical studies of real organizations. The source of the increasing fragmentation in US organization theory is not genuine scientific development, but rather a push for novelty fuelled by individual academic career interests. Influential also is the tendency for organizational scholars, even if working in schools of business or management, to seek approval from disciplines such as sociology or economics which carry with them attitudes and values quite antithetical to business and management.

1

Fragmentation of the field

The focus of the present work is US theories of organizational structure. By organizational structure is meant the set of relationships between people in an organization, including the authority relationships and control systems, and including also the informal organization. Prior to the contemporary period of intellectual fragmentation, there was a unifying theoretical paradigm in US organizational structural theory, and this was structural contingency theory (e.g., Lawrence and Lorsch, 1967; Thompson, 1967). This held that organizations adapted their structures in order to maintain fit with changing contingency factors such as size, technology and strategy, so as to attain high performance (Chandler, 1962; Blau, 1970). The implied role of management was vague but positive. Managers orchestrated this adaptation of organizational structure to its changing contingent circumstances, reflecting in turn changes in the environment, and thereby sought to maintain a high performance for their organization (Chandler, 1962; Blau, 1970). However, managers lacked accurate knowledge to guide their efforts and so research on organizational structure, when fed back through education and the like, would assist management attain structural fit more quickly and more exactly, thus avoiding performance loss for the organization (Woodward, 1965). Academics were to be collaborative partners with management. And both management and academic research were seen as rational collective enterprises. The study of organizational structure was guided by the unifying framework of the contingency approach, and the task of theory-building and empirical research was to refine this approach (e.g., Khandwalla, 1973, 1977; Reimann, 1974).

However, structural contingency theory came under increasing attack in the USA from about 1970 onwards as part of a development which has been hailed as a break-up of the paradigm. From around the mid-1970s, there arose not one but several new paradigms, each challenging structural contingency theory and offering a view on organizations and organizational structure which differed radically from structural contingency theory (see Davis and Powell, 1992). The newer organization theories in the USA mainly decry or deny structural contingency theory and its attendant picture of organizational rationality and managerial benevolence. Four major new paradigms in US organizational structural theory can be distinguished: population-ecology theory (Hannan and Freeman, 1977; Aldrich, 1979), institutional theory (Meyer and Rowan, 1977; Zucker, 1977), resource dependence theory (Pfeffer and Salancik, 1978) and organizational economics (meaning here agency theory and transaction cost theory) (Williamson, 1975; Jensen and Meckling, 1976). Each of the newer paradigms explicitly or implicitly repudiates structural contingency theory.

There are interconnections among these four theoretical views as well as sharp differences.

Population-ecology theory holds that the primary mechanism of organizational change is not purposeful adaptation by the individual organization, as held by structural contingency theory, but rather the Darwinian process of selective death and birth, so that change occurs at the population level with maladapted organizations dying out and being replaced by better-adapted young organizations (Hannan and Freeman, 1977). Population-ecology theory is pursued through a research literature which contains its own technical vocabulary, mathematical models and novel statistical procedures (Hannan and Freeman, 1989), making it a research paradigm to a degree inaccessible to many other organizational scholars.

Institutional theory holds that organizational structures are not primarily shaped by the task environment contingencies, but rather by the need to fit with preconceived notions in the wider community about forms of organization which are legitimate, effective and rational (Meyer and Scott, 1983; Powell and DiMaggio, 1991). Thus organizations are presented to outsiders as conforming normatively, sometimes via surface-level or facade structures only loosely connected to the operating levels, which retain different structures (Meyer and Scott, 1983). Since institutional theory is mounted largely as a rejection of structural functionalism and structural contingency theory, the emphasis is on normatively prescribed structures which are different from the structures actually required for operational effectiveness.

Resource dependence theory holds that organizations are dependent upon external resources and seek to manage them through a variety of means (Pfeffer and Salancik, 1978). It is premised on a rejection of the idea that the organization is a rational instrument for goal attainment (Pfeffer and Salancik, 1978), which is central to structural functionalism and to structural contingency theory (Parsons, 1961; Chandler, 1962; Donaldson, 1985a). A closer examination reveals that the theory is a political model of organizations that gives primacy to maintenance of autonomy by the organization (Pfeffer and Salancik, 1978).

Organizational economics is composed of agency and transaction cost theories of organization (Jensen and Meckling, 1976; Williamson, 1985). These are both based on the discipline of economics, using its concepts and language. Agency and transaction cost theories have in common that both draw upon the model of men and women as untrustworthy, devious and pursuing their own self-interest to the detriment of the organizational collective (Jensen and Meckling, 1976; Williamson, 1985). In agency theory this refers to the agents misusing the discretion which has been delegated to them by the principal to benefit the agents themselves while deceitfully harming the interests of the principal (Jensen and Meckling, 1976). In organizational applications of agency theory, the principal is the owner while the agent is the manager who controls but does not own the corporation. Agency theory holds that losses to the principal can be stemmed by closely controlling the agent, through monitoring and sanctioning, or through bonding (Jensen and Meckling, 1976). Transaction cost theory similarly sees a failure of market discipline in the large corporation such that middle managers self-aggrandize through excessive salaries and perquisites and so on. This 'opportunistic' behaviour can be curbed by setting up a multidivisional structure in which corporate staff vigilantly monitor the divisions on behalf of the corporate centre – the M-form corporation (Williamson, 1970). Thus organizational economics theory sees managers as untrustworthy and as requiring controls from superordinate levels in the organization.

It has become quite conventional in the United States to distinguish different paradigms in organization theory and to see the field as a multiple paradigm science (Daft, 1980; Pinder and Moore, 1980; Ritzer, 1980; Davis and Powell, 1992). The newer organization theories may not refer to themselves as paradigms, but they function as paradigms in that they each take axioms radically different from structural contingency theory, and from each other, and construct a distinct set of theoretical ideas in their own language, often accompanied by distinct methodologies and rules of evidence (Aldrich, 1992). Thus theories are paradigms in the Kuhnian sense that they are mutually antithetic theory statements and languages, which tends to make them incommensurable with each other. Each paradigm has its own set of adherents, that is, there are distinct paradigm communities (Kuhn, 1970). It is logically possible to break down the incommensurability and link ideas across the paradigms into integrated theories (Lawrence and Dyer, 1983; Kaufman, 1985; Singh et al., 1991). However, this process is resisted by each of the theory communities, which to a degree choose to develop their ideas in a way that makes them most different from the other theory schools and thus preserves their distinctiveness and thereby their status as a paradigm (Aldrich, 1992). This leads to several problems for present-day organization theory.

The present malaise in organization theory

Contributing to a discussion of modern trends in organization theory, Aldrich (1992: 17) confesses at the outset:

Indeed, I considered at least two alternative titles for my paper: 'Confessions of a disillusioned positivist', and 'Pursued by the post-modernist panic'. The first title reflects my sense that the promise of the 1960s – when organizational sociology began a substantial expansion – remains unfulfilled. The major research programs generated by enthusiastic teams of investigators ultimately did not spawn the long-term cumulative growth of theorizing and research glimpsed as a possibility in 1970.

Aldrich sees organization theory research as not having built up a solid, cumulative body of knowledge, and thereby having failed the expectations of the science-building sixties. There is therefore no coherent, integrated body of knowledge to be taught to students and to offer as guidelines to managers with pressing, practical problems.

The difficulty in American organization theory lies not at the localized level of a particular theoretical proposition or methodology or study, but at far more fundamental levels. The field is constituted by several mutually incompatible theoretical paradigms. They each negate rather than build on earlier work, especially of the structural contingency theory sort. We see three levels of problem here. *The first problem is the fragmentation into distinct paradigms and consequent lack of an integrating theoretical framework. The second problem is that each of the paradigms is itself limited and flawed. The third problem is that the rejection of the previous paradigm of structural contingency theory which each newer paradigm makes is overdone and in error.* The task of this volume is to give critiques of the excessive proliferation of paradigms, and of each of the main, newer theoretical paradigms of organizational structure and their rejection of structural contingency theory. Our inclination will be towards synthesis of the various paradigms into a more unified view, and the possibilities for such integration will be addressed. However, this integration is far from a ready or easy task.

In contemporary American organization theory the newer theoretical perspectives which will be examined here are those which have rejected previous structural contingency theory and which thereby have become major theoretical paradigms. This does not cover all recent American developments, many of which seek to build on structural contingency theory and thus facilitate cumulation and integration of the field. A long list of fruitful, scientifically sound and programmatically incrementalist contributions from contemporary American organization researchers could be made (see pp. 13–15). Important as such work is, nevertheless much of modern American work is in the vein of the newer paradigms. The latter work takes a high profile, catching attention and creating drama. And the newer paradigms tend to stand out and dominate the landscape, capturing interest and defining the contours of the field. Accordingly, our discussion will focus thereon to seek to challenge their definitions of the field of organization studies.

The context

The main forms of intellectual endeavour are shaped by the guiding preoccupations of the intellectual communities within which the discussions take place. At the risk of considerable oversimplification, some preliminary observations on contemporary organization studies can be made by distinguishing between a European and a North American tradition.

In European organization studies of the past two decades, a dominating agenda has been politics (Mannheim, 1936). Numerous European writers on organizations have had as their primary *animus* and drive the programme of the 'New Left'. This has meant that the primary mission of professional intellectuals has been to criticize organizations as capitalist and therefore immoral (Salaman, 1979). The allied critique of organization theories is that they are capitalist in origin, effect and moral colouring (Clegg and Dunkerley, 1977, 1980). This left-leaning political programme has underlain the highly critical tone of much writing and the explicitly neo-Marxist nature of some analysis (Clegg and Dunkerley, 1980). It has also had an influence on less politically extreme contributors (Child, 1969, 1972a; Silverman, 1970; Burrell and Morgan, 1979; see Donaldson, 1985a).

In North America the dominating agenda has been different and is centred on individualistic competition over careers. As Durkheim (1964) explained, specialization is promoted by the desire of each person to differentiate themselves from the mass and thereby to create their own niche in which they enjoy a monopoly. One would predict from Durkheim that the country with the largest number of professional researchers into organizations, the USA, would display the largest degree of competition and of attempts at differentiation. As expected, one finds that in America the organization analysis scene is multidimensional, complex and rapidly changing. The overwhelming impression is of pluralistic diversity. Given the American national ethos of the virtue of America being a pluralistic society, calling any branch of American scholarship 'pluralist' hardly invites critical scrutiny. However, the present degree of pluralism in US organization theory is excessive and harbours severe problems of incoherence, lack of cumulation, cynicism, faddism and despair that anything of lasting worth can be accomplished.

Further, the aspiration for novelty is fuelled in America by the strong value placed on the new rather than the old, and on the future rather than the past. Anthropologists (Kluckhohn and Strodtbeck, 1961: 15) have remarked on this as a characteristic of American society compared with others. In part this may reflect a society whose prevailing public tone is optimism and progressivism. European commentators (e.g., de Tocqueville, 1945) have long remarked on the rapid, restless pace of life in America, and the constant waves of new experiments and fashions. In some ways, this signifies a healthy creativity and a throwing off of Old-World inhibitions but it may also lead to faddism. The eminent Russian *émigré* sociologist, Pitrim Sorokin, was moved to write critically of fads and fashions in American social analysis (Sorokin, 1956). He also criticized the American readiness to forget earlier work in the rush to present innovations that were often not new discoveries and were inferior to the earlier work which they would supplant. In similar vein, observers of the USA have warned of the dangers that social thought in such a democratic society will fluctuate wildly as public opinion changes, being at once socially responsive but lacking long-run responsibility to the society (Bloom, 1987).

Rieseman (1950) paints a picture of contemporary American society as mobile and rootless, composed of individuals who are bereft of strong personal character, the inner-directed personality of an earlier America, and are rather 'other-directed': tuned into the norms of whichever group they are temporarily members, their sensors finely calibrated to pick up changing tastes and demands as signalled through vigilant and ever-present mass communications media.

The problem of novelty-seeking in organization theory

One can apply the Rieseman–Sorokin analysis to US organization theory. As one reads the literature of the middle and late eighties on organization structure, a highly critical treatment of structural contingency theory and its associated findings and methods seems almost to be *de rigueur* (Zey-Ferrell and Aiken, 1981). Few Assistant Professors would risk their reputation or the chance of acceptance of their own work by prefacing it with a positive appreciation of previous research in the structural contingency mould. When the intelligentsia discourse with each other on matters of organization structure, the shared appreciation of structural contingency theory is critical. To advance any other evaluation is to be seen as an *ingénue* – strong temptation then to see the structural contingency theory paradigm as in crisis or defunct, that a new paradigm is needed and to declare oneself for a new paradigm.

In US organization theory there are many new paradigms and newer ones are introduced frequently. Since around 1967 at least fifteen new paradigms have been launched, all with implications for the explanation of organizational structure: interorganizational theory (Evan, 1966), ethnomethodology (Garfinkel, 1967), enactment theory (Weick, 1969), cybernetics (Hage, 1974), transaction cost theory (Williamson, 1975), agency theory (Jensen and Meckling, 1976), population-ecology (Hannan and Freeman, 1977), institutional theory (Meyer and Rowan, 1977; Zucker, 1977),

Marxism (Goldman and Van Houten, 1977), resource dependence theory (Pfeffer and Salancik, 1978), organizational symbolism (Smircich, 1983), organizational cultures (Fine, 1984), feminism (Ferguson, 1984), emotionalism (Sutton and Rafaeli, 1988) and post-modernism (Mumby and Putnam, 1992). On average a new paradigm is offered every second year.· This paradigm proliferation process is mitigated to a degree by textbooks which tend to conserve previous contributions and change only incrementally, gradually incorporating the new paradigms (e.g., Daft, 1986; Bedeian and Zammuto, 1991).

Pfeffer (1993a: 616) comments on the increasing lack of unity in organization theory:

Theoretical and methodological diversity may be adaptive as long as there is some agreement over fundamental goals and on a set of rules to winnow the measures, methods, and theories on the basis of accumulated evidence. In the study of organizations, there appears to have been more agreement on these issues in the past than there is at present, when almost every aspect of the research process is contested.

A diversity in ideas and in methodology can be useful to the field as long as the diversity can be resolved at some point. The question is whether the social structure and organization of the field encourage resolution of diverse ideas or the continued particularistic advancement of separate agendas, often with explicitly political undertones. At present, I believe that the field encourages the development and advancement of differences and separate agendas rather than attempts at integration or resolution. More than 10 years ago, I (Pfeffer, 1982: 1) argued that 'the domain of organization theory is coming to resemble more of a weed patch than a well-tended garden. Theories ... proliferate along with measures, terms, concepts, and research paradigms. It is often difficult to discern in what direction knowledge of organizations is progressing.' The situation has not changed, and, if anything, there are [sic] now more diversity of ideas and measures and more contention over the rules for organizational science than there were [sic] a decade ago.

Pfeffer (1993a: 612) explains this increasing fragmentation, in part, by the value placed on novelty and professional rewards for proliferation rather than consolidation:

Journal editors and reviewers seem to seek novelty, and there are great rewards for coining a new term. The various divisions of the Academy of Management often give awards for formulating 'new concepts' but not for studying or rejecting concepts that are already invented.

Two other American academics, Mone and McKinley, have written in similar vein. They state that there is a 'uniqueness value' that governs the organization studies literature (Mone and McKinley, 1993: 284). This 'prescribes that uniqueness is good and that organization scientists should attempt to make unique contributions to their discipline' (284). They document the presence of this uniqueness value in the statements of authorities (e.g., Weick, 1969; Davis, 1971; Astley, 1985a), editors of leading journals (e.g., *Administrative Science Quarterly*, *Academy of Management Review* and *Organization Science*), in the review forms used to rate journal submissions and by special issues of journals that are aimed at encouraging unique work (286ff.).

Mone and McKinley (1993) see positive benefits of this uniqueness value, such as innovativeness, adequate representation of complexity and freedom of inquiry. However, they see also disbenefits of disciplinary fragmentation, lack of standard concepts that frustrates generalization, information overload on readers of the literature and lack of replication that precludes validation. The uniqueness value is seen as being self-reinforcing, through rewards and through altering individual beliefs about the meaning of ' "good" ' research (Mone and McKinley, 1993: 292). The result is a field fragmented into a number of paradigms which thereby becomes less influential than it might be:

we view the lack of integration across paradigms as a threat to advances in organizational knowledge. Perhaps business and government decision makers rely infrequently on organization scholars not because of our lack of relevance, fresh methods, and up-to-date topics (as suggested by Daft and Lewin, 1990; Lawrence, 1992) but because of the status of the findings in organization studies. This status could be partially attributable to the consequences of the uniqueness value ... [This value] may be channeling behaviour in directions that are dysfunctional for the field. (292)

Mone and McKinley (1993: 293) also identify a possible divergence of interests between the individual scholar and the field, expressing the concern that individuals may gain at the expense of the field.

The value of novelty will encourage some organizational academics to champion new paradigms, thereby becoming the thought leaders. Simultaneously the value placed on novelty and the other-directed conformity ethos will cause other organizational academics to become enthusiastic, uncritical followers of the new paradigms. To the degree that these social processes influence the American academic community, there is reason to fear faddism, superficiality, conformism and a calculating type of product differentiation lacking any genuine intellectual grounding. This implies that contributions will not individually stand up to probing analysis, and that collectively such contributions will not cohere in a cumulative body of knowledge.

There are real costs to a proliferation of paradigms in a field. The development of a new paradigm in an existing field is conventionally welcomed as healthily increasing pluralism, which can potentially lead to quantum leaps in theoretical understanding through paradigm revolution (Kuhn, 1970). Ultimately one can never predict new knowledge (Popper,

1945), so the only way to ascertain whether a new perspective will be fruitful is to pursue it. Any rejection of a new approach *a priori*, before it has been given a fair trial, would be unscientific and also incompatible with democratic ideals. While accepting all of this, it has to be recognized that the advantages of new paradigms and an increasing intellectual pluralism also entail some disadvantages.

All human beings are boundedly rational in their cognitive processes (Simon, 1965), possessing limited amounts of time, attention and information-processing capacity – and this even applies to academics. The more new paradigms, and the more frequently a field has to learn and appraise a new paradigm, the less intellectual capacity is available for prosecuting the existing paradigm or paradigms. Paradigm attention is a zero-sum game. This means that paradigm proliferation shifts resources from paradigm consolidation towards novelty. At worst a field moves from sustained, systematic study to a succession of mere fads. This delays the development of a firm body of knowledge – with detrimental consequences for the standing of the profession (Mone and McKinley, 1993; Pfeffer, 1993a). With the constant rush to the next new paradigm the consequence is half-finished research programmes, as exemplified by structural contingency theory, where decades of research have left a literature widely perceived as containing unresolved theoretical problems and empirical inconsistencies (e.g., Pennings, 1975; Kimberly, 1976). Reference to such problems is a standard argument for embarking upon the next new paradigm (e.g., McKelvey and Aldrich, 1983) but this argument can be self-defeating, precluding the completion of any research programme.

Moreover, a field with a large number of paradigms is difficult for newly entering professionals to master – doctoral students are also boundedly rational. Doctoral students 'are confronted with a morass of bubbling and sometimes noxious literature. Theories presented are incompatible, research findings inconsistent, and the general body of knowledge often indigestible.' (Zammuto and Connolly, 1984: 32) In practice there will be a tendency for them to learn only some of the paradigms with any degree of depth and sympathy. Faced with such bewildering diversity, they may well be tempted to learn only the newer, seemingly more exciting and promising paradigms at the expense of the old (which often have all that attendant, tedious empirical literature 'which never got anywhere'). In this way, older paradigms, however truthful, can fall into disuse through failure to pass on the cultural traditions from one generation to the next. Thus in turning to the evaluation of any new paradigm in our field, we would do well to be mindful of the inherent costs of paradigm proliferation, as well as, of course, the potential benefits.

Further, all the talk of new paradigms has produced a kind of academic inflation in US organization theory. The construction of a new paradigm is more important than work within an existing paradigm, which is categorized as mere 'normal science'. Thus arises an invidious comparison between the authors of the new paradigms as major contributors and the normal scientists as minor contributors. This flows through into publishing decisions, becomes the basis of professional reputations and leads to differential rewards. Hence there is encouragement for members of the field to play the paradigm-mongering game and to eschew making cumulative, incrementalist contributions (Astley, 1985a). When one works cumulatively, valuing positively preceding contributions, then a new contribution is virtually certain to be at best incremental, that is, an addition to the existing body of knowledge. However, if one argues that all existing prior work is in error and seeks to overthrow it in a paradigm revolution, then the new contribution is revolutionary, dramatic and is implicitly compared against a baseline of nought, making it a great contribution. This may be termed the strategy of zero-based cumulation in social science. Thus the announcement of a paradigm revolution in organization theory has built into it a new definition of the status of contributions in the field which is self-serving for the interests of the paradigm revolutionaries.

American organization theory, and most especially the theory of organizational structure, for this is the focus of our inquiry, presently displays some of these problems. In this book we will offer a critique of the four newer organizational theory paradigms that appear to be most influential on scholarly work in the United States at present (resource dependence, population-ecology and institutional theories, and organizational economics; see Davis and Powell, 1992). There follows in this chapter a short delineation of the similarities and differences among these four newer paradigms. But before that we need to review briefly the preceding organizational structural theory paradigm, structural contingency theory, in order to understand what the newer theories challenged and to appreciate its place in the contemporary US organizational structural literature.

The structural contingency paradigm

Until approximately the late 1950s, the theory of organizational structure was dominated by classical management theory with its idea that there was one best way to structure all organizations – through a hierarchical, highly formalized arrangement in which organizational life was governed by detailed plans and systems laid down centrally (Brech, 1957). A secondary view was contained in the human relations movement which took a more individual-centred view and advocated participation through communication and shared influence (Likert, 1961). Around the early sixties these two views became synthesized into the contingency theory of organizational structure which held that the organizations should be more centralized or more participatory depending upon their contingent circumstances. More specifically, the degree of formalization and centralization which was optimal for an organization was a function of its operational technology (Woodward, 1958, 1965), rate of environmental change (Burns and Stalker, 1961; Lawrence and Lorsch, 1967), and size (Pugh *et al.*, 1969b). Also, the choice of the optimal apex structure (a functional or multidivisional structure) was held to be determined by the strategy (Chandler, 1962) or size (Williamson, 1970). Similarly, the extent to which lateral co-ordinating devices or, in the extreme, fully fledged matrix structures were required, was also held to be determined by contingency factors such as the rate of environmental change and product diversity (Lawrence and Lorsch, 1967; Galbraith, 1973; Davis and Lawrence, 1977).

Common to all these different structural contingency theories was the idea that the fit between the structure and the contingency factor affected organizational performance – with a fit raising performance and a misfit lowering performance. Again, throughout these structural contingency theories of the sixties there was a notion of deliberate adaptation by organizational management. Managers were seen as first setting the contingency variables, such as technology, desired innovation rate, size and product diversity, as part of setting the strategy of the organization, and then as adopting the structure which was most appropriate given the contingency variables (Burns and Stalker, 1961; Chandler, 1962; Woodward, 1965). Usually the organization was seen as having been in fit between contingencies and structure, until a change in a contingency produced a misfit and consequent performance problems; this led to the adoption of a new structure leading to a new fit, thus restoring performance (Chandler, 1962; Woodward, 1965). Thus organizational structure was secondary to strategy as primary and structural changes followed strategy change in time (Christensen *et al.*, 1978). Organizations were seen as rational, purposeful systems in which structures were instruments chosen to implement strategies effectively. By implication, organizational management, as the main maker of both strategic and structural decisions, was acting rationally on behalf of the organization, i.e., action was collectively rational.

The main inefficiency that occurred within this scenario was the performance lost while the organization was in misfit between the old structure and the new value of the contingency factor. This time lag was seen in part as arising from incomplete knowledge by management, so that it became aware of the need for structural change only after some time in misfit. The utility of structural contingency research was in identifying which structures were required to fit with each contingency so that, through education, managers would be better informed and make faster, more certain structural adaptations as part of their strategic change programmes, thus minimizing misfit and maximizing performance (Woodward, 1965). It is this set of ideas which will be referred to herein as structural contingency theory.

Thus the structural contingency theory views management in a positive way as the controllers who orchestrate the adaptation of the organization to its environment through implementing better-fitting structures. Within the structural contingency theory literature a particularly positive role is accorded to management in the writings of Chandler. In a long series of historical studies he has advanced the view that management has played a vital role: first in building the large, multifunctional corporation in response to expanded market opportunities made possible by new transportation (Chandler, 1977); then in adopting new structures suited to the new strategies such as diversification (Chandler, 1962, 1964, 1982) and in building transnational corporations (Chandler, 1980) (see also McCraw, 1988). For Chandler (1983, 1990) the development of a hierarchy of professional managers, without connection to the owners, is essential to the development of the modern corporation; he identifies professional managers as responsible for the success of large corporations in Germany and the United States and the lack of professional managers as responsible for the relative failure of large corporations in the United Kingdom. Thus structural contingency theory is a pro-management paradigm.

While much of the pioneering structural contingency theory research was conducted in Britain (Woodward, 1958, 1965; Burns and Stalker, 1961; Pugh et al., 1963, 1968, 1969a, b; Emery and Trist, 1965), there were major contributions also from the USA (e.g., Chandler, 1962; Hage, 1965; Hage and Aiken, 1967, 1969; Lawrence and Lorsch, 1967; Perrow, 1967; Thompson, 1967; Blau, 1970). Indeed the term contingency theory applied to organization theory is believed to have originated with Lawrence and Lorsch (1967).

Structural contingency theory constituted a research paradigm in that there was a core theory (the idea of a structural contingency fit which affected performance) and a style of empirical research which featured comparisons of structures and contingencies across organizations. Within this broad paradigm there was scope for development in the contingencies identified, the structural aspects to which they were related, the performance outcomes examined, and refinements in concept and method.

This structural contingency type of research programme was energetically pursued in the USA during the seventies and eighties and continues into the nineties, constituting a considerable body of structural contingency theory research (Price and Mueller, 1986). The concept of task interdependency as a contingency (Thompson, 1967) has been refined and researched empirically (Van de Ven et al., 1976; Gerwin, 1979). The relationship between the organization and the environment has been conceptually refined (Duncan, 1972; Downey et al., 1975; Kimberly, 1975; Bourgeois, 1980; Astley and Van de Ven, 1983; Dess and Beard, 1984; Hrebiniak and Joyce, 1985). The ideas that information-processing underlies contingencies such as uncertainty and diversity and that information-processing needs give rise to the required organizational structures have been developed theoretically and empirically (Galbraith, 1973; Egelhoff, 1982, 1988a; Daft and Lengel, 1984). The concept of a product life-cycle contingency has been developed (Utterback and Abernathy, 1975; Abernathy and Utterback, 1978). Whereas sixties contingency theory discussed organizational growth and development, subsequent theorists have theorized and researched organizational decline (Ford, 1980a, b; Whetten, 1980; Cameron et al., 1987; Sutton and D'Aunno, 1989). The idea of a connection between size and the more bureaucratized, differentiated structure which nevertheless produces economies of scale in administration (Blau, 1970; Blau and Schoenherr, 1971) has led to a continuing stream of research (e.g., Goldman, 1973; Beyer and Trice, 1979; Lenz, 1980).

Similarly, the idea that technology affects organization structure (Whisler et al., 1967) has continued to be critically discussed and empirically researched in the USA (Khandwalla, 1974; Blau et al., 1976; Reimann, 1977, 1980; Robey, 1977; Gerwin, 1979; Reimann and Inzerilli, 1979; Lincoln et al., 1981). The organizational design implications of innovation have continued to receive attention (Hage, 1974, 1988; Tushman, 1978; Schoonhoven et al., 1990). Within the multidivisional structure, variations have been identified that correspond to differences in degree of product diversification (Lorsch and Allen, 1973; Pitts, 1974, 1976, 1977; Hill et al., 1992). Research has been undertaken on the critical issue of whether or not the fit between a given contingency and a structural variable affects organizational performance, and there has been an increasing tendency to examine multivariate models of more than one contingency, structure or performance variable (Khandwalla, 1973, 1977; Pennings, 1975; Schoonhoven, 1981; Alexander and Randolph, 1985; Drazin and Van de Ven, 1985; Gresov, 1989). Structural contingency theory has been extended to the study of investment banks (Eccles and Crane, 1988), into the future to theorize newly emerging structures such as network organizations (Miles and Snow, 1986; Hage, 1988) and also into the past to probe the origins of modern corporate structures (Chandler, 1977). Moreover, the early work on multinational organizational structures (Stopford and Wells, 1972) has been pursued and extended (Davis, 1972; Egelhoff, 1982, 1988a, b; Daniels *et al.*, 1984, 1985; Ghoshal and Nohria, 1989). While this review is illustrative rather than exhaustive, it does demonstrate that structural contingency work is ongoing in terms of conceptual, theoretical, methodological and empirical developments.

From this continuing work we can see that the structural contingency theory paradigm is alive in the USA. However, it is no longer nearly as all-embracing or unquestioned as it was in the sixties. In the seventies, eighties and nineties, there has been a persistent calling into question of structural contingency theory (e.g., Mayhew *et al.*, 1972; Freeman and Kronenfeld, 1973; Pennings, 1975; Kimberly, 1976; Starbuck, 1981; McKelvey and Aldrich, 1983). Moreover, several newer theories have arisen as rival accounts of organization and organization structure, challenging the explanation offered by structural contingency theory. Their popularity reflects in part a sense that structural contingency theory was invalid or severely limited in its validity. The pull towards new paradigms has been reinforced by a push away from the once common shared paradigm of structural contingency theory. Structural contingency theory has broken down as the unifying framework guiding research in the USA.

The newer sociological paradigms of organization

The period of the late sixties and the early seventies was a time of ferment in the United States, with active opposition on university campuses to the war in Vietnam. The war and its excesses were linked to the establishment and to established ideas in social science research (Chomsky, 1969), creating a mood hostile to sociological functionalism and to what was seen as scientism. In society at large there was growing support for a counter-culture. In universities this led to moves to overthrow existing paradigms. There was a tendency in radical sociology to see society as dominated by powerful elite classes (Mills, 1956). In sociology, and, by extension, organizational sociology, there was growing adherence to the view of organizations as being constructed by human beings and as serving the interests of some people more than other people, as being the subject of conflict, of political action, and as being built upon and sustaining power relations (Benson, 1977; Goldman and Van Houten, 1977). Organizational sociology came to see organizations as places wherein elites dominated other members and where organizations colluded with other organizations to maintain domination in society (Perrow, 1979, 1986). The core theory of organizations shifted its emphasis from the functionality of structures to seeing structures as political. Managers were no longer seen as builders of functionalist strategies and structures in the Chandlerian manner.

With this world view, a new generation of theories of organizations was spawned, differing among themselves but reflecting a common origin in the political model of organizations. In particular, three new paradigms arose in the United States in the seventies which all shared elements of the political view – resource dependence theory, institutional theory and population-ecology theory. Each is propounded as a distinct theory with somewhat distinct assumptions, languages and research bases (Pfeffer, 1982; Scott, 1992), yet all are in a way political models.

Resource dependence theory holds that organizations need certain resources and will tend to comply with resource suppliers, thereby granting power to those who assist resource supply, either as external providers or as internal facilitators (Pfeffer and Salancik, 1978). This shapes the main parameters of political action. However, within these constraints organizations manoeuvre to maintain their autonomy through a variety of stratagems including mergers, diversification, interlocking directorates, collusion and so on. There is attention to perception and information manipulation, as tactics. Thus the model is at heart political.

Institutional theory holds that organizations are to a considerable extent shaped in their structures by the need to fit not with task contingencies, but with the demands and expectations of the wider institutional environment stemming from cultural norms, standards set by professional bodies, requirements of funding agencies and so on (Powell and DiMaggio, 1991). By complying, or by appearing to comply, through erecting a structure that is just a facade disconnected from how work is organized, the organization obtains approval, legitimacy and continuing support from powerful superordinate organizations and from society (Meyer and Scott, 1983). Again the key exigency is really political rather than functional, in the usual functionalist sense of task efficiency and effectiveness.

Population-ecology theory stresses how organizational form and structure is shaped through organizational birth and death rather than through adaptive change by individual organizations (Hannan and Freeman, 1989). However, the core theoretical argument of why internal adaptive change by organizations fails to occur or lacks sufficient frequency or speed, refers to the internal power system. Successful extant organizations, especially where these are large, routinize operations and formalize procedures to ensure reliability of performance. This leads to rigidities and to an internal social organizational structure in which powerful vested interests resist adaptive change. Again we arrive at a core model which involves political power. Population-ecology is functionalist in part, accepting that misfit between organization and environment will endanger organizational health, but it denies the functionalist proposition that organizations and their managements frequently make successful adaptations through changes in structure. Thus population-ecology is functionalist, but not individual organizational adaptive functionalist. The population-ecology model buys into the critical treatment of organizations and their management which became entrenched in sociology as a result of its radicalization.

Thus each of the three newer sociological paradigms arising in American organization theory gains its strength in part from the way it adheres to the political model and so discounts the functionalism of the sixties-style structural contingency theory. In this way, the three newer paradigms within organizational sociology reflect shifts in the mother discipline of sociology.

The break with the structural contingency paradigm

These three theories present themselves as new departures and distance themselves from earlier theories, especially structural contingency theory. There is a repeated tendency in the newer theories to criticize structural contingency theory for its focus on the internal structure of the organization (Pfeffer and Salancik, 1978) and for its postulate that organizations frequently select structures better adapted to the task contingencies (Hannan and Freeman, 1989; Powell and DiMaggio, 1991). In none of the three newer theories is there much attempt to accommodate previous structural contingency theory or to present the newer theory as complementing the older theory by adding to prior work so that a more complete explanation of structure is obtained. The approach is not the eclectic or synthesizing or integrative one of building upon an earlier model and showing how the new model explains more variance in organizational structure or in other dependent variables. The underlying process is not integrative; rather, it is dialectical, being the postulation of opposites. Hence each of the three newer organizational theories potentially constitutes a paradigm revolution. The old structural contingency theory with its supposedly erroneous adaptive functionalist base-assumption is to be swept away and replaced by a more adequate political model of the organization struggling to wrest resources from its environment.

Thus the paradigm-revolutionary nature of the newer organizational theories means that there is a disjunction or break in the way the field thinks about organizations. This poses problems of integration and cumulation. At the theoretical level there is no scheme which unifies old and new (that is functional and political) and makes the field coherent by offering a picture of how all of these variables and processes go together. Nor would it be easy to somehow construct such a unified theory as the base-assumptions are antagonistic, e.g., internal structural adaptations of task organization (structural contingency theory) versus the absence of such adaptation (population-ecology theory). This is the price of paradigm revolution in any science, as in the physics of light where the corpuscular model paradigm is incompatible with the wave model paradigm (Kuhn, 1970). Paradigm revolution becomes a major impediment to serious integration of thought – unless one paradigm completely triumphs over the other, that is, the paradigm revolution is successful.

At the empirical level, paradigm revolution prevents cumulation of research results across paradigms. Seeing how much more variance can be explained by using two rather than just one paradigm is discouraged by the underlying theoretical antagonism of the rival paradigms. For example, institutional theory research sometimes includes an independent variable or variables, said to be drawn from structural contingency theory, but rather than seek to explain more variance thereby, the point has been to show how such variables fail to account for the dependent variable, which instead is explained by the institutional theory variable (Tolbert and Zucker, 1983; Baron et al., 1986). This is the nature of the struggle between paradigms.

Again, differences in levels of analysis between the empirical work of different paradigms make their addition difficult. For instance, in structural contingency theory research, contingency variables are used to explain variations in structure at the *organizational level*, whereas in population-ecology theory research, variables such as the number of organizations in the population are used to explain variations in the death rate of organizations at the *population level*. Thus disjunctions in theory and method attendant upon paradigm revolution make cumulation and addition of their contributions difficult.

So far we have focused on the similarities among the three newer organization theory paradigms of resource dependence theory, institutional theory and population-ecology theory, in order to show how they display a common root in the rejection of functionalism and in the avowal of the political view of organizations. However, while sharing common elements, the three newer theories differ from each other in definite ways.

Paradigmatic differences between the newer theories

Both resource dependence theory and institutional theory have notions of the organization taking actions to improve its survival chances by making changes either internally or in external relations with the environment. Resource dependence theory sees a reorientation of the internal organizational power structure in order to better facilitate the acquiring of external resources (Pfeffer and Salancik, 1978). Institutional theory sees that the organization adopts structural elements which better fit with the preferences of the surrounding institutional system (Powell and DiMaggio,

1991). In contrast, population-ecology theory has, as its central idea, organizations failing to adapt to their environments and thereby dying out, and thus it focuses upon the idea that organizational change comes at the population level through organizational births and deaths (Hannan and Freeman, 1989). Thus resource dependence and institutional theories see individual organizations as adapting, whereas population-ecology theory differs, seeing individual organizations as not adapting, or as adapting insufficiently.

Resource dependence theory asserts that organizations can control their environments through building interorganizational relationships such as mergers, joint ventures, vertical integration, interlocking directorates, cartels, trade associations and the like; in other words, by active external relations work to change the surrounding organizational field (Pfeffer and Salancik, 1978). In contrast, institutional theory sees the institutional environment as less open to influence by the organization and as thereby imposing difficult-to-resist conformity pressures on the organization (Powell and DiMaggio, 1991). Thus there is a difference perceived in the plasticity of the environment.

Again, resource dependence theory sees the internal power structure as adjusting to changing environmental demands by empowering the internal group best able to deal with these new demands; thus, the internal power structure is adaptive and a source of organizational adaptiveness (Pfeffer and Salancik, 1978). In contrast, population-ecology theory sees the internal power structure as perpetuating the status quo and as resisting the organizational changes needed to reflect changing environmental demands and so bringing organizational death (Hannan and Freeman, 1989). Hence the internal power structure is maladaptive and a source of organizational demise. Thus there is a difference between resource dependence and population-ecology theories in whether intraorganizational power is seen as functional or dysfunctional.

Lack of integration of the three newer sociological paradigms

As we see from the above, there are differences between the three newer organization theories. The way resource dependence, institutional and population-ecology theories relate to each other reflects their status as separate paradigms. While there is some tendency for each theory to cite and quote the others, on occasions approvingly (e.g., DiMaggio and Powell, 1991; Singh et al., 1991), this is done sparingly. None of the three newer theories offers any extended statement of how it relates to either of the other two in any complementary way or how they may be fashioned into an integrated model. Given the differences in core theoretical propositions and assumptions, such integration would be difficult if not impossible without substantial dilution of the position of each of the newer theories.

It would be logically possible to construct an integrative framework by taking pieces of each of resource dependence, institutional and population-ecology theories and rendering them in diluted form. For example, one could argue: 'Organizations tend to a degree to adopt interorganizational linkages which facilitate their acquisition of needed resources; however they also tend, to a degree, to adopt structural elements from the institutional environment to ensure legitimacy and support; both these mechanisms tend to help survival to a degree, however these adaptations are insufficient for some organizations and so they die out, especially in demanding environments where presently occupied niches are fast disappearing.' Thus the intellectual strategy would be to render all of the core propositions of all three theories operative, but only to a degree and in contingent fashion. Such an exercise in theoretical synthesis may have much to commend it. However, the point is that it would require each theory to soften its stance and to partially retract its theoretical assertions, that is, to compromise. In the process each theory would become less distinct and lose its separate identity. The three theories would no longer each be prominent outcroppings in the literature. It is hardly surprising, therefore, that they prefer to remain distinct and resist accommodating one another through compromise and synthesis.

Further, there are other obstacles to the integration of the three newer theories. Each has a somewhat distinct language which would not aid ready inter-theoretical discourse and would pose the problem of which language would be used in any new integration. Moreover, population-ecology theory uses mathematics whereas the other two theories are non-mathematical, and this could be a barrier to communication between theories and between theory communities. There are also differences in methodology. The analyses offered by institutional theory are sometimes qualitative in nature (e.g., DiMaggio, 1991), as may be thought fitting for a theory much concerned with symbols and myths. The analyses offered by resource dependence theory make extensive use of quantitative methods to measure resource dependencies and their results (Pfeffer and Salancik, 1978). The unit of analysis is typically the organization. Population-ecology theory uses extremely sophisticated, novel statistical methods to analyse data on populations of organizations, covering long historical periods (Hannan and Freeman, 1989). It is not obvious that a synthesis of methodologies could be readily achieved across the three theories in empirical studies intended to be integrative. Again, it may be logically possible but it is difficult to see how three different traditions and sets of conventions could be combined without substantially altering each.

As we have seen, each of the newer theories differs from the others in core theoretical propositions, assumptions about organizations, language and methodologies. Each of the theories conforms rather closely to the definition of a theoretical paradigm advanced by Kuhn (1970). As three paradigms of organization, each theory is quite separate from the other two. Moreover, because the paradigms each signify a disjunction in thought, they are not easy to synthesize and their adherents tend to resist integration and synthesis. Thus the theoretical framework in organization studies is divided up not only between structural contingency theory and newer theories; rather, the newer theories themselves each mark out a division in thought about organization. This makes for fragmentation in organization studies.

The organizational economics paradigm

Thus far we have traced the recent evolution of theory within that branch of organization theory composed of organizational sociology, for it is the sociological influence which has been strongest on theoretical developments in organization theory in the sixties and seventies. However, in the United States in the seventies, new organizational theorizing also came under the influence of economics, and this became increasingly influential during the eighties and into the nineties.

Barney and Ouchi (1986) term this collective movement 'organizational economics'. They are explicit in offering this as a new paradigm in organization theory; the title of their work is *Organizational economics: towards a new paradigm for understanding and studying organizations*. In terms of impact upon organization theory, the most important strands within organizational economics to date have been agency theory and transaction cost theory. Accordingly, it will be convenient to have one term to cover both agency and transaction cost theories and in this volume we will use the term 'organizational economics'. (We also recognize that there are other approaches to organizations which are inspired by economics and which are classifiable as organizational economics, such as theories of comparative advantage (Porter, 1985), but these will not be examined here.) Hesterly *et al.* (1990) use the term organizational economics in this way and see it as a 'paradigm' that possesses 'a common set of axioms that define a unique perspective on the role and determinant of organizational forms'. This they see as offering advantage over the lack of clarity and parsimony in conventional organizational and management science, as well as offering new insights unavailable from pre-existing theories (Hesterly *et al.*, 1990: 415).

Agency and transaction cost theories share the common concern of theorizing dishonesty and cheating by managers. In agency theory this is conceived of as managers as agents pursuing self-interest to the detriment of the interests of the owners or principals of the companies, such as shareholders, thus creating 'residual loss' (Jensen and Meckling, 1976). Principals will seek to curb residual loss by monitoring and sanctioning managers through installing control systems and incentive schemes. An important type of control system is a powerful board of directors that is independent of management, being composed of outsiders who control the executives on behalf of the shareholders (Fama and Jensen, 1983). A type of incentive is having a management shareholding scheme to align managerial interests with owner interests. Managers as agents may also seek to reassure principals that they will act in their best interests by bonding schemes wherein wayward managers would forfeit some of their own wealth if they did not serve the owners well. Where effective schemes of monitoring and sanctioning or of bonding are absent, managers will cheat the owners through excessive salaries, benefits, perquisites and on-the-job leisure, and in other subtler ways such as corporate diversification or risk aversion.

In transaction cost theory such problems are discussed as market failure. The growth of the large corporation with its tiers of managers encourages and facilitates loss of control of lower- and middle-level personnel by top management; this allows middle management to indulge their personal interests through empire-building and sacrifices organizational perfor-mance (Williamson, 1970, 1985). The structural solution is to restore controls over middle management by rendering them more accountable through the creation of the M-form corporation, a multidivisional struc-ture with multiple profit centres under a vigilant head-office corporate staff which makes managerial performance visible and brings it under organiza-tional discipline (Williamson, 1970, 1985). Again, in transaction cost theory, where two firms are vertically integrated and either the supplier firm or the purchasing firm makes investments in assets specifically to service this transaction, the economic relationship becomes one of bilateral monopoly rather than arm's-length perfect competition between many buyers and many sellers (Williamson, 1975, 1985). In this way, market failure occurs and one firm may cheat the other, leading each firm towards costly manoeuvring to protect itself and so incurring transaction costs which would be unnecessary in a well-functioning market. These costs can be avoided by having the two firms combine so that the managers in each unit are subject to a common hierarchical authority. Thus hierarchy replaces market (Williamson, 1975).

Organizational economics shares with the newer sociological theories of organization a political model. There are conflicts of interest between agent and principal in agency theory and between one firm and another in transaction cost theory (Perrow, 1986: 220). Moreover, in organizational economics power is required in the form of hierarchical controls over managers. Thus there is some overlap of conceptual framework between organizational economics and politically oriented organizational sociological theories.

Paradigmatic differences between organizational economics and organizational sociology

Once again there is a rather wide divergence between the theoretical stories offered by organizational economics and by the three newer organizational sociological theories. For example, agency theory and transaction cost theory both advocate that if lower-level organizational members are using delegated authority to pursue their own interests at the expense of the interests of the organization as seen by top management, then top management should instigate new controls to investigate, reveal and sanction (i.e., punish) such deviancy (Jensen and Meckling, 1976; Williamson, 1985). In contrast, institutional theory argues that such 'control loss' is endemic in institutional organizations, such as US schools, wherein schools and school-teachers typically enjoy considerable autonomy and act to a degree oblivious of the official programmes set on high (Meyer and Scott, 1983). Any increase in controls and inspection would just make public this extensive deviancy and would undermine public belief in the myths about the public education system (Meyer and Scott, 1983). It would require schools to try to comply with a myriad of inconsistent policies and regulations which, in turn, would undermine their ability to operate even moderately effectively (Meyer and Scott, 1983). Hence for institutional theory, unlike organizational economics, control loss is beneficial, and lower-level autonomy and invisibility are to be maintained. Again, while population-ecology emphasizes population adaptation, organizational economics sees adaptation by individual organizations. Once again, resource dependence theory sees vertical integration as a means to increase control over resources whereas organizational economics sees it as a way to minimize transaction costs.

A further disjunction between organizational economics and organizational sociology is seen in its language and methods. Organizational economics uses the language of economics: interest alignment, residual claimants, rents and such terms, whose meaning might not be familiar to someone trained in sociology rather than in economics. Again the mode of reasoning and exposition follows economics, being highly formalistic and utilizing mathematical symbols and diagrams of a kind largely foreign to sociology (Jensen and Meckling, 1976). These all work against communication between organizational economics and organizational sociology.

Thus in core theoretical propositions, language and methods, organizational economics is quite distinct from the newer organizational sociological theories, and also from the older organizational sociological structural contingency theory. The organizational economics literature does not feature any extended attempts to synthesize and integrate with the organizational sociological theories, either new or old. Indeed the organizational economics literature generally ignores most organizational sociological or organizational psychological contributions, keeping mainly within the economics camp (see chapter 6). Thus organizational economics is yet another new paradigm within US organization theory. There seems little prospect of ready integration of this new paradigm with any of the other organization theory paradigms.

Negative view of managers

The view taken of managers and management is more negative in these newer theories than is the vague but positive model of managers implicit in most structural contingency theory (and in the explicitly positive model in the Chandlerian version). In resource dependence theory it is explicitly stated that managers make little difference to organizational success and that their role is often mainly symbolic, as heroes of success and scapegoats for failure, but in neither case really validly so (Pfeffer and Salancik, 1978). In institutional theory, managers construct facade structures to fool powerful external bodies but make little contribution to real productive work at lower levels, keeping their distance from it (Meyer and Scott, 1983). In population-ecology theory, it is the environment which is proactive and managers resist change to the point where adaptation by the organization fails to be forthcoming and the consequence is organizational death (Hannan and Freeman, 1989).

In organizational economics the characterization of managers is even more negative. In agency theory, managers are untrustworthy, always trying to cheat their owners, the principals, and requiring to be curbed by stiff measures, including a strong dose of hierarchical discipline (Jensen and Meckling, 1976). In transaction cost economics managers are again deceitful and lazy shirkers requiring strong controls by head office, many of whose staff are appointed expressly to sniff out the deficiencies lower down (Williamson, 1985). Again, when two firms are vertically related the managers in one firm cannot be trusted not to cheat the managers in the other firm, and so the two firms must be merged so that a third set of managers, the new overarching management level, can keep these two sets of managers honest (Williamson, 1975). Thus in organizational economics, managers are, unless curbed, deliberate cheats, idlers, liars and not to be trusted. Relative to population-ecology, resource dependence and institutional theories, organizational economics goes beyond them all in the extent to which it castigates management, not as lacking knowledge or discretion, but as using knowledge and discretion to cheat the organization, its principals and clients. Hence the model of managers in organizational economics is even blacker than that in the three newer organizational sociological theories. Since organizational economics has come to prominence in US organization theory more latterly, this means that the model of managers in US organization theory is becoming progressively bleaker. In organizational economics the anti-management tendency within academic organization theory reaches its current apogee.

Schematic summary of differences between organization theories

Each of the paradigms carries very different value-oriented assessments of organizations and managers. The differences between the five paradigms may be summarized by considering three levels of analysis: the society, the organization and the individual manager levels. At the societal level, the issue is whether the organization is seen as being functional or dysfunctional for society. At the organizational level, the issue is whether the organization makes adaptive change or not. And at the managerial level, the issue is whether the managers of the organization work to further or to undermine the interests of the organization as a whole. From the above discussion it is possible to capture the differences between the five paradigms by charting each of them on the three different levels. One may code the position of each paradigm on each of the three levels as being either mainly positive or mainly negative. The five paradigms each take unique combinations of positions on the three levels. The five paradigms on the three levels are shown schematically in figure 1.1.

Structural contingency theory sees organizations as adapting in ways which are functional for society and for the organization, under the guidance of their organizational managers. Hence structural contingency theory is positive at all three levels. Institutional theory sees organizations as moderately functional for society and as making adaptive changes, under the guidance of their organizational managers. Hence institutional theory is moderately positive societally and more fully positive at lower levels. Resource dependence theory sees organizations as adapting in ways which are anti-social but beneficial for the organization (e.g., cartels), under the guidance of their organizational managers. Hence resource dependence theory is negative societally and positive at lower levels.

Organizational economics, both in agency theory and the M-form (multidivisional structure) thesis of transaction cost economics, sees organizations as functional for society and as making adaptive changes, but this

Level	Characteristic	Structural contingency theory	Institutional theory	Resource dependence theory	Organizational economics	Population-ecology theory
Societal	Functionality of organization for society	Positive	Moderately positive	Negative	Positive	Positive
Organizational	Organization makes adaptive change	Positive	Positive	Positive	Positive	Negative
Managerial	Managers further interests of their organization	Positive	Positive	Positive	Negative	Negative

Fig. 1.1. Positive or negative views taken by theories.

is despite the deliberate attempts by managers to maximize their personal interests at cost to the organization. Hence organizational economics is positive at societal and organizational levels and negative at the managerial level. Population-ecology theory sees organizations as functional for society but as failing to adapt, and their managers as resisting adaptive change. Hence population-ecology is positive societally and negative at lower levels.

Only structural contingency theory is positive at all three levels. Population-ecology theory is the most negative in the sense of being negative at more levels than the other theories. Resource dependence theory, institutional theory and organizational economics are intermediate, varying in which level is negative (or less than fully positive).

Problems of application

The question 'How should I organize my company (or government department)?' which a manager or management student might put to organization theory draws several answers which are widely different and mutually contradictory. Structural contingency theory advises the organization to fit its structure to the task contingency to yield operational effectiveness. Institutional theory advises that organizational management should build a facade structure which panders to the encircling institutions and their expectations. Organizational economics advises tight control of managers by owners and headquarters. Resource dependence theory advises avoiding fixation upon internal organization, which little affects performance, and instead concentrating on external relations with other organizations. Population-ecology theory states that organizational survival is a function of ecological factors over which managers have almost no control, such as whether the organization is in an industry with many or few other organizations. Thus modern organization theory offers no consistent advice to practitioners and indeed offers no consistent story about organizations and how they survive and prosper. This is the inevitable result of a field becoming composed of a number of distinct paradigms which are mutually contradictory.

Such fragmentation of organization theory poses a host of problems regarding the credibility of the field and why the field should continue to be pursued and continue to receive resources and support from society (Pfeffer, 1993a). The last thirty years of organization theory research in the USA have seen not the creation of an increasingly strong, well-established, consistent, refined and validated body of knowledge, but rather an increasingly fragmented and incoherent jumble of mutually inconsistent ideas. It is conventional to laud this growing pluralism as increasing 'richness', but the question is whether US organization theory is now too rich a mixture to be stomached by organizational researchers, students and managers.

Thus American organization theory became during the 1980s a set of conflicting paradigms. The breakdown of the older, sixties-style, structural contingency theory as a unifying paradigm led, not to its replacement by a new unifying paradigm, but to a jostle of conflicting, mutually contradictory paradigms.

Attempts at synthesis

There have been a number of attempts at synthesis of the organizational structural theoretical paradigms in the United States. Lawrence and Dyer (1983) produced a model which seeks to combine structural contingency and resource dependence theories. Aldrich (1992) has sought to combine population-ecology, institutional and interpretist theoretical approaches. Kaufman (1985) has offered a theoretical discussion which synthesizes population-ecology and institutional theories. Hage (1980) has made a synthesis between structural-functional and power-conflict theories of organization. This list is not exhaustive. It indicates that attempts are being made in the USA to merge the differing theories, thereby moving them away from being full-fledged paradigms and hence reducing the fragmentation of the field. Worthy as each of these efforts towards reintegration is, none of these syntheses seems to have become generally accepted and none has captured the field by providing a synthesis which is the new standard theoretical approach. Thus, while it would be appealing to hail one or other of the attempts at synthesis as having led to a new integration, such a claim would be premature.

Moreover, there is little sign that the differing, major US organization theories are abandoning their status as distinctive paradigms to any serious degree. For example, the later population-ecology writings, such as Hannan and Freeman's (1989) and the collection edited by Carroll (1988), are fairly much hard-core population-ecology analyses with only limited moves towards integration with the other paradigms. Again, the later collection of institutional theory writings edited by Powell and DiMaggio (1991) is overwhelmingly hard-core institutionalist and displays little evidence of integration with the other organization theory paradigms.

There seems little enthusiasm among the core proponents of each of the newer paradigms for a dissolution of their paradigms into a new unifying theory of organizations. Nor is this reluctance surprising, for such a surrender of distinctiveness and autonomy would compromise cherished beliefs and would also reduce the profile and other benefits of paradigm entrepreneurship.

Aldrich (1992: 36) comments on the extent to which a cumulative scientific approach has not been followed in organization studies, such that the field has become, instead, a scramble for product differentiation between theorists:

What would a strict positivist conclude after observing the relation between research and theory in our field? Too often theoretical developments appear driven primarily by responses to other theorizing, rather than by the accumulation of empirically tested hypotheses and well-grounded generalizations. Organization studies resembles many other social sciences in the way that it systematically disdains the two processes central to scientific endeavour: attempted replication of previous findings, and publication of negative findings. Instead, we are treated to 'new' concepts and 'positive' findings, as authors try to differentiate their products from their potential competitors.

Aldrich (1992: 29ff.) has offered an attempted synthesis between three contemporary US organization theories – ecological, institutional and interpretive theories. However, he notes also that each theory is championed by its own community that resists integration and preserves distinct theories and methods (37):

all of the perspectives I have reviewed have achieved significant standing today because, at their core, they have groups of dedicated researchers working on empirical research to test hypotheses derived from the perspectives. They read one another's papers, hold conferences, and issue edited volumes collecting recent empirical work (Carroll [1988]; Frost *et al.*, 1985; Pondy *et al.*, 1981; Powell and DiMaggio, 1991; Singh, 1990; Zucker, 1988). In the process of constructing theory groups they have bounded themselves, and organizational boundaries can be extremely difficult to surmount. The groups work very hard at emphasizing how they differ from one another, and investigators have a stake in stressing their incompatibilities.

Thus attempts at forging a new synthesis to reintegrate the field of organization theory have not been successful. The paradigms strive to retain their distinct status from one another. This is prompted by the strong forces within the US academic system for novelty and product differentiation.

Thus the rise of several distinct paradigms of organization theory has fragmented the field and no synthesis is presently effective. Accordingly we will critically examine the paradigms and seek a new integration.

Plan of the book

Structural contingency theory holds that organizations adapt to their environments by adopting an internal organizational structure that fits their contingency factors (e.g., strategy) which in turn reflect the environment. The structural contingency theory of organizations adapting to their environments will be briefly considered in chapter 2.

It will be convenient to consider the four newer organization theory paradigms in the order of the degree to which they explicitly reject structural contingency theory, beginning with the greatest rejection and then considering in turn the paradigms that make a lesser rejection: population-ecology theory, institutional theory, resource dependence theory and organizational economics.

The most radical challenge to structural contingency theory is from population-ecology theory which calls into question the structural contingency theory axiom that adaptation is primarily by changes in on-going organizations. Accordingly, it will be appropriate to examine the population-ecology theory first of the newer organization theory paradigms, in chapter 3.

Institutional theory agrees with structural contingency theory that adaptation to the environment occurs within on-going organizations, but institutional theory argues against the structural contingency theory view that adaptation is to the task environment and instead holds that organizational adaptation is to the institutional environment. Thus institutional theory is a challenge to structural contingency theory, but a somewhat lesser challenge than population-ecology theory, and so it will be appropriate to examine it second of the newer organization theory paradigms, in chapter 4.

Resource dependence theory argues that the internal emphasis of structural contingency theory is misplaced in that organizational prosperity is more influenced by the environment. Thus resource dependence theory seeks to redirect organizational analysis away from the internal organization and towards interorganizational phenomena (e.g., mergers, co-optation). Structural contingency theory becomes largely irrelevant to be replaced by an interorganizational research programme. Accordingly, it is appropriate to examine resource dependence theory third of the newer organization theory paradigms, in chapter 5.

Whereas structural contingency theory identifies the structures needed to fit the task contingencies (e.g., strategy), organizational economics holds that organizational structures need to be designed to stem the recalcitrance of managers whose fundamental motives are in conflict with the interest of the organization. This leads to prescribed structures whose nature and purpose differ from organizational structures prescribed by structural contingency theory. The differences between organizational economics and structural contingency theory are more subtle and therefore organizational economics is examined last of the newer organization theory paradigms, in chapter 6.

At the theoretical level, it is desirable to move towards a unified organization theory, to reverse the present fragmentation of the field and to have a coherent image of organizations to offer students and managers. Steps towards this goal can be taken. Integration can be obtained within the domain of organization structure through synthesis of selective elements of the different paradigms which can be brought together in a logically consistent manner. The core explanatory model for organizational structural phenomena is structural contingency theory. However, to this core can be added certain complementary theoretical ideas from the other paradigms to produce a fuller, synthesized explanatory model of organizational structure, in chapter 7.

A lesson for the future is that US organization theory would be well served to concentrate henceforth on the steady build-up of a science of organization structure through continuous improvement rather than through the present 'permanent paradigm revolution' ethos. This necessitates a deliberate alteration in priorities away from novelty, as the main value, towards validity. More specifically, research in organizational structure needs to be conducted with an emphasis on cumulation by systematically filling out a programme of inquiry, and several suggestions are offered in this regard in chapter 8.

Conclusions

The present real-world problem of declining American economic performance finds its complement in the decline in intellectual analysis of management organization in American academic circles. The rational process of building a science of organization in an orderly manner has been replaced to a significant degree by an increasing profusion of paradigms – a passing parade of fads and fashions. Several new theories are offered as new paradigms: resource dependence theory, institutional theory, population-ecology theory and organizational economics. This plurality of paradigms fragments the field and prevents the cumulation of knowledge. Attempts at synthesis to date have been less than completely successful. The social and academic context in the United States tends to heighten these problems. Moreover, these variegated modern American organization theories share a view of management which is increasingly negative, varying from ineffectual through to deceitful.

2 Structural contingency theory of organizational adaptation

Structural contingency theory argues that individual organizations adapt to their environment. The environment is seen as posing requirements for efficiency, innovation or whatever, which the organization must meet to survive and prosper (Hage and Aiken, 1970). This in turn leads the organization's management to adopt a strategy for the organization which in part reflects the environment but is in part also a managerial statement of organizational objectives given the comparative advantage of the organization (Christensen et al., 1978). These organizational strategies, together with extant organizational resources, lead in turn to the organization adopting particular levels of size, technology, diversification and other factors, each of which is considered to be a contingency variable in structural contingency theory (Chandler, 1962; Woodward, 1965; Perrow, 1967; Blau, 1970; Pugh and Hickson, 1976).

Each of the main structural contingency theories identifies a contingency factor (or set of kindred factors) and delineates which organization structure is needed in order to operate effectively at each level of that contingency factor. For instance, Chandler (1962) argues that as firms increase their level of the contingency of product diversification so they need to increase their level of decentralization and move from a functional to a multidivisional organizational structure. Thus when product diversification is low, the functional structure constitutes a fit which leads to high performance – because it is simple, low-cost and promotes economies of scale through specialization. When product diversification is high, the multidivisional structure constitutes a fit which leads to high performance because it caters for complexity by allowing co-ordination of each separate product market (Chandler, 1962). Equally, when product diversification is low, the multidivisional structure constitutes a misfit which leads to low performance, because it is expensive and destroys scale economies. When product diversification is high, the functional structure constitutes a misfit which leads to low performance because it retards rapid response to each product market, impairing flexibility and innovation (Dill, 1958; Utterback and Abernathy, 1975). Thus structural contingency theory posits that organizational performance is affected by the fit or misfit between the structure and the contingency.

Structural contingency theory holds also that organizations adapt their structure by moving out of misfit, with its consequent low performance, and into fit, in order to restore effectiveness and performance. Thus much structural change is seen as being positive and productive, for the organization. These ideas, that there is a fit between structure and contingency which affects performance, that structural change is an adaptive move from misfit into fit, and that effectiveness and performance are thereby improved, are common ideas across all of the major structural contingency theories. However, these theories differ in regarding the nature of the contingency factor as, variously, strategy (Chandler, 1962), technology (Woodward, 1965), technical and market change (Burns and Stalker, 1961), or organizational size (Blau, 1970; Williamson, 1970).

A change of the contingency variable moves the organization out of fit into misfit – and hence from equilibrium into disequilibrium. The structural change process is seen as being led by shifts in contingencies, such as increasing diversification, increases in sophistication of technology, increases in rates of technical and market change and increases in organizational size, with structural change following as a secondary adaptive change to restore equilibrium (Chandler, 1962; Woodward, 1965). Thus from these classic contributions one can abstract the structural-adaptation-to-regain-fit model (SARFIT). This states that the adaptive cycle is: organization initially in fit, then increase in contingency variable produces misfit and reduces performance, and then structure is changed adaptively from misfit to a new fit which restores equilibrium and performance (Donaldson, 1987).

Given this theoretical model of how individual organizations make structural adaptations, the question is whether there is empirical evidence to support each component part. There is held to be a fit between the organizational structure and the contingency which affects organizational performance. There is the idea that a change by the organization in its contingency variable causes it to move from fit to misfit. There is the idea that misfit causes structural change. There is also the idea, key for our present concern, that the organization by changing its organization structure moves from misfit into fit and thus it is adaptation, and thus organizations do make internal adaptive moves. Each of these four propositions can be shown to be empirically valid.

Strategy and structure

We will demonstrate the validity of this structural contingency theory model, in its SARFIT formulation, by considering research on the Chandlerian structural contingency theory which connects strategic diversification with apex managerial structure, in the sense of the distinction between functional and multidivisional structure. This is one of the original, major structural contingency theories and so is central to that tradition, and it has been the most comprehensively researched of any of the structural contingency theories.

Chandler (1962) contributed the seminal study of strategy and structure mainly through a detailed examination of the business history of several large US corporations. These studies have all the merits of rich description and led to the postulation of the basic model of fit between strategy and structure. They also revealed the dynamic process whereby strategic change caused the shift from fit to misfit and the subsequent structural change caused the shift from misfit to the new fit. Thus the rich, descriptive, early studies were valuable for the theory formulation. However, such qualitative case histories leave open the issues of the generalizability of their findings and of whether the narrative correctly disentangles cause and effect given the problems of simultaneously occurring factors in clinical cases. In order to attain greater precision and confidence in generalizability, we need to take the theory developed from the cases and subject its hypotheses to tests, using comparative, quantitative methods from large samples of corporations. Such a programme of empirical testing has been conducted and the results will now be reviewed.

Fit affects performance

The first proposition stated that there was a fit between the contingency of strategic diversification and the structural aspect of divisionalization which affected performance. Numerous studies have been conducted of the effect of divisionalization on performance, with mixed results (Poensgen, 1974; Armour and Teece, 1978; Steer and Cable, 1978; Teece, 1981; Cable and Dirrheimer, 1983; Buhner and Möller, 1985; Hoskisson and Galbraith, 1985). However, these are not tests of the contingency theory that it is the *fit* of divisionalization to diversification which leads to higher performance. Simply divisionalizing would not necessarily lead to higher performance as it might be a misfit if the organization had an undiversified strategy. There have been studies of the effect of strategy–structure fit on performance (Rumelt, 1974; Grinyer *et al.*, 1980; Hill, 1988). The study by Grinyer *et al.* (1980) failed to find any effect of strategy–structure fit on performance; however fit was being measured at a single point in time and so organizations switching between fit and misfit would confound the analysis. The study by Hill (1988) attained mixed results, with some findings being the opposite of the contingency theory expectations. The results of Rumelt

(1974) were equivocal. The study by Donaldson (1987), based on a re-analysis of the US corporations studied by Rumelt (1974) used a stronger treatment design and showed that organizations which were in strategy–structure fit for a period of ten years enjoyed, as a result, higher subsequent financial performance than those in misfit. Thus there is evidence from the time ordering of the variables in the research design that fit was the cause and performance the effect. Moreover, the effect of fit on performance held after controlling for industry (dichotomized as science versus non-science), strategic diversification and change in strategic diversification.

A subsequent study of large New Zealand corporations by Hamilton and Shergill (1992) took a similar approach. Again fit was associated with higher performance after controlling for several factors including industry (by numerous dummy variables), risk, leverage, and so on. Corporations which were in fit and remained in fit over a period of years showed superior growth rates to those which were in misfit and which remained in misfit over the same period. Since the superiority in performance occurs after adoption of the structural fit, this is evidence that fit is the cause and performance is the effect. The New Zealand study replicates the US study and also provides evidence that these results generalize from the United States to New Zealand, and thereby from large to smaller corporations (since large New Zealand corporations are smaller than large US ones). A further study of US corporations supports the positive effect of strategy–structure fit on performance (Hill *et al.*, 1992). Thus the proposition that there is a fit between undiversified strategy and functional structure and diversified strategy and multidivisional structure, and that this overall fit model positively affects performance, receives empirical support from the research to date.

The idea that organizations adapt their structure leads to the hypothesis that undiversified firms will tend to retain the functional structure and that diversified firms will tend to have adopted the multidivisional structure and thus that diversification would be associated with divisionalization. There have been quite a number of empirical studies which test for positive association between diversification and divisionalization: all find the association (Channon, 1973; Rumelt, 1974; Dyas and Thanheiser, 1976; Pavan, 1976; Khandwalla, 1977; Suzuki, 1980; Grinyer and Yasai-Ardek-ani, 1981). These cross-sectional associations are held to arise by the causal processes postulated by structural contingency theory and SARFIT, that is, by structural adaptation to escape from misfit caused by earlier change in the contingency variable, i.e. divisionalization caused by diversification. However, some writers have suggested that, by contrast, divisionalization causes diversification (Hall and Saias, 1980). This would produce an association between diversification and divisionalization which would not constitute support for the structural contingency or SARFIT model. And this would not be evidence of structural adaptation to the contingency. Thus a direct test is required of the dynamics of organizational change in the second and third propositions.

Contingency change causes misfit

The second proposition states that organizations move from fit into misfit between structure and contingency as a result of a change in the contingency factor while retaining the existing structure. Donaldson (1987) re-analysed the data from five studies of strategy and structure, each of a different country: France, Germany, Japan, the UK and the USA (Channon, 1973; Rumelt, 1974; Dyas and Thanheiser, 1976; Suzuki, 1980). Combining the data for the five countries, of the eighty-seven corporations which moved from fit into misfit, 83 per cent changed their strategy, overwhelmingly by increasing diversification (Donaldson, 1987: 14). Thus an increase in the contingency variable of diversification is the major source of disequilibrium and of movement from fit into misfit. The proposition that the cycle of structural adaptation is initiated by a shift in the contingency variable is supported.

Misfit causes structural change

The third proposition is that misfit causes structural change. There were 585 corporations that were in misfit between structure and strategy and of these 39 per cent subsequently changed only their structure (Donaldson, 1987: 14). By comparison, there were 619 corporations that were in fit and of these just 9 per cent subsequently changed only their structure. Thus corporations in misfit are four times more likely to change only their structure in the ensuing period than those corporations in fit. Hence misfit is a cause of structural change. In contrast, change in the contingency variable is not a direct cause of structural change (13). Change in the contingency variable leads to misfit (as was shown above), so contingency change indirectly causes structural change through the intervening stage of misfit. Thus the evidence supports the first two stages of the SARFIT model: contingency change causes misfit which in turn causes structural change.

The immediate trigger for structural change is the disequilibrium of misfit and the problems of disorganization that result, such as delayed decision-making, co-ordination difficulties and lower performance. Organizations in misfit were more likely to move into fit if they were suffering from low performance (Donaldson, 1987: 18). It is the lowered performance resulting from misfit that stimulates structural adaptation to regain fit and performance, as Chandler (1962) found.

Structural change leads to new fit

The fourth proposition is that organizations in misfit regain fit when they change their structure so that such structural change is therefore structural adaptation. Of corporations changing only their structure, 72 per cent moved from misfit into fit and only 5 per cent moved from fit into misfit; thus structural change is adaptive (Donaldson, 1987: 14). Overwhelmingly, structural change involved adopting the divisional structure which fitted the more diversified strategy already adopted.

In summary, all four propositions of structural contingency theory are empirically supported and they validate the SARFIT cycle: organizations move out of fit into misfit by a change in their contingency variable, misfit leads to lower performance, and so to structural change as the organizations shift out of misfit into the new fit through structural adaptation, thereby regaining performance.

Divisionalization not a cause of diversification

This investigation of the dynamics and time ordering argues against the interpretation that diversification and divisionalization are associated in these data because divisionalization leads to diversification. If this were so then structural change would precede strategic change, i.e., corporations would divisionalize before diversifying. Yet the published primary studies show that corporations overwhelmingly diversify first and divisionalize later (Channon, 1973; Rumelt, 1974; Dyas and Thanheiser, 1976). Moreover, the idea that divisionalization leads to diversification rests on the belief that once a corporation has adopted the divisionalized structure it is more likely to diversify subsequently than is a corporation which retains a functional structure. Scott (1971) argued this theoretically, and Rumelt (1974) produced some evidence in favour (but only for the fifties, not the sixties). However, there are methodological problems with the Rumelt study (Donaldson, 1982a: 910). Donaldson (1982a) re-analysed the data of Rumelt (1974) using an improved method and also re-analysed data from four other national studies of strategy and structure (Channon, 1973; Dyas and Thanheiser, 1976; Suzuki, 1980). The results fail to support the idea that firms which are divisionalized are more likely to diversify subsequently than are those which are functionally organized. Thus the association between diversification and divisionalization in these studies is not produced by corporations first divisionalizing and then diversifying. This reinforces the findings that diversification leads to divisionalization, i.e., corporations first change their contingency variable and then make a structural adaptation by divisionalizing.

Lack of alternative contingency adaptation to attain new fit

Child (1972a) argued that organizations in misfit could regain fit by adjusting their contingency factor rather than their structure, thereby avoiding structural adaptation. However, the empirical analysis fails to support this speculation. In 95 per cent of organizations in misfit which regained fit, structural adaptation was involved (Donaldson, 1987). Overwhelmingly, organizations in misfit regain fit by adaptation of their structure to their contingency, not by adaptation of their contingency to their structure.

Thus the empirical evidence on the topic of strategy and structure strongly supports the contention that divisionalization is a structural change made as an adaptive response to the contingency change of diversification. The statistical, comparative, quantitative research on large numbers of corporations bears out the original theoretical insights and qualitative case studies of Chandler (1962). The research stream overall shows that many organizations make adaptive moves by reorganizing their internal structures to attain better effectiveness and performance. Moreover, these studies are of the largest corporations in their respective countries, that is, Fortune 500 type corporations, which would include the wealthier and more successful corporations (see also Fligstein, 1985). These findings run completely contrary to the assertion of population-ecology that adaptation to the environment by organizations is unlikely, especially for large, successful organizations which supposedly will be inured in their habits and governed by inertia and resistance to change (Freeman and Hannan, 1989).

Thus, overall in the area of strategy–structure research, there is support for the idea that individual organizations make adaptive changes by adjusting their internal organizational structure, and that this is driven by changes in the contingency variable producing in turn misfit, disequilibrium and poor performance, which in turn eventually leads to structural change.

Size and bureaucracy

In the topic area of size and bureaucracy, another area of structural contingency theory, there is also evidence of structural adaptation at the level of individual organizations. Theory holds that as organizations grow in size, that is, numbers of people, the organization faces recurrent decisions around personnel, administrative and work issues and many tasks become routine through the division of labour and repetition. Such a work system can efficiently be handled by a bureaucratic structure in which work and administrative roles are specialized, there are formal role definitions, tasks are predefined, there are standard operating procedures and there is extensive documentation (Weber, 1968; Blau, 1970; Astley, 1985b). In terms of the Aston research programme, bureaucracy is characterized by functional specialization, standardization and formalization. Thus increasing size leads to increasing bureaucracy and this is functional, aiding predictability, efficiency and speed, though at the cost of some reduction in flexibility. Given that many organizations contain some degree of repetition and routine internally, and that they face requirements to control costs and attain some degree of efficiency, it will be functional for many organizations to adopt some degree of bureaucracy in many areas of their operations and administration (Child, 1984).

There have been two research projects which have tested the proposition of a fit between increasing organizational size and increasing bureaucratization of the organization structure. Both Child (1975) and Khandwalla (1973) found that the set of firms in which increases in size were matched by increases in degree of bureaucratization of the organizational structure displayed higher performance than the set of firms which deviated from the fit line. These findings are consistent with the theory that the fit of bureaucracy to size affects performance.

The implication is that as the organization increases in size it will increase commensurately the degree of bureaucratization of its organization structure, in order to maintain fit. Hence larger organizations would be expected to show greater bureaucratization than smaller organizations, and thus samples of organizations which had been internally adapting their organizational structure to their size would show a positive association or correlation between size and bureaucratization. Numerous surveys of organizations have shown a positive association between size and bureaucracy. This holds for each major component of bureaucracy: role specialization, functional specialization, standardization and formalization. The positive associations between size and each of the Aston measures of specialization, standardization and formalization have shown a high degree of consistency from study to study and the correlation is typically quite high (Pugh and Hickson, 1976). Two independent meta-analytic reviews have shown that across many studies, size is consistently, positively related to specialization and formalization (Donaldson, 1986a; Miller, 1987). Also, size is consistently related to standardization (Donaldson, 1986a). These results support the notion that many organizations, across many settings, display structures which are congruent with the idea that those organizations are adaptively increasing their level of bureaucratization as they grow in order to retain fit between size and bureaucracy.

Task uncertainty and organic structure

A further area of structural contingency theory is the relationship between the contingency of technical and market change and organization structure. Burns and Stalker (1961) distinguish between the mechanistic structure, which is characterized by formalization of roles, hierarchical direction and concentration of power and knowledge, and the organic structure, which is characterized by ongoing role definition through mutual agreement and decentralized power, knowledge and initiative-taking. They argue that the mechanistic structure is effective in a stable environment but that under conditions of technical and market change the organization needs to innovate and hence faces uncertain tasks which require an organic structure for their accomplishment. Empirical studies have shown that higher rates of innovation in organizational outputs are associated with more uncertain tasks facing members and with a more organic, less mechanistic structure (Hage and Aiken, 1967; Harvey, 1968). Moreover, a more organic structure leads to greater innovation rates in the subsequent period thus demonstrating that organic structure is a cause, and innovation an effect (Hage and Dewar, 1973). Thus there is a fit between uncertainty and structural organizations which affects innovation performance. As organizations vary between needing to minimize costs or maximizing innovation, so their criteria of performance effectiveness shift accordingly and they need to adopt a lesser or more organic structure to attain fit. Thus research to date supports the theory that there is a fit between uncertainty and organicness which affects innovation performance.

In view of the fit between uncertainty and organicness, organizations which were internally adapting would increase the degree of 'organicness' of their organization structure commensurate with increases in their internal task uncertainty which would in turn reflect increases in the environmental rate of technical and market change. The implication would be that a survey of organizations would show a positive association between task uncertainty and organic structure. Numerous studies have found a positive association between task uncertainty and degree of organicness of organization structure and quite consistently so (Gerwin, 1979). Thus the evidence supports the proposition that there is a rather widespread tendency for organizations to adapt their organization structure as regards organicness to shifts in the task uncertainty contingency.

Thus for the topic areas of strategy–structure, size–bureaucracy, and uncertainty–organicness, three sets of contingency–structure relationships which have been central to the structural contingency theory literature, there is evidence consistent with the proposition that many organizations have made and are making structural changes which constitute an internal adaptation of their organization, that is, adaptation exists at the level of the individual organization.

Structural contingency theory receives empirical support and is a valid theory of organizational structure and structural change. While being a valid theory it is not a novel theory. Let us now turn to the four more novel theories of organization and examine the validity of each of them.

3   A critique of population-ecology theory

Introduction

American organization theory has witnessed the rise of a new theory called population-ecology theory. This was created around the mid-seventies (Hannan and Freeman, 1977) and grew in strength throughout the late seventies and the eighties (Aldrich 1979; Hannan and Freeman, 1989), developing its approach, gaining increasing numbers of adherents and widening its influence over organization theory. Population-ecology is presented by its proponents as a theory distinct from prevailing organization theories such as structural contingency theory. It differs radically in several key regards, including emphasizing selection rather than adaptation, and the population (or group) of organizations rather than the individual organization.

Population-ecology theory is a distinct class or family of theories within organization theory, that is, it is a separate metatheory of organizations. Indeed, the basic ideas have been developed in such a way as to emphasize the difference from previous conventional organization theory. In this way population-ecology is a new paradigm within organization theory, rather than an incremental development building on previous organization theory. There is considerable novelty in its contribution, and much which is innovative and provocative. The development of population-ecology theory is a prime example of the formulation and assertion of new paradigms in organization theory so common in recent times in the United States. As such, it fragments the discipline and prevents unification. Moreover, population-ecology theory takes a dismal view of organizations, as failing to adapt, and a bleak view of their managers, as resisting change. Thus the influence of population-ecology on organization theory leads to problems of novelty-seeking and disciplinary fragmentation, and provides an erroneous and negative depiction of organizational management. All of this tends to reduce the value of organization studies academically, for socially responsible knowledge generation, and for practising managers.

Population-ecology theory is a label applied to their work by a number of writers such as Hannan, Freeman, Aldrich and others. Pre-existing structural contingency theory emphasized that individual organizations adapt their own characteristics to their environment (e.g., Thompson, 1967). Population-ecology emphasizes the broader perspective of populations, holding that adaptation of a population of organizations comes about by the environment selecting for survival those organizations which are well adapted and rejecting those organizations which are maladapted (Hannan and Freeman, 1977). Population-ecologists argue that adaptation by individual organizations is severely limited and that selection is an important process in shaping the organizations which are left existing in the world (Hannan and Freeman, 1977).

Aldrich (1979) states that there are three important types of process: variation, selection and retention. Variation refers to those processes which create variations in organizational form among organizations. Variation is not necessarily primarily a process of rational adaptation and includes processes such as random chance. Selection works on this variation among organizations with the environment selecting against those organizations which are not in fit with their environments. Such misfitted organizations die out leaving in existence the organizations which are in fit with their environment. The organizational forms of the survivors become set through processes of retention so that the organization will continue to be in fit with its environment and so continue to survive – until the environment changes significantly when that organizational form will become misfitted and no longer be able to survive.

Population-ecologists repeatedly argue the need to study the population of organizations as the unit of analysis and to examine population growth dynamics that incorporate the births and deaths in the population (Hannan and Freeman 1989). Adaptive creativity in society is seen to come not so much from existing organizations making internal innovations and developments, but rather from the newly entering organizations, that is, from the new births. The important new varieties of organizational form come from the variation in organizations which exists at the time of their creation, not from their subsequent intra-organizational adaptation. This idea leads population-ecologists to argue for the study of births, which they rightly argue was neglected in earlier organization studies (e.g., Woodward, 1965; Blau and Schoenherr, 1971). This, in turn, leads to the development in population-ecology of theories of organizational birth and to their empirical study (Singh *et al.*, 1986; Hannan and Freeman, 1989). Population-ecologists also study the mortality of organizations (Hannan and Freeman, 1989).

The term population has a particular meaning within population-ecology writing. The world of organizations is divided into numerous populations of organizations of distinct types (e.g., labour unions or semiconductor firms). Each population arises because there is a corresponding ecological niche which will provide resources for growth of a population of organizations which are specifically adapted to that niche, i.e., the characteristics of the organizations are such that they can utilize the resources of that specific niche (Hannan and Freeman, 1989). The environment is thus considered as being made up of numerous distinct niches. Organizations specialize to a degree by having developed competences which fit with that niche, i.e., highly situationally specific skills, repertoires of behaviour and management systems adapted only for their niche, e.g., the airline industry (McKelvey and Aldrich, 1983).

Organizations which are adapted to their environment tend to institutionalize, retain and reproduce their form, which in turn promotes their growth and survival as long as the environment remains static. However, this same institutionalization, which produces reliable performance of existing effective behaviour, constitutes a strong inertial force against organizational change, if ever the environment changes in such a way as to render existing organizational routines obsolescent and counter-productive (Hannan and Freeman, 1984). The result is that organizations, especially if previously successful and large, fail to respond adaptively to environmental changes and fail to survive (Hannan and Freeman, 1984). The new opportunities presented by the environmental change are met by new organizations being born which possess from birth a form better suited to the new environment.

The distinctiveness of the paradigm

Rejection of structural contingency theory

Hannan and Freeman (1977) begin their classic statement of population-ecology theory by making a critique of the then prevailing contingency theory such as espoused by Chandler (1962), with its emphasis on adaptive learning by organizations and rational adjustment of structure to the situation by managers and others. They see this degree of adaptive organizational change as unlikely for many reasons: organizational assets are specific to current tasks, organizational leaders have incomplete information on their organization and environment, political resistance, normative restraints on change, legal and fiscal barriers to entry and exit, limits on legitimated mission and the difficulty of finding a state which is adequate for long in an interactive environment of many players (Hannan and Freeman, 1977: 931). They then argue that a more fruitful approach may be derived by borrowing biological notions, especially that the adaptation of a population may come about through failure of organizations to fit their environment and hence for them not to survive. Thus attributes of a population of organizations may be the result of differential survival as well as adaptation by individual organizations. Indeed Hannan and Freeman (1977: 930) contend that 'there is no reason to presume that the great structural variability among organizations reflects only or even primarily adaptation'. Population-ecology challenges the structural contingency theory of adaptation by individual organizations, asserting instead population adaptation through birth and death. Therefore any observed tendency of organizations to be adapted to their environments is more likely to be the result of this selection process than to have been brought about through adaptation by individual organizations. This means that population-ecology theory is quite different from and rivals structural contingency theory. Population-ecology theory is highly novel and it is a dramatic challenge to conventional organization theory of the structural contingency type.

It might have been expected that population-ecologists would have more moderately asserted that there are selection processes as well as adaptive processes operating in organizations, i.e., that both traditional adaptation theory and their newer selection theories are valid. However, population-ecologists have not taken such a moderate stance; they have asserted validity problems with adaptation theory and repeatedly propound their selection theory in conjunction with a critical attack on adaptation theory (e.g., Hannan and Freeman 1977, 1989). As well, population-ecology research has not combined the study of organizational births and deaths with the study of adaptive changes by on-going organizations.

Logically there is room for theoretical agreement between structural contingency theory and population-ecology theory. Both structural contingency theory and population-ecology theory are sub-types of structural-functionalism, so common parentage bodes well for complementarity. Structural contingency theory could be used to specify which structures fit with which environmentally produced contingencies and thereby produce a fit between organization and environment. For example, a diversified firm needs a divisional structure to be in fit; if a diversified firm retains a functional structure it is in misfit. And population-ecology could hold theoretically that the misfit of an organization to its environment leads to lower performance and hence reduced probability of survival. Continuing the example, a diversified firm with a functional structure is in misfit and therefore has a reduced probability of survival. Population-ecology could then study organizational mortality as the result of intra-organizational characteristics which constitute misfit of the organization to its environment as specified by structural contingency theory. In this way population-ecologists could complement structural contingency theory by providing the studies of organizational mortality which conventional structural contingency research omits. Thus population-ecologists could study survival processes in populations of organizations but using a theoretical framework in common with structural contingency theory, i.e., lack of survival is explained by misfit of organization to environment. However, population-ecology theory has *not* been developed in this way, so it remains a logical possibility but one not realized in practice.

The population-ecology model, in its most distinct form, emphasizes the explanation of structure through selection by the environment, that is, structure is determined by the fit or not of extant structures to the material situation. Little is granted to management in the way of being able to pick the required structure, because of the uncertainty of their cause–effect knowledge (i.e., lack of valid design knowledge) compounded by the tendency of the environment to shift and thus to be ever changing the required structure, so frustrating intelligent management choice of structure (Hannan and Freeman, 1989). Instead structure is seen as the outcome of chance, through the managers blindly varying the structures, only some of which will 'hit lucky', and of structural inertia, that is, lack of change, with the misfitted structures being constantly eliminated by environmental culling of those organizations.

Linkage with sociology

In presenting population-ecology theory Hannan and Freeman (1989) position it as renewing links between organization theory and sociology. They depict these links as having once been strong around the nineteen fifties, in work such as that by Selznick (1949). However in the sixties, contingency-approach organization theory fell under the influence of management schools and managerially oriented theory, such as structural contingency theory, weakening organization theory intellectually and separating it from sociology. Hannan and Freeman present population-ecology as a new rapprochement between organization theory and sociology which will reinvigorate and make organization theory more valid.

The new, closer connection with sociology is depicted in several aspects of their population-ecology theory by Hannan and Freeman (1989), including the de-emphasis on managers as being capable of sound structural choices and the emphasis on institutional and normative factors promoting inertia in organizations (Hannan and Freeman, 1984). Also invoked as a distinctly sociological type of insight by Hannan and Freeman (1989) is the model of the organization not as a unitary entity but as composed of various interest groups, which leads in turn to political processes determining organization strategy and structure, which again tends towards inertia rather than organizational adaptation. Again, the notion of organizations as tools to implement the strategy set by top management is criticized as a managerialist view and eschewed in favour of a recognition of the recalcitrance of organizations, which again supports their argument about the prevalence and strength of inertia.

More broadly, Hannan and Freeman (1989) argue that organizations are intermediary processes whereby power is exercised and mobilized and whereby social change is effected or resisted. In this way they locate organizations as key units in the sociological analysis of societal change. Ingeniously, Hannan and Freeman make the argument that if organizations were perfectly pliable tools they would transmit social change perfectly, and so they would make no contribution to change process. Thus it is the inertia and resistance to adaptation of organizations which makes them of interest to students of societal change, which is to say, to sociologists. The argument about organizations as being of central interest in the understanding of power mobilization is in the opening paragraph of Hannan and Freeman (1989), and much of the early and end sections of their book are taken up with advancing the claim to the sociological nature of their inquiry. Thus their theoretical programme is part of a conscious attempt to reclaim organizational analysis for sociology out of the hands of management studies. (While Hannan and Freeman use power concepts they only embrace radical sociology to a degree which has meant that ecological analysis can still be attacked by a more full-blown type of radical sociology in which power and conflict are the mainstays of explanation (see Dawson, 1980; Perrow, 1985a, 1986).)

This sociological orientation gives added force and meaning to the way in which Hannan and Freeman (1989) invoke intra-organizational mechanisms such as inertia, blind chance, politics, normative traditions, etc. to counter a mechanism of rational organizational choice guided by an integrated, informed and conscientious management. Organizations and management are to be depicted as irrational and incapable of more rational, purposeful action because such a rational model in structural contingency theory is managerially oriented. This would not allow a rapprochement with sociology, that is, the contemporary variant of sociology with its penchant for conflict and focus upon societal change (or the reasons for the failure of radical societal change). An organization theory paradigm which was to appeal to a radically oriented sociological audience would have to distance itself from the idea of rationality in organizational management.

Thus despite the potential openness of population-survival theory to a broad set of more middle-range theoretical elements which are logically consistent with population-survival theories, the middle-range mechanisms chosen by Hannan and Freeman (1989) are of the irrational-organization and anti-management type. Hence despite the population-ecology perspective being basically functionalist, the population-ecology theory advanced by Hannan and Freeman, under the influence of radical sociology, rejects the functionalist tradition of ascribing deliberately created functionality and rationality to organizational structural change in the manner of structural contingency theory.

An organization which is not subject to political factionalism, and which is managed conscientiously and rationally with intelligent decision-makers selecting valid adaptations, nevertheless could still have a maladapted structure, through lack of knowledge and a rapidly changing environment making its adaptive moves obsolete. Uncertainty in knowledge and rapidity of environmental changes are invoked by Hannan and Freeman (1989), and these alone would lead to some environmental selection, that is, culling, and hence to population-level adaptation through selection; this would thus still allow a distinct population-ecology theory. Such a theory construction route was not taken because of the need to distance from managerialist models of rationality and the need to be acceptable to the discipline of sociology. Thus we find in population-ecology the additional theoretical elements of politics, power, normative institutionalism, blind variation and chance – all elements of the irrationalist view of organizations. And these are the elements which make population-ecology theory the opposite of structural contingency theory. This helps to make population-ecology theory a distinct paradigm separate from the prior organizational theory of structural contingency.

Within the population-ecology literature a number of different strands can be identified. Three different elements in the population-ecology literature will be identified here: the root biological metaphor; Aldrichian historical population-ecology; and the population arithmetic of Hannan and Freeman (1989). (A further element is community ecology theory but since its focus is interorganizational rather than intra-organizational it will not be considered here (Astley, 1985c, 1987).)

Root biological metaphor

The first strand is the basic biological metaphor of selection in the manner of Darwin. Biology and population studies are held to be a protean source of theoretical ideas, models and methods of study which now are to be applied in the sociology of organizations as a conscious exercise in cross-fertilization between disciplines (Aldrich, 1979; Hawley, 1986). The population-ecology literature often presents itself as drawing guidance and inspiration from biology (Hannan and Freeman, 1977; Aldrich, 1979). This includes mathematical models of biological population dynamics. However, population-ecologists also explicitly identify the limitations on such borrowings and note where they need to modify these biological theories in recognition that organizations are not biotic creatures (Hannan and Freeman, 1989).

The issue of how far sociological analysis can use biological metaphors validly has ever attracted criticism in sociology. Not surprisingly, population-ecologists have been criticized for their use of biological terms (Young, 1988). Again not surprisingly, Hannan and Freeman (1989) insist that their use of the biological metaphor is a carefully circumscribed and selective one. Indeed, Hannan and Freeman repeatedly note ways in which their analysis builds upon but develops in different ways from the biology on which they draw. Since Social Darwinism has right-wing connotations it is unpopular with sociologists. It is to be expected that Hannan and Freeman would seek to distance their work from Social Darwinism. This is consistent with their sociological orientation.

In her critical review of population-ecology theory, Young (1988) points out that whereas the base metaphor is biological, much of the substance of the propositions advanced by population-ecology theorists such as Hannan and Freeman (1989) is in fact drawn from sociological theory, such as that by Stinchcombe (1965). Indeed, the fact that Hannan and Freeman use as the title of the book which draws together much of their work, not *Population-Ecology* but *Organizational Ecology*, may in part reflect a desire to emphasize the sociological rather than the biological flavour of their work. This is consistent with our view that the main thrust of population-ecology theory is to consciously create a sociological theory of organizations.

Thus the biological theory is a root metaphor and source of analogy but the population-ecology theory of organizations is not presented as governed by these same laws of biology nor as always a close parallel. With this biological inspiration population-ecologists mount their argument that selection is more important than adaptation in organizations and that selection has been neglected by earlier organization theories. Population-ecology as an organization theory then becomes a call for the study of populations of organizations and of selection processes therein (Hannan and Freeman, 1989).

Historical population-ecology approach

Aldrich (1979) builds on this base model by arguing that selection in organizations works through the triple processes of variation, selection and retention. He develops a number of causal sub-processes within each of these major processes. This collection of sub-processes is quite eclectic, drawing upon ideas from sociology and psychology. The major commonality in this potpourri of theories is that the theories tend not to be the mechanisms posited within the pre-existing organization theories such as structural contingency theory. In particular the formulations tend to eschew theories which claim that organizations act rationally under the guidance of their managers. There is emphasis instead on political processes, cognitive limitations on decision-making and the like. It is almost as if there is an underlying premise to construct the detail of population-ecology theory so that it is as radically different as possible from pre-existing organization theory, that is, to ensure that population-ecology theory is a new paradigm rivalling the older organization theory. Thus from the base metaphor in biology through to its detailed theoretical propositions, population-ecology theory is constructed to be different.

In the Aldrich (1979) writings there is also something of a political flavour with industrial development depicted in quasi-Marxian terms as increasing economic domination and the like. The bulk of Aldrich's book fleshes out his thesis with a wealth of social historical material. Hence the Aldrichian branch of population-ecology may be called historical population-ecology. Much of his work is about how organizations impact upon each other, i.e., interorganizational analysis. Much again is about change in the technology of production and its effect upon the development of an industry, favouring some organizations over others, etc. There is little about the internal organization and its management. That is to say, there is little discussion of the details of internal organization structure or of administrative systems, or of how managers might make more correct decisions about how they organize the enterprise. There is an absence of discussion of optimal spans of control or structural differentiation or departmentation or specialization or centralization in anything like the sort of terms or detail usual in a book about organizations in their environments. There is a lack of prescriptive advice on offer. Hence population-ecology is developed by Aldrich into a vaguely leftish, semi-irrationalist theory of how organizations are moulded by their environments, in which there is little interest in internal management organization or how the managers of the organization could assist the organization to better adapt to its environment. This makes of Aldrichian population-ecology a distinct, specialized and challenging contribution to the theory of organizations. The work is highly acceptable as an academic contribution to organization studies and would find favour as a sociological counter to overly managerial theories which might be too simple in their views or in their prescriptions. However, the work seems deficient as a serious study of organizations, their internal structures and their adaptive actions, especially regarding internal restructuring at the hands of management.

In summary, Aldrich (1979) takes the basic biological metaphor of population-ecology and develops a highly eclectic theory which has the thrust of a novel paradigm distinct from older paradigms and which makes no attempt at integration with preceding theory.

The population arithmetic approach

Another distinct strand of population-ecology theory is that associated with Hannan and Freeman (1989). They made early and seminal contributions to population-ecology, writing some of its original statements (Hannan and Freeman, 1977). Since their approach is the most widely received form of population-ecology and is the most distinct from other organizational theory paradigms, our discussion will dwell on the contribution of Hannan and Freeman. Pfeffer (1993a: 613) comments favourably that this type of population-ecology work constitutes a highly developed research paradigm, displaying a high level of cohesion and consensus around methods, variables, literature and problems. Hannan and Freeman (1989) have delved deeply into biological population theory including highly abstract mathematical models. This makes parts of the writing of Hannan and Freeman esoteric – to the point where they border on the inaccessible for the average social scientist. Young (1988) has criticised population-ecology for the lack of precision of its concepts, which makes empirical testing difficult (for a reply, see Freeman and Hannan, 1989).

Problems with the biological metaphor

Population-ecology theory frequently invokes the metaphor of biological theory à la Darwin's theory of evolution and related theories. The proposal of Hannan and Freeman (1989) is that organizational theorists should consciously borrow from biologists their models of natural selection of organisms in environments. This is an exciting and potentially fruitful idea. However, when population-ecologists invoke Darwinian natural selection theory they invoke a model with several specific attributes: discrete organisms, genetic inheritance, random mutation, biological reproduction, organisms which are born and die, high rates of birth and death and so on. To apply Darwinian natural selection theory to organizations implies that analogies of each of these biological characteristics can be found for organizations. However, this is no easy task. Hardly has this process of theoretical translation from organisms to organizations begun than difficulties start to appear.

Take the first characteristic of Darwinian natural selection theory: the subjects are discrete organisms which are born and die. Yet organizations may merge so that two organizations become one. Or again a division may be divested from a corporation and become a free-standing company. Animals do not merge or divest bits of themselves. Female organisms have children but the children are new, whole organisms. Human mothers do not 'spin out' a major organ, such as the heart, to become a whole new entity, while the mother continues living, but conglomerates do spin out a product division which becomes free-standing (see Davis and Powell, 1992: 353).

Hannan and Freeman (1977) grapple with this issue. They discuss the different properties of small and large organizations. They then have to recognize that many large organizations grow from being small organizations. But this is troubling as this smacks of adaptation and is inconvenient for their approach which needs to treat small and large organizations as belonging to separate categories, i.e., as if they were two different populations of distinct organisms. Hannan and Freeman (1977) escape from this impasse by suggesting that such big organizations be viewed as having once been little organizations which have died as little organizations and have been born again as large organizations. Thus scarcely has population-ecology been initiated than it is having to ascribe to organizations processes which have no reality in organizational life and are wholly fictional. How fruitful is a theory which, before it can explain any existent phenomena, has to invent phenomena which do not exist? (Similar problems occur with other aspects of the Darwinian theory, though they are less explicitly discussed in population-ecology and so an analysis will be deferred until later (see pp. 71–6).)

The domain of the theory

An issue arising in regard to population-ecology theory is the domain of the theory in the sense of the organizational phenomena to which the theory applies. Population-ecologists often use the term organizational form to refer to the subject of their theory. Organizational form is a vague term yet one which suggests that a breadth of organizational characteristics are subsumed therein and hence are subject to the theory.

Hannan and Freeman (1989) often use the terms 'strategy' and 'structure' in referring to the phenomena that their theory is to explain. However, Hannan and Freeman (1989: 79) at one point offer a more restrictive definition of the subject of population-ecology, that is, of organizational form, as core organizational features which are relatively immutable. This is consistent with their interest in organizational inertia and lack of organizational adaptation leading to environmental selection. They suggest that the core characteristics of an organization are its stated goals, forms of authority, core technology and marketing strategy, and that these are relatively immutable and form the basis of selection–survival processes in organizations. They distinguish these core organizational characteristics from more peripheral aspects such as 'structure in the narrow sense of numbers and sizes of subunits, number of levels in authority structures, span of control, patterns of communication, and so forth'. Also excluded are linkages with the environment such as interlocking directorates and joint ventures. These non-core aspects are held to be more plastic and less subject to inertia:

Earlier (Hannan and Freeman 1984) we suggested defining organizational forms in terms of four core characteristics: stated goals, forms of authority, core technology, and marketing strategy. Although these four properties encompass much of organizational strategy and structure, they do not come close to exhausting the dimensions of structure that interest social scientists. In particular, the list does not include structure in the narrow sense of numbers and sizes of subunits, number of levels in authority structures, span of control, patterns of communication, and so forth. Nor does it contain what Scott (1987) calls peripheral structures, the detailed arrangements by which an organization makes links with its environment and tries to buffer its technical core, for example, by forming inter-locking directorates and joint ventures.

We think that organization charts and patterns of specific exchanges with actors in the environment are more plastic than the core set. The former aspects tend to change as organizations grow and decline in size, as technologies change, and as competitive and institutional environments change. They can be transformed because attempts at changing them involve relatively little moral and political opposition within the organization and in the environment, since they do not raise fundamental questions about the nature of the organization. In short, inertial forces on these aspects of structure and on peripheral or buffering activities tend to be weaker than those on core features. (Hannan and Freeman, 1989: 79)

Stated thus, population-ecology theory does not purport to explain structural phenomena such as structural differentiation in either the Blau (1970) or the Lawrence and Lorsch (1967) senses, nor much of structure in the sense studied by technology theorists à la Woodward, Thompson, Perrow and Van de Ven, bureaucracy in the Aston sense and so on. In other words, organization structure as usually considered in the structural contingency theory literature seems to be defined as outside the scope of population-ecology theory. Similarly, 'forms of authority' sounds like the broad sociological categories of the basis on which authority rests, such as professional, bureaucratic, traditional, charismatic, property ownership, etc. (Weber, 1968). Thus most of the structural change within existing organizations such as more differentiation, more formalization, wider spans of control, divisionalization, etc. are excluded as being mere modifications within a particular form of authority, i.e., within the bureaucratic form of authority. Such a narrow definition of the object of inquiry virtually precludes population-ecology theory from being a theory of organization structure rivalling structural contingency theory. Indeed, population-ecology theory becomes a theory of only certain aspects of a firm such as technology and marketing.

However, elsewhere in Hannan and Freeman (1989) the phenomena being explained include: communications, complexity of interlinkages between organizational sub-units (1989: 88), whether the organization is centralized with a short hierarchy or decentralized with a more extended hierarchy (81), and so on. These structural attributes are conceptually those which traditional structural contingency theory discusses as centralization, differentiation, and so on. Thus it seems that the scope of population-ecology theory is not just form of authority but includes many of the structural variables found in structural contingency theory. Indeed, without such a more inclusive definition of organization structure, Hannan and Freeman (1977, 1989) cannot position their work as a new contribution to the sociology of organizations offering a new explanation of phenomena already explained by earlier organization theory (e.g., Chandler, 1962). If there is no overlap in the object of study then a theory of selection in no way challenges or rivals a theory of adaptation, and thus the opening critique of Hannan and Freeman (1989) would be beside the point. Thus Hannan and Freeman in fact employ their theory to explain aspects of structure beyond just the form of authority, including much of structure as understood in structural contingency theory. Moreover, this is the way the literature on organization structure has received population-ecology, using it, for example, to explain multidivisional structure (Fligstein, 1985).

The rationale offered by Hannan and Freeman (1989) for their definition of organizational form is that only the core characteristics of organization are subject to high degrees of inertia. Yet this is contradictory to the theory of inertia where inertia arises through the creation of an organizational system which is reliable, based upon high reproducibility and accountability (Hannan and Freeman, 1984). The requisite structure is the bureaucratic system of organization with its rules, regulations, narrow job definitions, specialization, hierarchy, delegation of authority and so on, in short, the machine bureaucracy (Mintzberg, 1979) and the highly structurally differentiated organization (Blau and Schoenherr, 1971). Thus the theory of inertia implies that selection will be visited upon large, bureaucratic, routinized structures. Hence the inertial organizational form which is at the heart of the theory of population-ecology must include in its definition organizational structure in many of the dimensions previously studied. Thus the meaning of organizational form in population-ecology theory is wider than the narrow formal definition of organizational form which Hannan and Freeman (1989) offer.

This inconsistency over the definition of organizational form seems to sit uncomfortably with a theory which tends to present itself as the height of analytic precision and scientific method in organization studies. It may be that when the situation arises in which a definition of organizational form must be given, the difficulty of actually claiming that organization structures do not change adaptively inside organizations, given previous supporting evidence about adaptation (e.g., Chandler, 1962; Woodward, 1965), leads population-ecologists to demur about the explicitly claimed domain of their theory. No such inhibition, however, applies at other places in their writings, where the polemic against adaptation theories is given vent (Hannan and Freeman, 1977, 1989). This illustrates the difficulty of constructing and maintaining credibility around a new paradigm whose central tenets are already known to be false at the time of its construction. The cost of paradigm-hood is internal incoherence.

The population arithmetic research programme

Hannan and Freeman have led a research programme of organizational ecology work undertaken by themselves, their colleagues and their students (e.g., Carroll, 1985; Carroll and Huo, 1986; Tucker *et al.*, 1990; Swaminathan and Wiedenmayer, 1991; Hannan and Carroll, 1992). Hannan and Freeman (1989) open with a metatheoretical argument giving a critique of adaptive theories of organization such as structural contingency theory and arguing the need for a selection-based population-ecology theory. The population-ecology theory is elaborated in terms of organizational inertia and other concepts in ensuing chapters. Emphasis is placed on explaining organizations as the products of external factors in the environment of the organization, rather than by internal factors (which would include management), and emphasis is placed also on studying populations of organizations rather than individual organizations. Drawing upon Durkheim and others, Hannan and Freeman go on to theorize that survival of an organization in an environment is affected by the number of resources and the number of other organizations competing for those resources. This is developed into a mathematical model of some sophistication. Essentially the distribution of organizational forms is explained by environmental support and competition. In this way, the general theoretical perspective is rendered much more specific in a theory of population dynamics whose exposition and testing forms the latter part of the book, and the core of the empirical work of Hannan and Freeman.

Hannan and Freeman (1989) argue that earlier organization studies over-emphasized adaptation by individual organizations and assert that organizations in fact make only limited adaptations and that there is a necessity to study survival processes to truly understand organizational change. Whereas this theoretical platform might be thought to lead to studies of survival and culling in populations of organizations to study how misfitted organizations die out and are replaced by better-fitting organizations, in fact this is not how their research programme unfolds. Instead the introductory theoretical argument about the importance of survival and of adaptation at the level of the population turns into a study of the dynamics of population growth. Population size is explained by rates of entry and exit of organizations into and out of the population, that is, birth and death rates of the population of organizations.

Theory of organizational vital rates These organizational birth and death rates in a population, that is, rates of organizational founding and mortality in the language of Hannan and Freeman (1989), are collectively termed by them 'organizational vital rates' (i.e., life process rates). The vital rates are affected by the population, especially its size, i.e., number of other organizations in the population – which is called 'population density' by Hannan and Freeman. Thus this is a theory of how the size of a population of organizations changes as a result of the rates of birth and death (entry and exit) in that population; these rates are in turn determined by the size of the existing population. Thus population size determines subsequent population size, through the intervening variables of entry and exit rates, which are themselves determined by population size. The number of organizations in a population is caused by the prior number of organizations in the population, i.e., *N* causes *N*. This is not a tautology, as present population size drives exit and entry rates at a later date, which in turn drive population size at a still later date. However, it is a theory of the limited phenomena of population size and organizational birth and mortality rates. This population dynamics is a narrow topic. The theory constructed for its explanation is also a narrow one, i.e., population size. The approach taken by Hannan and Freeman and their colleagues in empirical work may better be termed *population arithmetic*.

In greater detail, the model of the dynamics of organizational population by Hannan and Freeman (1989) is as follows. Rates of organizational founding and mortality are both held to be density-dependent, that is, influenced by the number of other organizations present in the population immediately prior to either the founding or mortality of the focal organization. Density-dependence exerts a curvilinear effect on the rate of founding, which rises and then falls as population density increases, and also on the rate of mortality, which falls and then rises as population density increases. The initially rising founding rate and the initially falling mortality rate, as density first increases, are both due to increased legitimation of that organizational form and to associated increases in the availability of resources. The subsequently falling founding rate and the subsequently rising mortality rate, as density increases further, are both due to increasing competition between organizations in the population for increasingly scarce finite resources, e.g., for customers between business firms in the same industry. Thus the density of an organizational population, that is, the total number of organizations within a single population, can only grow to a limiting value, which is set by the resource limitations of that ecological niche and is termed the carrying capacity of that niche for that organizational population.

Empirical studies Hannan, Freeman and their colleagues and students have made a series of studies to test their ecological theory. These studies are characterized by the way the entire population of organizations of a certain type over the entire history of that type is carefully reconstructed. The population history contains records of organizational foundings and mortalities (where they have occurred) for all the organizations in the population. This is longitudinal study on a massive scale. The researchers have faced and overcome many problems in their feat, which in itself is a distinguished contribution within organization studies. These data are then subject to analysis involving the construction of mathematical models and their statistical estimation in a process which is both sophisticated and careful, and which has been refined through numerous iterations (see Hannan and Freeman, 1989).

Hannan and Freeman (1989) report results from three separate empirical studies which test their model of organizational vital rates. The three populations studied are US national labour unions, US semiconductor firms selling only to the industrial user (i.e., the 'merchant' manufacturers) and newspapers in the San Francisco Bay area. For all three populations, density affects rates of organizational mortality in the curvilinear way hypothesized in the organizational ecology theory. For the two populations of labour unions and newspapers, density also affects the rate of organizational founding in the curvilinear way hypothesized by the theory. Within the population of semiconductor firms, the sub-population of firms which are subsidiaries of larger firms display the theoretically expected curvilinear relationship with density, but not the sub-population of firms which are independent producers of semiconductors.

Overall, the results of these three studies provide a high level of support for the organizational ecological theory that population density affects the vital rates of founding and mortality. The consistency of the findings provides evidence of a high level of generalizability of these phenomena, for findings generalize across business firms and labour unions, across hi-tech and lo-tech, and across profit-oriented and not-for-profit organizations.

Also, as Hannan and Freeman (1989) point out, the findings about competition between organizations hold in non-market (unions) as well as market (semiconductors, newspapers) settings. Thus Hannan and Freeman claim, with considerable justification, that the results of these studies are encouraging evidence for the validity and fruitfulness of organizational ecology. Further support for the curvilinear effect of density on mortality comes from the study of trade associations by Aldrich *et al.* (1990).

Singh *et al.* (1991: 402), in an analysis of voluntary social service organizations in Toronto, also found a curvilinear effect of density on the rate of organizational foundings, though the density effect was not significant. However, in regard to mortality rates, Singh *et al.* (1991: 411) note that their findings contradict the usual population-ecology findings of mortality rates falling then rising with density: in their study mortality rises, then falls and then rises again as density increases. Thus the study is an exception to the other studies of organizational mortality.

The population-ecology approach to the study of organizational mortality has been used to analyse types of competition (Barnett and Carroll, 1987; Barnett, 1990). The exploration of the effects of competition on vital rates is extended by Hannan and Freeman (1989) to the study of the effects of competition from one sub-population on another. Hannan and Freeman also find several other relationships in their studies and again these display encouraging degrees of generalizability across the populations studied. The vital rates are affected by population density, but also by more short-run effects. Both founding and mortality rates tend to show wave-like bunchings across the years. In all of these analyses, Hannan and Freeman are careful to introduce controls for other factors which affect, or could be held to affect, the dynamics of each of their populations.

Hannan and Freeman (1989) also investigated how mortality rates vary by the age of the organization. They note that for biotic creatures, increasing age leads to increasing mortality rates. However, for organizations, increasing age leads to decreasing mortality rates. The mortality rate drops sharply over the first few years of organizational existence and then declines more gradually. Freeman *et al.* (1983) write of this phenomenon as a 'liability of newness' in that new organizations are prone to failure due to inexperienced personnel, lack of tried procedures, etc. The liability of newness and declining mortality with organizational age is found in all three population studies by Hannan and Freeman (1989). However, in a study of savings and loans organizations, Rao and Neilsen (1992) found that organizational mortality increased with age and then decreased with further ageing. Thus the mortality–age relationship was curvilinear and exhibited not a liability of newness but 'a liability of adolescence' (Rao and Neilsen, 1992: 460).

The final major finding in the empirical studies of Hannan and Freeman (1989) concerns their organizational theory of niche width. Hannan and Freeman distinguish between specialist organizations which depend for survival on a narrow range of inputs and generalist organizations which can survive on a broader range of inputs. They also distinguish between fine-grained and coarse-grained environmental changes. Fine-grained environments have frequent changes whereas coarse-grained ones have less frequent changes as they remain in any one state for a longer period. A specialist organization can survive changes in a fine-grained environment because a period in which the environment turns unconducive for that organization never lasts too long before the environment returns to a more conducive state. However, a coarse-grained environment means that there are lengthy periods in which the environment is unconducive for the specialist organization and it consequently will fail, whereas a generalist organization will be able to survive such a lengthy period as it can find acceptable levels of resources even in a less munificent environment. Therefore generalist organizations are held to survive better than specialist organizations in coarse-grained environments. Hannan and Freeman find support for this theory in their empirical tests in studies of both restaurants and the semiconductor industry. In restaurants, specialist firms are those such as fast-food restaurants offering a limited range, e.g., hamburgers, whereas generalist firms are those offering a fuller menu of different dishes and having a chef who provides the resource for producing a broad range of dishes. A coarse-grained environment is operationalized as one subject to larger temporal variations in sales revenue.

In summary, Hannan and Freeman (1989) find some evidence of general laws of population dynamics. Founding rates of organizations are influenced by population density, recent founding rates and competition between different types of similar organizations (i.e., competition between sub-populations). Population density reflects contrasting forces of legitimacy and competition. Thus competition works within sub-populations and between sub-populations. Similar remarks apply to mortality rates. Additionally, mortality rates are a declining function of organizational age and are also affected by the fit between organizational generalism and coarseness of grain of the environment.

A critique of population arithmetic The theory of organizational vital rates is a little more complex than an explanation of them by population size: there are curvilinear relationships, timing effects and ageing effects, and there are cross-effects of one sub-population's size on another's. However, this is mostly just the elaboration of a simple model in which population size begets population size. Absent from either theory or empirical work is examination of internal organizational characteristics such as organization structure, administrative systems, human resource management practices, culture or social interaction patterns. Absent also is any sense of what management might be doing or might do in future to aid the survival chances of their organization. Absent again is any study of how organizational mortality results from lack of adaptive organizational change and from the inertial forces which the theory of Hannan and Freeman asserts dominates organizations.

Any inquiry into processes of organizational inertia would require an investigation into the internal power, politics and decision-making systems of organizations and thus would again require inquiry within the organizations studied about their internal characteristics. Yet Hannan and Freeman (1989) explicitly state that their population-ecology theory eschews such preoccupations with the internal organization in favour of an external focus on the environment, on the population and thereby on the ecology of organizations. Given such a restrictive view it is difficult to see how the approach can empirically study organizational inertia and the other internal organizational processes which the theory of population-ecology uses to explain why organizations fail to adapt.

Thus the later work of Hannan and Freeman (1989), i.e., the population density theory and associated empirical work, does not obviously constitute a logical working through of their original theory and programmatic writing about the necessity to understand survival and selection based on organizational inertia and the lack of intra-organizational adaptation. It is almost as if Hannan and Freeman had gone afresh to the well, that is, to the biological theories of population, and created from this a theory of organizational population dynamics which is a distinct topic area in the organizational literature with no direct or necessary linkages to the earlier theory about organizational inertia and lack of organizational adaptation. The population dynamics theory deals in organizational births and deaths. But there is neither theoretical argument nor empirical evidence adduced to establish the earlier thesis that mortality reflects failure to adapt based upon organizational inertia, nor that newer entrants to the population provide a source of wide variation on which selection works, nor that creative change in the population comes from newer organizational entrants being better adapted to the new environment than the old organizations that died out.

There are elements in their findings which might lend themselves to such selection–survival arguments, for instance, that among national labour unions, craft unions precede industrial unions, but once industrial unions are established they flourish while craft unions decline in numbers. Nevertheless the empirical analyses of Hannan and Freeman (1989) are noticeable for a lack of any systematic attempt to test their selection–survival propositions through their inquiries. An exception is their investigation of how organizations which attain a fit between the generalism of their product lines and the variability of their environments have lower mortality rates than these organizations in misfit. Subsequently, Hannan *et al.* (1990) and also Barnett and Amburgey (1990) have examined the role of the size of the organization in density and competition. Isolated instances apart, Hannan and Freeman (1989) avoid explaining the survival of individual organizations by reference to their internal characteristics. Indeed, far from identifying organizations which survive and comparing them with organizations which fail, in order to reveal characteristics of the internal organization which would explain survival in terms of better fit between organization and its environment, there is almost no analysis at the level of individual organizations and their environments. The analysis is focused on the aggregate level of the population. Mortality is examined as the *rate* of organizational mortality, that is, the number of organizations failing to survive in any one year. The questions of which organizations these are and why those organizations rather than some other organizations in the population fail are mostly ignored in the analysis.

The neglect by Hannan and Freeman (1989) of organizational-level factors as causes of organizational mortality has been criticised by Petersen and Koput (1991a). They argue that the decrease in organizational mortality occurring with the initial increase in density that is supposedly due to increasing environmental legitimacy is actually due to unobserved heterogeneity, i.e., to differences between the organizations themselves. This says that the initially declining mortality is caused not by the external ecology but by internal organizational factors. More specifically, Petersen and Koput hold that differences in frailty between organizations mean that the frailer organizations are selected out and the population is increasingly composed of hardier organizations. As the population becomes hardier so the mortality rate declines. Thus the Darwinian process of selection of the fittest leads mortality to decline. This is an ingenious argument, for the decline in mortality is explained by the selection–survival mechanism itself, rendering the legitimacy postulate superfluous. Hence the selection–survival mechanism inherently produces a declining mortality rate with no need to postulate an independent causal force that comes from outside that mechanism. Thus the causal explanation of organizational mortality through legitimacy may be false. There is some debate as to the robustness of the simulation used by Petersen and Koput (1991a) (see Hannan *et al.*, 1991; Petersen and Koput, 1991b), but selection for survival logically implies a declining mortality rate. Here the sociological orientation of Hannan and Freeman (1989) may have led them to the idea of an effect of legitimacy whereas a more thoroughgoing positivism would have led to the expectation that selection would affect the organizational mortality rate.

Petersen and Koput (1991a: 406) give several examples of organization-level variables that have been neglected in population-ecology research yet which might lead to differences in frailty between organizations. By extension, frailty might occur because of misfit between the organizational structure and the contingency factors of the organization. Thus increasing structural fit might be an intra-organizational cause of the initial decline in the rate of organizational mortality as population size grows.

Similarly, organizational mortality rates rise at higher levels of population density due to increasing competition between members of the population for limited resources (Hannan and Freeman, 1989). Such a theory is one describing a general pressure experienced in common by all organizations. The theory does not differentiate between organizations by stating that some organizations will succumb to this pressure before others due to their internal characteristics. The ecological perspective deployed by Hannan and Freeman means focusing upon gross aspects of the environment (how many other organizations each has to compete with) and neglects the issue of how this environment interacts with specific features of the organization to determine organizational survival.

The empirical research does not study adaptation by organizations and does not demonstrate that population adaptation occurs by misfitted organizations dying out and being replaced in the population by newly born, better-fitting organizations. Organizations that die are not necessarily misfitted to their environment, since an organization could be in fit to the environment and yet die as a result of competitive pressure or limits in the resources and carrying capacity of its ecological niche. Thus population adaptation remains undemonstrated empirically. It follows that there is no evidence that population adaptation through births and deaths is as important as adaptation by individual organizations.

The organizational mortality studies tell us little about survival as the result of organizational selection by the environment for organizations adapted to their environment. The later theory and empirical work of Hannan and Freeman (1989) is not a logical fulfilment of their earlier theoretical statements about population-ecology and the importance of survival over adaptation. Thus the later work of Hannan and Freeman cannot be used to support the validity of their original criticisms of the then prevailing theories of organizational adaptation such as structural contingency theory. This discontinuity between the general assertions and the empirical work of Hannan and Freeman means that their population-ecology theory is much less of a coherent approach than it may first appear. There is continuity in the use of biological theory, biologically inspired terms (population, mortality, vital rates, etc.), esoteric mathematical models, emphasis on population and insistence upon the external perspective on organizations. But there is also discontinuity in that the original claim about the importance of selection over adaptation is never substantiated. The paradigm remains merely a posture of opposition to more mainstream organization theory views about adaptation. The research is not a programme which explicates and establishes the original thesis.

The restricted focus of the empirical work and theory of Hannan and Freeman (1989) mean that there are problems also in it contributing to organizational sociology and to managerial practice.

Relationship to organizational sociology The detailed theory-building and empirical work in population-ecology is premised around the external study of organizations rather than of their internal characteristics and indeed much of the focus is upon the population and its rise and fall. Almost nothing is said about internal organizational features such as organization structures or administrative systems or even about strategies (Davis and Powell, 1992: 354). Those organizational characteristics which are entered into the analysis are mainly given aspects of an organization which would be relatively fixed at founding and not readily changed, such as whether a firm is independent or a subsidiary or whether a union is craft or industrial. It is instructive to note that in the entire volume of Hannan and Freeman (1989) there is not a single organization chart, such is the lack of interest in questions of internal organization.

Similarly, in discussing their finding that increasing organizational age leads to decreasing organizational mortality, Hannan and Freeman (1989) note the possibility that this might mean that poorly adapted organizations or more poorly managed organizations fail when young and that the longer-lasting organizations are better in their adaptation or their management; yet Hannan and Freeman do not pursue this to identify what such factors might be – indeed they discuss such an interpretation as a kind of alternative, plausible explanation against which they would wish to protect their view that age and maturation *per se* are a cause of longevity. Yet questions of which internal organization characteristics of structure or strategy, etc. cause survival are central to any structural-functionalist theory of organization, including structural-functionalist theories of organizational structure (e.g., Etzioni, 1975). Moreover, which internal organizational characteristics lead to survival is of considerable interest to any sociological treatment of organizations, wherein questions of the structure of authority, power, status, communications, values, beliefs, perceptions, sociability, etc. within organizations and their effects upon survival have long been central to the sociology of organizations (Weber, 1968).

However, none of these internal characteristics is either studied or even figures in an articulated way in the specific ecological theoretical proposition. Indeed central to the explanatory efforts of Hannan and Freeman (1989) is a model in which the number of organizations being founded (or failing) in any one year is predicted by the number of other organizations in that sub-population, plus the number of organizations in some other sub-population and the number of organizations being founded or failing in the previous year. This is a core model of stark simplicity, bereft of any variables of a kind usually considered either sociological or organizational. There is precious little information here about these organizations which would register their nature as social human organizations rather than as inanimate objects. The core model is reminiscent of the approaches dubbed social arithmetic – the implication of such epithets being that the 'arithmetic' overwhelms the 'social'.

Similarly, many organization structure theories have been interested in the fit between structure and environment, that is, finding out what is the appropriate structure to give survival in each different environment. Contingency theorists have argued that structure needs to fit strategy or structural differentiation needs to fit size or organicness needs to fit task uncertainty, etc. (Burns and Stalker, 1961; Chandler, 1962; Blau, 1970). However, the studies by Hannan and Freeman (1989) shed no light, in terms of any of the pre-existing structural contingency theories, on which structure fits with which environment thereby to raise survival chances of organizations. Thus there is no link made between these studies and structural contingency theory, the prior structural paradigm.

The Hannan and Freeman (1989) studies do, however, examine the survival benefits to an organization of a fit between generalism and coarseness of grain of the environment. This is an interesting theory and set of findings, which potentially contributes to organization theory about environmental–organizational fit. However, the internal characteristic of organizations studied is the range of products and the supporting production technology which makes the range possible. The internal organizational characteristics of generalism might be classified as concerning product diversification strategy or production technology. It is not a characteristic of the organizational structure nor its administrative systems nor its human resource management practices, though these may be involved in some way unidentified by the research. Thus the intra-organizational characteristic whose fit with environmental grain coarseness affects organizational survival is not an attribute of the social, human organization or organization structure in any sociological sense.

Given the peculiarly inanimate way in which the organization is treated, in the specific ecological propositions and in the empirical studies, this may help us to understand why there is the repeated insistence throughout the volume by Hannan and Freeman (1989) that the ecological approach *is* a sociological approach. The authors needed to make this assertion given the tenuous nature of the connection between population-ecology and sociology.

This broad scope of population-ecology poses a real issue for it as a theory of organization structure. Hannan and Freeman (1989) present it as a sociological theory in the context of theories of organization theory and theories of structure. They also use the phrase 'strategy and structure' in discussing the phenomena to which their theory applies. However, while strategy covers quite a number of phenomena, even the concepts of strategy and structure cover only a fraction of all the different characteristics of an organization and its relationship with its environment, any of which can affect survival chances. Organizational survival may result from any organizational characteristic that helps fit with the environment and these may include characteristics other than organizational structure or strategy, such as marketing, product, manufacturing, design, finance and quality of management. Thus the factors that make for organizational survival and that could therefore be selected by the environment are not necessarily the factors such as organizational structure and strategy that organization theory emphasises. Thus there is no guarantee *a priori* that the effect of environmental selection on organizations will result in particular strategies or structures. An ecological approach comes with no in-built requirement that the phenomena that it explains will turn out to be either structure or strategy. The theory is so open that it could include just about anything. This increases the onus on population-ecology theory to demonstrate empirically that population adaptation (i.e., ecological selection) explains organizational structure and strategy. Moreover, for population-ecology to contribute to sociology the variables selected by the environment need to be shown to be sociological (i.e., aspects of organizational or social structure) and not inanimate variables such as technology, etc.

While the density-dependence effects display some generality they are not generalizable in other respects and this limits their explanatory value. The relationships between density and founding rates are curvilinear. However, Hannan and Freeman (1989) point out that the point of inflexion in the curve of founding rates, that is, where it turns from rising to falling, varies markedly from population to population, and even from sub-population to sub-population within a population. Thus the maximum value of founding rates appears to be situation-specific and not to be generalizable. In any case, Hannan and Freeman advance no argument about generality either theoretically or empirically. This means that the inflexion point or maximum value of the founding rates is *ad hoc* and not predicted by theory.

This situation reduces the theoretical interest of the explanatory effort. The rate of founding of organizations in a population must turn down at some value of the population density, otherwise the annual rate of founding of organizations of that type would increase indefinitely. This is impossible, so the founding rates must have a point of inflexion. Thus the density-dependence theory about founding dynamics, once it states that the founding rate initially rises with density, must say that the founding rate has some point of inflexion at some value of population density. By leaving open the location of the point of inflexion, organization ecology theory is really stating that the relative strength of the two opposing forces of legitimation and competition on founding rates is unknown. Such *ad hoc* argumentation is a deficiency from the viewpoint of scientific theory.

Relationship to managerial practice Organizational ecology has limited explanatory abilities. The narrow focus of the variables and the limited predictions of the theory do not make it a very managerially useful theory of organizations. Hannan and Freeman (1989) offer little or no managerial implications of their work. The absence of a focus on intra-organizational variables means also that there are few variables which managers could control to affect the fate of their organization. Perhaps managers could try to use this model to time the founding of their organization, that is entry into an industry. But the managers would really need to know in advance the inflexion point for the carrying capacity of their product-market niche, that is, when the environment would change from supportive to hostile. However, the absence of a predictable, general inflexion point precludes informed managerial action.

Once the organization exists, its chance of survival, as revealed by population-ecology analysis, is governed by the number of other organizations and the age of the focal organization. None of these variables is apparently much under the control of organizational management: organizations and their managers sit as passive victims waiting for the grim reaper.

Hannan and Freeman (1989) insist that this external focus of causality in explaining survival is precisely the special contribution of population-ecology. Moreover, the lack of managerial implications in their work is consistent with the avowed intent of organizational ecology to rescue organizational analysis from the supposedly baleful influence of management theory and management schools under which it had fallen and to thereby regain organizational analysis for sociology. In the event, population-ecology seems to lack any developed sociological analysis or any developed analysis of how organizations are organized or to what effect. The only output of organizations in population-ecology is that they go on existing, which hardly meets concerns such as competitive efficiency, innovation, safety, environmental friendliness, social responsibility, wealth generation, quality, employment record or humaneness.

Rate of organizational change relative to the environment

In articulating population-ecology theory, Hannan and Freeman (1989) introduce a qualification which renders the theory seemingly more plausible but which does so by blunting its thrust as a well-integrated paradigm.

The central thrust of population-ecology theory is that such a theory is needed in place of traditional adaptation theory because organizations change little. However, later, Hannan and Freeman (1989: 70) state that organizations do change but the maladaptation arises through the organizational rate of change being too slow for the environmental rate of change:

Claiming that organizational structures are subject to strong inertial forces is not the same as claiming that organizations never change. Rather, it means that organizations respond relatively slowly to the occurrence of threats and opportunities in their environments. Therefore, structural inertia must be defined in relative and dynamic terms. It refers to comparisons of the typical rates of change of the processes identified in the previous paragraph. In particular, structures of organizations have high inertia when the speed of reorganization is much lower than the rate at which environmental conditions change. Thus the concept of inertia, like fitness, refers to a correspondence between the behavioral capabilities of a class of organizations and their environment.

Yet there is a theoretical problem here because this statement runs foul of another theoretical stricture by Hannan and Freeman (1989). They insist that it is unhelpful to treat organizations as existing in some undifferentiated environment when that environment in reality is itself composed of other organizations: competitors, suppliers, and so on. But surely each of these organizations is itself, according to the theory, subject to the laws of population-ecology theory, namely it is governed by inertia and so is changing neither very much nor very rapidly. Thus in a world composed of inertial organizations, how can any one organization be faced with a rapidly changing environment?

For an organization whose environment is composed of large and therefore inertial organizations (according to population-ecology theory), such a focal organization faces limited environmental change. Therefore, for these focal organizations, if they can change, their rate may be adequate to match the slow rate of change in their environment and therefore their relative rate of change is fast enough for them to be able to adapt to their environments. Therefore organizational structure would be shaped by adaptation of individual organizations and not by selection by the environment. Hence population-ecology theory would not apply in the situation of an environment composed of large organizations – a major domain limitation.

The second type of case would be an organization whose environment was composed of small organizations which according to Hannan and Freeman (1989) are inherently more flexible and less subject to inertia than larger organizations. An environment composed of smaller organizations would be thus characterized by higher rates of change. Moreover, apart from environmental change originating within each of the environing organizations, over time there would also be changes caused by changes in the composition of the set of environing organizations. According to Hannan and Freeman, compared with large organizations, small organizations are subject to higher birth and death rates. This fact would be expected to introduce constant change into the set of organizations composing the environment of any one organization. Thus organizations facing an environment of smaller organizations would face a higher rate of environmental change than organizations in an environment composed of larger organizations. However, if the focal organization was small and therefore flexible there would be the chance that its rate of change would be fast enough to match in relative terms the environmental rate of change, and therefore the focal organization could make adaptive change. Therefore, for small organizations facing environments composed of other small organizations, structural change would often be accomplished by individual organizational adaptation and accordingly the role for explanation of change through population-level differential survival would be less.

Consider then the case of the large organization in an environment composed of small organizations. The environment would change rapidly but the focal organization being large and inflexible would change little (according to population-ecology theory); therefore relative organizational change would be little and not adequate to produce adaptation and, therefore, population-level survival processes would govern structural change. This is the only scenario which is internally consistent with the proposition, advanced by Hannan and Freeman (1989: 70), that organizations can change and yet fail to change enough relative to their environments, and so fail to adapt. Hence the only scenario within population-ecology theory which allows such relatively inadequate intra-organizational change is the scenario of a large organization confronting an environment of small organizations.

This means a whale confronting minnows. It means that the large capitalist corporation is a near helpless victim of change wrought by fast-moving small firms, a Goliath surrounded by Davids. Yet this is not at all the image of the corporate world advanced throughout by Hannan and Freeman (1989). Such a scenario would break with the semi-radical political view of the corporate world which is the received view in much of contemporary sociology. It is this opposite scenario which Hannan and Freeman invoke repeatedly with their image of large firms enjoying long life expectancy based on collusive arrangements with the environment, protection by government regulation, and ossified, institutionalized expectations of the professional bodies, banks, funding agencies and governments. This is a world of corporate stability and coy mutuality, the world of latter-day revisionist Marxian critiques of big business as monopoly capitalism (Baran and Sweezy, 1968). This is an environment in which as Hannan and Freeman (1989) state, large firms are reinforced for being reliable, accountable and reproducible, i.e., business as usual.

The image of the large corporation as a Goliath constantly endangered by fast-moving Davids is more a theoretical argument of those liberal economists who insist that those large organizations which look like monopolies and oligopolies are really hard-pressed by competitors from the dynamic small business sector or other large firms, and that their markets are not captive but contestable (Baumol *et al.*, 1982). This imagery is more the line of the University of Chicago Economics Department than it is of the left-leaning sociologists. Thus founders the attempt by Hannan and Freeman (1989) to construct an argument that organizational change can fail to be adaptive because of a low rate of change relative to the environment. It logically means that the domain of population-ecology theory shrinks just to large organizations in environments of small organizations, a severe limitation in scope, and one whose ideological connotations are liable to embarrass some organizational sociologists. The proposition that large organizations in an environment of small organizations are peculiarly subject to ecological selection is contradicted by the lower mortality of larger organizations than smaller ones (Hannan and Freeman, 1989). Thus the attempt to make the theory more realistic results only in incoherence.

Summary of problems of population-ecology

In summary, population-ecology theory draws on a biological root metaphor. It asserts that organizational change occurs through selection rather than adaptation. In the Aldrichian version the theory is elaborated in eclectic fashion via the statement of various mechanisms underlying the variation–selection–retention process. In Hannan and Freeman (1989) the argument for selection is buttressed by the theory of organizational inertia. However, the later theoretical work largely ignores either environmental selection or organizational inertia. Instead they draw again on biology for the basis of a theory of population dynamics which is distinguishable from their original concerns and which is not a fulfilment of their earlier programmatic proclamation about the need to study selection. While population-ecology theory spans the eclectic theory and often qualitative case history material presented by Aldrich, on the one hand, and the starkly narrow mathematical–statistical exercises of Hannan and Freeman on the other hand, there is a common rejection of individual organization adaptation or any notion that management frequently guides such an organizationally rational process. Above all, the varieties of population-ecology maintain the theory to be distinct from other theories of organization such as structural contingency theory and thereby preserve the status of population-ecology as a distinct paradigm.

Some fifteen years or more after the announcement of the population-ecology theory of organizations one might have hoped that its proponents would have documented their assertions about selection processes shaping organizations. One would have hoped that the relative validity of theories of selection and adaptation might have been established empirically. One might have anticipated the creation of a contingency metatheory which would identify which organizational phenomena are shaped by survival and which by adaptation. Any progress towards such a goal would mean that previously neglected selection effects would have been articulated and brought within an integrated organization theory together with the more conventional adaptation processes, thereby enhancing organization theory. Yet there seems to have been little or no progress made towards such a goal. In particular, population-ecologists have not contributed towards such a resolution. Not only have they been disinclined to incorporate adaptation into their empirical studies, they have not prosecuted the study of selection in their work. Empirical tests of their assertions about environmental selection would run the risk of revealing them to be false. Theoretical and empirical work combining selection and adaptation approaches would break down the identity of population-ecology as a distinct paradigm. Thus a task for others is the study of the relative prevalence of selection and adaptation and the articulation of a metatheory which incorporates both processes. This is what is required if the field is to attain integration as a coherent body of knowledge.

Integration of population-ecology and agency theories

Rao and Neilsen (1992) present an attempt to integrate population-ecology and agency theories in an investigation of organizational mortality of savings and loan associations (SLAs). They examine the effects on the mortality of SLAs of ecological factors such as the density of competitors and the regulatory environment as well as organizational age and size. A large number of SLAs are studied over several decades and the type of data and method of analysis are of the population-ecology type. To this is added a theoretical argument, drawing upon agency theory, that governance structure affects the extent of residual loss and therefore competitive efficiency. Residual loss is argued as inherently greater in mutual than in stock-based SLAs where stockholder property rights lead to greater discipline upon management (Rao and Neilsen, 1992). The results lend support in that organizational mortality is greater in mutual than stock SLAs. Thus by examining an internal organizational feature – in this case, the governance structure – the effect of this organizational feature on mortality can be identified.

Given that governance is of concern in agency theory, the inclusion of the organizational governance variable in the population-type study allows an integration between the population-ecology and agency theory approaches. This study is to be welcomed both as extending population-ecology studies to reveal the effect of intra-organizational factors on population vital rates and also as a step towards integration of population-ecology and agency theories. It remains to be seen whether a more integrative approach such as that of Rao and Neilsen will become the norm among proponents of the population-ecology paradigm.

Problems in applying the Darwinian metaphor to organizations

The Darwinian theory of natural selection contains three necessary and related ideas: reproduction, genetic inheritance and high birth and death rates. These refer to mechanisms in nature that allow natural selection to work. Yet these mechanisms are largely absent in organizations, rendering the Darwinian theory mainly inapplicable therein.

In nature, creatures come into being through reproduction, i.e., through prior creatures replicating themselves. The design of the newborn creature is determined by genetic inheritance so that it is a reproduction of its parents. Those members of the species which survive long enough to reach reproductive adulthood pass on their particular genes. Their offspring are shaped by the genes of their parents and so will be very like their parents. Natural selection produces evolution because reproduction is genetic and therefore offspring are very like the survivors of the previous generation, rather than the unfit creatures who were culled. In the absence of inherited genes, offspring would not reflect the form taken by their parent and might equally be like the members of their species which did *not* survive and were culled before reproductive age. Thus newborn creatures would be no more adapted to the environment than the previous generation.

Thus the form taken by biological organisms such as plants or animals is determined by their genes. The organisms are an exact outcome of the code of their genes. There is no such mechanism for organization structures. The immediate determinant of organizational forms is the decisions of their managers. These are shaped by contingency factors such as size or product diversity and by goals such as the desired level of innovation, but none of this is genetic. The decision processes are, relative to genetic inheritance, quite plastic. This is shown by the way organizations can change their structure radically over their lifetime from small, centralized firms dominated by an owner-manager to large, decentralized, multidivisional conglomerates. New organizations are not formed by reproduction and genetic inheritance. They are started independently or as a spin-off from an existing corporation or government. There is no genetic code which determines, from conception, the whole form of the organization for life. Organizations are influenced by the ideas of their founders and of successive managers, but these can vary considerably over the organizational life-cycle. The play of ideas and influence upon the structure of an organization is inherently variable and fluid.

The absence of genetic reproduction of organizations means that new organizations do not faithfully reproduce the form taken by the successful organizations (the survivors) of the previous generation. Doubtless managers will attempt to learn lessons from knowing which of the previous 'generation' of organizations survived and which failed, but this is inherently less certain than having your parents' genes inside you. With the absence of genetic reproduction, new organizations have some probability of taking the form of the organizations which failed. Thus the population 'learns' only to a limited degree. The newly forming set of organizations *may* even have, on average, organizational forms *less* suited to the environment than the presently surviving organizations. Thus without the mechanism of genetic reproduction there is no theoretical reason why a population of organizations in a constant environment should converge towards the most appropriate form for the niche. Thus 'organizational evolution' is not nearly as determinate and environmentally crafted as is natural evolution.

The rate at which members of a species are born is much higher than that needed for steady-state replacement of the adult population. This over-abundance of births seems wasteful of nature until the naturalist recognizes that the multitude born provide a wide field of variant creatures most of which will be culled fairly rapidly (Boorstin, 1983). There can be rapid selection of the fittest through high rates of mortality of the unfit because the high birth rate constantly supplies new members of the population. Thus the multitudinous young provide culling fodder to facilitate rapid evolution through high rates of mortality of the maladapted.

Thus the proposition that rates of births and deaths in a population be high flows directly from the idea of natural selection. If the characteristics of a population are shaped by differential survival, the more members of the population that are culled the stronger the resultant population reflects the survival process. If only a few members are culled, then the population at the end of the period will closely resemble that at the start – differential survival will have had little effect. If many members are culled, the resultant population will strongly bear the marks of the survival process. If mortality rates are high then after several periods there will be few members of the population left for further culling. Thus an influx of new members of the species is needed in order that the high mortality rate can continue, and allow selection to continue strongly. High birth and death rates are necessary for natural selection to work strongly and quickly in shaping the characteristics of a population. Low birth and death rates mean that survival pressures will exercise a weak pressure in the medium term and a strong pressure only over the long term.

For natural selection to explain organizational change, the rate of change in the population due to natural selection must be as high as the rate of organizational change. High rates of change due to natural selection will occur where there are high birth and death rates for organizations. Thus the population-ecology approach to explaining organizational change becomes more plausible if high rates of birth–mortality can be established for each particular population of organizations.

For certain sections of the organizational population there seems little sign of these overabundant birth and death rates. The upper reaches of the corporate world show considerable stability. For US corporations, Chandler (1977: 371) shows that:

Of the 278 largest industrials in 1917, ... only 14 had been liquidated, dissolved or discontinued by 1967. All others that were no longer independent enterprises had been incorporated into the hierarchies of existing companies.

Hence there is a low death rate of large firms.

For large corporations the new births are these corporations which become large enough to join the large-size category. Fligstein (1990a: 65) shows that the number of new entrants to the largest hundred US corporations is an average of only about twenty each ten years and that this held over a sixty-year period, 1919–79. This means that, on average each year, only about two firms 'die' or leave that population and only about two firms are 'born' or enter into that population. In fact fifty firms remained in the largest hundred corporations for the entire sixty-year period (64). Thus half the population membership is stable for over half a century. None of the change in this group of fifty can be attributable to ecological selection and all of the change in this group is adaptation by on-going organizations. The other fifty places in the largest hundred are subject to change in membership at an average approximate birth and death rate of only 4 per cent per annum. The slow rate of population membership change in this group means that little of the observed change in characteristics of the largest hundred such as technology, strategy or structure can be explained by ecological selection. Yet Fligstein (1985, 1991) demonstrates a large amount of change in strategy and structure among the largest hundred corporations over the sixty-year period: the proportion of corporations with the undiversified (i.e., dominant-product) strategy declined from 90 to 22 per cent (Fligstein, 1991: 326 and 327, table 13.1) and with the multidivisional structure increased from 2 to 84 per cent (Fligstein, 1985: 385).

To analyse in more detail how these changes came about we need to examine each decade the difference between those remaining on the list and those leaving or joining. For example, in the period 1948–59, nineteen of the largest hundred corporations increased their diversification strategy from the dominant-product to the related-products category; of these, eighteen cases were diversification by corporations which remained in the largest-hundred population and only one case was caused by changes in the population (eight of the corporations that joined the population were related-product at that time whereas seven of the corporations that left the population were related-products at that time, i.e., a net of one) (Fligstein, 1991: 330). Thus strategic diversification of this type among the largest US corporations was overwhelmingly due to change by members of the population (i.e., adaptation by on-going organizations) rather than to change in the membership of the population (i.e., population adaptation through maladapted organizations being less successful and so being replaced by better-adapted, more successful organizations among the population of the largest corporations). Similarly, in the same period (1948–59), thirty of the largest hundred corporations adopted the division-alized structure; of these, twenty-three cases were divisionalization by corporations which remained in the largest-hundred population and only seven were caused by changes in the population (thirteen of the corpor-ations that joined the population were divisionalized at that time whereas six of the corporations that left the population were divisionalized at that time, i.e., a net of seven) (Fligstein, 1985: 386). Thus divisionalization among the largest US corporations was preponderantly due to change by members of the population rather than to change in the membership of the population. Adaptive change in both strategy and structure among the population of the largest hundred US corporations was due far more to internal adaptation by individual organizations than to selection winnow-ing the population and altering its membership.

In this analysis we have termed as 'birth' and 'death', entry and exit, respectively, from the population of large corporations. Of course, corporations which enter the population of large corporations almost invariably have grown from being medium-sized corporations, so that they are not literally being born (i.e., founded), thus the birth rates quoted above are overestimates of the true birth rate. Similarly, as seen above from Chandler (1977: 371), few large corporations disband and so many of the 'deaths' included above are corporations leaving the list of the largest hundred corporations through merger or decline in size relative to those that remain on the list, so the death rate is also an overestimate of the true death rate. Hence, small as they are, the above quoted birth and death rates for large corporations overstate the true birth and death rates.

The high birth–high mortality scenario of Darwinism therefore fails to apply to large business firms. Thus population-ecology is not a valid explanatory theory for large corporate structures, because the underlying Darwinian premises are not met for large corporations in many industries. Thus adaptation in the population of large firms such as the technological and internal organizational changes therein cannot be explained by ecological selection to any great extent. Whether these sorts of changes among *small* firms are more the result of ecological selection would need to be demonstrated through empirical research.

In summary, population-ecology analysis of organizational change departs from the Darwinian model of natural evolution through selection in several, crucial ways. Organizational start-ups are not governed by genes. Therefore new organizations do not reflect previous survival processes as strongly as in natural selection. Explanation by survival is more compelling where birth and mortality rates are high in a population, as in Darwinian natural evolution. However, for some categories of organizational type, such as large corporations, birth and mortality rates are low. Given these differences between biological entities and organizations, population-ecology will never be as important in organization theory as Darwinian evolution is in the field of biology.

Evolution works in biology because of concrete biological mechanisms such as genes which are transmitted through reproduction. The population-ecology theory of organizations is devoid of such mechanisms as they do not exist for organizations. Yet without such mechanisms as genes the processes which produce evolution through selection cannot operate to nearly the same degree. Novel organization theories may take some inspiration from the natural sciences by drawing analogies with them. However, a *complete* set of analogous processes needs to be established before the explanation is compelling. Science works not only by drawing analogies and constructing metaphors (Morgan, 1980), but also by *discovering* real mechanisms and concrete things (Boorstin, 1983). There is more to social science theory-building than word play. One can say that

'The Moon is a balloon', but this does not make it so; it remains a hunk of rock. Analogies are suggestive, but discovery of real mechanisms is required for theorizing to be useful.

Validity of population-ecology compared with structural contingency theory

Population-ecology theory asserts that adaptation is mainly at the level of the population through birth and death processes, rather than through adaptation at the level of the individual organization. However, internal organizational characteristics are almost ignored in the present population-ecology empirical studies. Therefore population-ecology research has to date not demonstrated that internal organizational characteristics are shaped through population-level adaptation via birth and death. The idea that population adaptation is more important than adaptation by individual organizations is unproven. Even the more modest idea that population adaptation is a significant means of organizational adaptation is unproven. Population-ecology has yet to show the existence of population-level organizational adaptation, whereas structural contingency theory has shown individual organizational adaptation of organizational structure. Research shows that organizations do change their structures in adaptive ways (see chapter 2). For example, as organizations diversify they shift from functional to divisional structures (Chandler, 1962). As organizations face a need to innovate they adopt more organic structures (Burns and Stalker, 1961). And these structural adaptations are evident in large organizations that have enjoyed success. Thus there is evidence supporting the structural contingency theory of adaptive change in on-going (surviving) organizations. At present the structural contingency theory of organizational adaptation is better supported than the population-ecology theory of adaptation.

Structural contingency theory offers an answer to the question of the development of organizational structure. However, all of this is about organizations which already exist and changes which occur during their life. The birth of an organization, that is, the process whereby an organization comes into existence, and the preconditions which facilitate that, has been a topic on which traditional structural contingency theory has been silent. Therefore, organizational birth is a topic area about which population-ecology makes a distinct contribution. In this way population-ecology complements structural contingency theory to give a fuller organization theory.

Conclusions

Population-ecology theory draws from Darwinism the idea that organizational form is shaped at the population level through birth and death processes of organizations, rather than through change by individual organizations. Thus movement into fit comes about by population-level processes of survival rather than through individual organizational adaptation. This is a theory of change and adaptation which is different from the preceding organization theory of structural contingency theory, which deals in adaptive change being made by individual organizations.

Both structural contingency theory and population-ecology theory are functionalist theories which explain how fit between organization and environment is attained. Both also see the environment as demanding, and the organization bowing to its dictates as a given. With this relationship between structural contingency theory and population-ecology theory, they are potentially complementary. Population-ecology theory could draw upon structural contingency theory as one source of theoretical definitions of fit between organization and environment. The two theories could further complement each other in that structural contingency theory would explain those cases where fit is attained through adaptation by the individual organization and population-ecology theory would explain those cases where fit is attained by population processes of organizational birth and death. However, population-ecology has not developed in this complementary fashion; rather, it has been developed as a rival theory to structural contingency, and as a distinct paradigm, antithetical to structural contingency theory.

Population-ecology theory has been constructed in the manner of a radical sociological analysis, highly critical of established structural contingency theory and seeking to rescue organization theory from the clutches of management-oriented business schools. Hence population-ecology maintains an oppositional stance to ideas that individual organizations adapt and that this adaptation is brought about by managers acting rationally in the interests of the organization. Population-ecology theory sees organizational change as more random and blind in characteristic, and internal organizational management as political and self-interested so that inertia comes to prevail over adaptation. Thus it paints a picture of substantially irrational organizational management and organizational change.

The key assertions of population-ecology – that individual organizations fail to adapt, that organizational adaptation comes about at the population rather than the individual organization level, through misfitted organizations dying out and the birth of better-fitted organizations, that organizational change is blind variation, and that managers are politically self-serving and fail to guide their organizations in rational ways – all remain as assertions unproven by population-ecologists after more than a decade of research. Neither the qualitative-historical approach of Aldrich nor the quantitative approach of Freeman, Hannan and their colleagues has provided much in the way of crucial tests of these contentions.

The mainstay of quantitative research in population-ecology, rather, has been population arithmetic. This research is directed at showing that organizational births and deaths are affected by the number of organizations in the population and like characteristics of the population. There is evidence that these relationships replicate, with subsequent studies confirming the original findings, and generalize, with the original findings being shown to occur in other settings. Accordingly, such research contributes to organization theory through the study of a neglected topic, organizational births and deaths, and their explanation by environmental characteristics. However, this in no way tests the broader theoretical assertions about how fit occurs, the random nature of organizational change and the intra-organizational managerial processes, for internal organizational characteristics are largely unexamined. Specifically, internal organizational structure is not studied as to its role in organizational deaths.

Thus the attack on structural contingency by population-ecologists, though widely taken seriously, remains empty rhetoric. In contrast, structural contingency theory provides evidence that adaptation into fit comes about by adaptation of individual organizations to their contingencies and their environment, and population-ecology mostly just ignores this work rather than offering a reasoned critique. At the present, there is little reason to see the attack on structural contingency theory by population-ecology, or any moves to replace structural contingency theory by population-ecology, as scientifically credible.

4   A critique of institutional theory

The core idea of institutional theory is that organizations are shaped by the institutional environment which surrounds them. Influential ideas are those which have been institutionalized, that is have been accorded legitimacy and have become the accepted way of thinking about organizational arrangements for organizations of that type. The legitimation process is often furthered through acceptance of those organizational ideas by key legitimating bodies in the society such as the state and the professions (DiMaggio and Powell, 1983; Zucker, 1987). The ideas become embodied in language and symbol, channelling thought to such an extent that other notions of how to organize become unthinkable and the normative concept of organization becomes taken-for-granted, precluding even the concept of alternative organizational forms (Zucker, 1987). The organization exists within an organizational field of other organizations of its type and one organizational form becomes institutionalized within that field as the legitimated form to which the organizations in the field conform through adaptation of their own form. This is a process of imitative or mimetic adaptation by one organization of elements from another (DiMaggio and Powell, 1983). Adoption of the legitimated structure by an organization helps it secure funding and eases its transactions with other organizations. The societally preferred structure may also be imposed on the organization by professional standards or by force from the state (DiMaggio and Powell, 1983).

Institutional theory is popularly known for its emphasis on organizations as being about ritual and symbol. This is the basis of the widely received critique by Perrow (1985b) which is entitled 'Overboard with myth and symbols' and which laments the lack of attention to organizational and social realities in institutionalism. While sharing the concerns of Perrow, the present critique comes from the functionalist, contingency theory direction and so adds other criticisms to those made by him.

The distinctiveness of the institutional paradigm

The nub of institutional theory is the idea that organizations are social systems whose shape is influenced by the wider social, cultural and symbolic systems in which they are located, rather than tools structured for effective work. Scott (1987) states that these two views of organizations are essentially complementary and thus that organizations are both institutions and instrumentalities. This accords well with, indeed is, the traditional structural-functional view that organizations both have instrumental goal-attainment aspects and are socio-cultural systems of norms, values and shared meanings (Parsons, 1951). Nevertheless, analyses conducted within the institutional school assert that many organizational structures are to be understood not as rational adaptations to their contingencies in the technical-instrumentalities mode, but by reference to normative suasion, imposition, legitimation requirements, myths, beliefs, thoughtways and such non-technical-instrumental factors (e.g., Meyer and Scott, 1983; Tolbert and Zucker, 1983; Baron et al., 1986).

Clearly, beliefs, norms and legitimation requirements, thoughtways and other socio-cultural phenomena could be consistent with technical-instrumental requirements. For example, one could legitimate the organization structure of a business by showing that it was the optimal structure to attain the goals of that organization. Similarly, beliefs and norms could embody technically optimal decision rules about structure – or the best available rules given limitations on present knowledge. There is no *a priori*, logical requirement that technical-instrumental and socio-cultural factors differ in their content.

Notwithstanding the statesmanlike rapprochement offered by Scott (1987), the typical arguments erected by institutionalists are along the lines that institutional explanations of organization structure are in conflict with technical-instrumental contingency type explanations, or institutional explanations are pursued independently with no explicit resolution of the two perspectives. Thus institutional theory – like the other newer organization theory paradigms – has the characteristics of a rival theory to structural contingency theory. In empirical work contingency explanations are argued to be inferior to institutional explanations (Baron et al., 1986). Institutionalist analyses tend to challenge functionalist, contingency theory by depicting organizations as irrational and their managers as duplicitous, as will be seen below.

DiMaggio and Powell (1991: 32) note some signs of increasing accommodation between institutional and other organizational theories, namely population-ecology and economic theories. However, these examples make up just two chapters (Orrù et al., 1991; Singh et al., 1991) in a book of sixteen chapters (Powell and DiMaggio, 1991) indicating the presently limited degree of integration between these organization theories. Thus institutionalism largely retains its status of a separate organization theory paradigm.

The institutional theory of organizations

At several places institutional theorists advance an ideationalist theory of society. Causative factors such as economic transactions are argued to be in turn the product of larger ideational factors which bring modern society and its organizations into existence. These ideationalist factors include the concept of the individual, Christianity and so on (Meyer and Scott, 1983; Friedland and Alford, 1991; Jepperson and Meyer, 1991). These are large questions. They concern society and are rightly the province of the sociologist. They point to the constellation of factors which undergird modern society and which have been discussed by sociological theorists (Parsons, 1966; Weber, 1968). It is less clear that they are central research questions for organizational analysis, which is more concerned with the variations between modern organizations rather than studying the societal parameters which set the bounds within which modern organizations are formed. Accordingly, most of the institutional organization theory literature (DiMaggio and Powell, 1983, 1991; Zucker, 1987, etc.) is focused on the organization and accounting for differences or similarities in comparative analysis. Since this is the generic province of organizational theory and research the discussion herein will do likewise.

DiMaggio and Powell (1983) theorize that organizations are shaped by powerful forces outside themselves by processes which include mimicry and compliance. Zucker (1987) propounds the idea of late adoption as being less functionalist than early adoption, and emphasizes the role of state compulsion. Meyer and Scott (1983) argue that while organizations are under strong pressure to conform to societal mores they only give the appearance of conformity, and maintain separate structures at operational levels. The work of DiMaggio and Powell may be grouped together with that of Zucker as the theory of institutional isomorphism. The work of Meyer and Scott is distinct and offers a loose-coupling theory of organizations. It will be convenient to consider these two groups separately, in that order. For each strand the main theory will be reviewed and then the supporting empirical evidence will be examined. Notwithstanding this separation, the two groups are interrelated, as will be seen.

After these two variants of established institutionalism have been considered, a more recent development in institutional theory will be analysed, the newly proclaimed cognitive turn. The attempt to forge a link between the institutional and population-ecology paradigms will then be examined. The analysis will finally reflect on the diversity of ideas in institutional theory and evaluate the research programme overall.

Institutional isomorphism: theory and evidence

DiMaggio and Powell (1983) argue that the trend towards increasing bureaucracy and efficiency spurred by competition, as described by Weber (1968), has changed. The trend towards increasing bureaucratization continues, but the spur is no longer competition and the search for efficiency. Bureaucracy has become the norm to which organizations increasingly conform as part of increasing homogenization of organizational structure. Much of this is occurring under pressure from the state and from the professions. DiMaggio and Powell (1983) use the term institutional isomorphism to mean that organizations of the same type, which compose what is termed an organizational field, come increasingly to resemble each other. Three sub-processes are identified: coercive, mimetic and normative isomorphism. Each will be considered in turn.

Coercive isomorphism refers to organizations adopting certain features because of pressure from the state, other organizations or the wider society. These pressures are of many sorts. They include force, legal compulsion, fear of suit, gaining legitimation, gaining funding, subordination to a parent organization, need to fit with a technical system (e.g., telecommunication interconnections), conformity to institutionalized rules, and need to be acceptable to powerful, hierarchically structured organizations and rationalizing ideologies. Such coercive means may be formal or informal and may lead to compliance or only to a ritualistic appearance of compliance (DiMaggio and Powell, 1991: 67).

Mimetic isomorphism refers to imitation of one organization by another (DiMaggio and Powell, 1991: 69). When uncertain about how to proceed, an organization may copy another. This modelling focuses on organizations seen as being 'more legitimate or successful' by the adopting organization (70). For an organization with a problem to seek the solution by taking some element from a successful organization would normally be called rational, especially under uncertainty, that is, in the absence of scientific knowledge about the most effective solution. Such a process is compatible with the functionalist theory of adaptation and with the idea of the diffusion of innovation within functionalism (Rogers, 1962). However, DiMaggio and Powell (1991) distance their view from functionalism by the stipulation that adoption may be prompted by the search for legitimation. This moves causality away from technical efficiency and towards ideology. They note that companies adopt quality circles and quality-of-work procedures to boost their 'legitimacy' and 'to demonstrate they are at least trying to improve working conditions' (DiMaggio and Powell, 1991: 69). Similarly, a television station adopted a consultant's recommendation to switch from a functional to a multidivisional structure. Its executives were sceptical of any performance benefits, but thought that financiers would recognize that the '"the sleepy nonprofit station was becoming more business-minded"' (70). Through such examples DiMaggio and Powell play up the idea of structural change as a search for legitimation rather than as being effective. By implication, the managers of the mimicking organization are more concerned with outside approval than with internal effectiveness of their organization.

The inclusion of both success and legitimation in the formal definition renders the theory ambiguous. By referring to success the theory could, on occasion, eschew criticisms that it was anti-functionalist. But it could then emphasize the legitimation aspect through theory statement and example, and thereby give a quite different depiction of organizations, and one that is anti-functionalist in operational effectiveness. Moreover, since many organizational structure decisions are uncertain because of the paucity of scientific knowledge, many decisions are liable to be influenced by imitation of successful organizations. However, the same element of subjectivity opens the door to scepticism about the effectiveness of any new organizational structure (DiMaggio and Powell, 1991). Some organizational members are likely to be more sceptical than others and this allows the interpretation that an organizational change is made to impress outsiders when it may have been made for reasons of operational effectiveness, and may be effective.

Only an analysis that examines the objective consequences of an adopted structure can establish whether it is successful or not and thus whether it is rational and functional. Otherwise what is described as legitimate may be successful and may be legitimate because it is successful. In such a situation assertions that the structure is ritualistic rather than rational become groundless. As will be seen, the institutional theory literature repeatedly fails to make analyses of objective effectiveness. This does not prevent strong assertions being made that structures are ritualistic and not operationally rational. This lacuna in the methodology of numerous institutional studies combines with the theory's ambiguity (around success and legitimacy) to make an argument which is quite slippery. It provides a ready means of rhetorically depicting organizations as ritualistic and irrational without scientific proof. Examples of these problems will be seen below in a discussion of the empirical literature.

Normative isomorphism is related to professionalization (DiMaggio and Powell, 1991: 70). Professional groups define their occupation cognitively and provide legitimation for their profession and for professional autonomy. The recent professionalization of administration extends the influence of professions to organizational form. Common models of organization are imbibed in professional training. Professional socialization combines with selection to homogenize the administrators and their outlook. While competition might intervene to promote adoption of effective structures, in some sectors, such as hospitals and others with professionalized personnel, market imperfections reduce effectiveness considerations and replace them with status competition which plays to professional criteria.

DiMaggio and Powell (1991: 71) argue also that the state reinforces the power of the professional bodies, making their preferences either more or less mandatory, and also that conformity to professional dictates is reinforced where professionals sit on funding committees (72). Again, DiMaggio and Powell point out that government recognition of certain organizations makes them role models for other organizations which seek legitimacy or which hope for funding (72). These causal mechanisms seem to be the same as the state power referred to under coercive isomorphism and the latter mechanism seems also to refer to the process of mimetic isomorphism. DiMaggio and Powell offer no discussion of these overlaps nor their significance for the structure of the theory, nor of how the distinctions they make between coercive, mimetic and normative types of isomorphism are to be maintained. This conceptual looseness seems to be a feature of institutional theory writing and sits oddly with work that would be taken as theory.

DiMaggio and Powell (1991: 73) make clear their basically anti-functionalist stance when they state of all three types of isomorphism:

Each of the institutional isomorphic processes can be expected to proceed in the absence of evidence that it increases internal organizational efficiency. To the extent that organizational effectiveness is enhanced, the reason is often that organizations are rewarded for their similarity to other organizations in their fields. This similarity can make it easier for organizations to transact with other organizations, to attract career-minded staff, to be acknowledged as legitimate and reputable, and to fit into administrative categories that define eligibility for public and private grants and contracts. None of this, however, ensures that conformist organizations do what they do more efficiently than do their more deviant peers.

Thus the benefits flowing from conformity are not of the internal operational kind with which both functionalism generally, and structural contingency theory more specifically, have traditionally been concerned.

DiMaggio and Powell (1991: 76) also write that to test their predictions about institutional isomorphism, that is, increasing homogenization: 'the best indicator of isomorphic change is a decrease in variation and diversity, which could be measured by lower standard deviations of the values of selected indicators in a set of organizations'.

Zucker (1987: 443) asserts that legitimated organizational forms are carried by language and symbols, becoming taken-for-granted, which precludes even the consideration of alternative organizational forms by their administrators. Also, Tolbert and Zucker (1983) advance a variation on the idea of mimetic adoption. They argue that organizations which adopt a feature after numerous other organizations have adopted it are more likely to do so out of conformity to a norm than are organizations that adopt the feature earlier out of considerations of operational effectiveness. Thus the proposition is that late adoption is more institutionalist and less functionalist than early adoption.

Having outlined and briefly discussed the organizational theory of institutional isomorphism, the empirical evidence which is adduced in its support will now be examined. The material will be considered under two headings, mimetic isomorphism and coercive isomorphism, as institutional studies of isomorphism fall mostly into these two classes.

Mimetic isomorphism

The studies of mimetic isomorphism, that is, of one organization mimicking another, may be grouped according to the four issues of increasing institutional isomorphism, late adoption, tradition and mimicry.

Increasing institutional isomorphism One of the findings in a study by Meyer *et al.* (1988) is increasing institutional isomorphism, that is, increasing similarity across the different states of the USA indicating the increased homogenization of the nation. This reflected the institutional processes of conformity and rationalization. In her review, Zucker (1987: 452) quotes these findings in detail:

Institutionalized fields limit the direction and content of change, causing 'an inexorable push toward homogenization' (DiMaggio and Powell, 1983: 148). For example, when measured by coefficients of variation, educational structures in 48 states converge dramatically over a 40-year time span (Meyer *et al.* 1987: tables 3 and 5): the ratio of superintendents to districts decreased variability across states from 1.05 to .29 and state education agency staffs from 1.43 to .80.

While this sounds like strong support for institutional isomorphism, a closer examination reveals the opposite picture.

Meyer *et al.* (1988: 150) present their results in terms of the coefficient of variation, which is the standard deviation divided by the mean. But for testing the institutional hypotheses, the real issue is the actual amount of variation. We want to see whether organizations become more like each other over time and this is what the standard deviation tells us. Therefore, as DiMaggio and Powell say (1983: 76), the standard deviation, and not the coefficient of variation, is the appropriate test. Let us therefore re-examine the findings of Meyer *et al.* (1988) using the standard deviation. It is possible to calculate the standard deviations of the educational structures of the US states from their tables 7-1 and 7-3 (Meyer *et al.*, 1988: 144, 152) and these are given in table 4.1.

Considering first the state agency staffs, the standard deviation in 1940 is 105 and the standard deviation in 1974 is 358. Thus the variation across states in the number of their staff has not decreased, it has increased. More specifically, it has increased to a maximum of 368 in 1970 and then declined a little to 358 in 1974. Thus there is a slight recent decline but set against an increase over the thirty-four-year period. Overall, it is truer to say that the number of people in the education agency staff of the different states is growing more dissimilar over the historical period. Homogeneity on this structural dimension is decreasing, not increasing, across states. There is no 'inexorable push toward homogenization' on this aspect of structure.

Similar remarks apply to another four of the six structural variables which Meyer *et al.* (1988: 152) presented as evidence of increasing homogenization across the states. The number of schools per school district has standard deviations which increase steadily over the years 1946 to 1980 from 2.73 to 5.60. Again, the number of principals per school has standard deviations which increase over those years from 0.170 to 0.348. Thus both these structural variables display not decreasing variation across states but the opposite.

Likewise, the number of students per school district has standard deviations which increase over the years 1946 to 1980 from 2,493 to 5,573. This variable peaks at 6,320 in 1970 and then declines slightly to the 5,573 figure in 1980. But overall the trend is increasing. Again, the number of students per school has standard deviations which increase over the years (1946–80) from 82 to 132. This variable peaks at 165 in 1970 and then declines slightly to the 132 figure in 1980. But once again the overall trend is increasing. For both students per school district and students per school the overall picture is of increasing differences across states.

Thus for these four structural variables, as for state education staffs considered above, the variation across states is mainly increasing, not decreasing, negating statements about increasing homogenization.

The last of the six structural variables presented by Meyer *et al.* (1988) is the number of superintendents per school district. This shows standard deviations which decline over the years (1940–74) from 0.38 to 0.24. These data do display a secular trend declining steadily from 1956 onwards. However, this decline (1940–74) of 37 per cent is far less than the decline of 72 per cent obtained for the coefficient of variation (i.e., 1.05 to 0.29). Thus on this variable the use of the coefficient of variation produces an impression of dramatic decline where the decline is only moderate.

Overall, of the six structural variables presented by Meyer *et al.* (1988) as

Table 4.1. *Differences in educational structure between US states*: standard deviations*

Aspect of educational structure	1940	1946	1950	1956	1960	1966	1970	1974	1980	Lack of isomorphism
State education agency staffs	105	164	248	239	256	328	368	358	—	Mainly increasing
Schools per school district	—	2.73	2.86	3.21	3.70	4.23	5.05	5.43	5.60	Increasing
Principals per school	—	0.170	0.212	0.244	0.264	0.288	0.283	0.314	0.348	Increasing
Students per school district	—	2,493	2,783	3,733	4,409	5,558	6,320	6,199	5,573	Mainly increasing
Students per school	—	82	95	127	142	149	165	150	132	Mainly increasing
Superintendents per school district	0.38	—	—	0.50	0.34	0.28	0.28	0.24	—	Decreasing

Notes: * 48 states (Alaska and Hawaii excluded).
— Data unavailable in original source.
Source: Meyer *et al.* (1988: 144, 152; tables 7-1, 7-3).

evidence of increasing homogenization, five actually mainly decrease in homogeneity over the historical period. These data reveal a pattern of increasing dissimilarity between states and are evidence against increasing, let alone inexorable, homogenization. The findings of Meyer *et al.* (1988) fail to support their theory of increasing standardization across states. The comment by Zucker (1987) in her review that their findings show dramatic convergence is without foundation.

Other scholars have begun to express scepticism about the empirical validity of the institutional theory assertion of increasing homogeneity of organizational forms among a particular type of organization caused by institutional isomorphism. They have sought to test the idea by examining the variance in organizational form to see whether it declines over time, in the way the theory predicts. In particular, Kraatz and Zajac (1992) have conducted an inquiry into liberal arts colleges. They note they are exactly the sort of organizations that institutional theory is held to apply to most strongly, and are the sort of organizations which figure prominently in institutional analyses, i.e., educational organizations (Meyer and Scott, 1983). Therefore an examination of these organizations is a fair test of institutional theory.

The institutional theory of institutional isomorphism holds that organizations of a given type tend over time to resemble each other more closely through the process of mimetic adoption. A form becomes the norm to which the other organizations conform by adjusting over time, producing increasing homogenization of organizational form. This implies a reduction in the variance of form over time. However, Kraatz and Zajac (1992) found that liberal arts colleges became more, rather than less, varied among themselves in form, thus contradicting the proposition about institutional isomorphism. Further, again contrary to institutional theory, the lower-status colleges showed no tendency to adopt the form of the elite colleges and in fact became more different from them. Whereas institutional theory asserts that organizations are structured according to ritual rather than rationality, in fact, the changes in the colleges were rational, being motivated by economic concerns, and rational in outcome in that adopting colleges were more likely to survive. Thus the changes by the colleges were rational, instrumental types of adaptation to their environments. Hence even in liberal arts colleges, institutional theory fails to explain structural change. These structural changes turn out to be explained by the functionalist, contingency type of theory of rational adaptation by the organization to its environment.

The idea of decreasing variance between organizations of a given type reflecting the convergence around a norm among organizations of that type turns out to be untrue in the Kraatz and Zajac (1992) study, just as it was not confirmed in the Meyer *et al.* (1988) study considered above. The institutional theory of institutional isomorphism is flawed.

Late adoption Tolbert and Zucker (1983) make a case for institutional explanation in their analysis of the historical adoption of civil service regulations as part of reforms of civic administration in the USA. They argue that early adoption of these practices by some cities was a rational attempt to solve problems while later adoption by other cities was a response to what had become institutional norms defining legitimate practice:

Early adoption of civil reform – before 1915 – appears to reflect efforts to resolve specific problems confronting municipal administrations, while later adoption instead is rooted in the growing legitimacy of civil service procedures, with the diffusion of societal norms serving to define local structure (Tolbert and Zucker, 1983: 22).

once historical continuity has established their importance (Berger and Luckmann, 1967; Zucker, 1977), changes in formal structure are adopted because of their societal legitimacy, regardless of their value for the internal functioning of the organization ... It is assumed that the adoption of an innovative measure may have little or no effect on the actual efficiency of organizational operations; its adoption fulfils symbolic rather than task related requirements. (Tolbert and Zucker, 1983: 26)

Tolbert and Zucker (1983) see structural change as oriented towards internal effectiveness for early adoptions, but towards institutional conformity for later adoptions. However, the evidence which they adduce in support really tests neither. The empirical evidence revolves around a model of the determinants of adoption (Tolbert and Zucker, 1983: 29). This model is shown to have explanatory power only for earlier adoption but not for later adoption. If this model specified the conditions under which adopting such civil service regulations would rationally improve internal effectiveness then this could offer a test of their theoretical argument. However, the model does not provide a set of contingent factors fixing under which conditions civil service regulations would solve internal effectiveness problems. The factors listed as determinants – size, age, city expenditures, and characteristics of the city population (proportions illiterate, immigrant and in manufacturing employment) – have as their principal rationale, a role as indicators of economic interests (Tolbert and Zucker, 1983: 30). Thus the fact that these variables predict adoption less among later than among earlier adopting cities is not evidence that the civil service regulations are less effective for later adopting cities, as no assessment is made of effectiveness for adopters, either late or early.

The study of the adoption of civil service regulations by Tolbert and

Zucker (1983) provides no test of the hypothesis that institutional factors, that is, the search for normative conformity unrelated to concerns for internal effectiveness, caused the adoption of administrative reforms among late adopters (see Davis and Powell, 1992: 361). On the contrary, the idea that effectiveness is promoted by insisting on selection by impersonal standards, such as written examinations (Tolbert and Zucker, 1983), rather than by favouritism, nepotism and patronage, is surely highly plausible. And if this indeed helps curb corruption and promotes internal effectiveness among city administrations which adopted early such civil service regulations, as Tolbert and Zucker argue, why should these reforms not also be beneficial for cities which are late adopters? The case for institutional theory is not made by the Tolbert and Zucker (1983) study.

A study of large US corporations by Rumelt (1974) finds a late adoption effect similar to that claimed by Tolbert and Zucker (1983). He interprets his data as showing that corporations adopted the multidivisional structure initially to regain fit after they had diversified, but that later adopters divisionalized out of deference to the norm that the earlier cases of divisionalization had created. Thus the early adoptions were cases of adaptation of structure to changes in the strategic contingency, whereas the later adoptions were cases of mimetic isomorphism. Rumelt (1974: 77) concludes that in the fifties adoption was rational, whereas in the sixties it became mimetic and norm-driven. The problem is that to distinguish rational from irrational divisionalization there needs to be a way to distinguish between those cases where divisionalization produced a fit with strategy from those cases where divisionalization made a misfit with strategy and thus lowered performance. Rumelt (1974) has no operational definition of fit and so could not classify the divisionalizing corporations as in fit or misfit.

Donaldson (1987) developed such an operational definition of strategy–structure fit and validated it empirically by showing that it predicted subsequent performance. Utilizing this definition on the data from Rumelt (1974), the proportion of corporations that adopted the divisional structure in the fifties for which their divisional structure was a fit was 97 per cent ($n = 97$ cases, coincidentally). Similarly, in the sixties the proportion of corporations that adopted the divisional structure for which their divisional structure was a fit was 100 per cent ($n = 15$). Divisionalization in the sixties was highly rational, and was no less rational than divisionalization in the fifties. In both the fifties and sixties divisionalization was overwhelmingly rational and in accordance with strategic diversification. When the data of Rumelt are fully analysed there is no evidence that later adoption is different from earlier nor that it is purely normative and mimetic. The late adoption effect of mimetic isomorphism is not present in the large US corporations. Like the study of city government by Tolbert and Zucker (1983), the Rumelt (1974) study of corporations, when more closely examined, does not really support the idea of a mimetic, late adoption effect. Neither of these two studies should be coded as support for the theory of mimetic isomorphism.

Another study of US corporations, restricted to the oil industry, was conducted by Armour and Teece (1978). They found that the multidivisional (M-form) structured corporations outperformed the functionally structured corporations, but only for an initial and not for a later period. Institutionalists are wont to quote this study as further evidence of the late adoption effect of mimetic isomorphism. This would mean that the earlier adoptions were for rational, effectiveness considerations whereas the later adoptions were in response to a norm rather than prompted by effectiveness. However, Armour and Teece (1978: 118) advance a different interpretation of their findings. Divisional structures outperform functional structures while divisionalization is still diffusing because there remain corporations which are inappropriately functionally structured. When the divisional structure has become well-diffused there are few corporations left which retain the inappropriate, functional structure. Then comparison of divisional with functional will show no performance difference because both structures are fits. Moreover, Armour and Teece (118) make the argument that the superior performance of the divisionalized corporations places competitive pressure on the misfitted functionalized corporations to adopt the divisional structure to regain performance, thus explaining why few corporations are left with the inappropriate functional structure. Armour and Teece offer an explanation of their findings which is not in terms of norms or mimetic isomorphism. Their explanation of the nil performance finding and the structural changes which brought it about are economic, with organizations seen as striving to curtail loss of profit. This scenario is consistent also with the structural contingency theory of corporations adapting structurally to regain fit and performance. Hence there is no need for recourse to the theory of mimetic adoption to explain these results.

Moreover, Armour and Teece (1978) offer an important insight into methodology. A nil relationship between a structure and performance may reflect that, in a contingency world, a comparison of structures which are fits for their respective contingencies will yield no performance difference. Such comparisons of one structure with another will yield performance differences only if one structure actually contains more misfits than the other. Given that earlier structural adaptations create fits which place competitive pressure on structures which are misfits, this causes structural adaptation so that eventually there is no performance difference between structures. In such a case a finding of no performance difference between structures reflects that adoption of more efficacious structures has occurred. The underlying difference in performance between the successful fits and the unsuccessful misfits has caused the structural adaptation. Thus a pattern of a positive effect of structure on performance in the early period and nil effect in the later period is to be expected for rational organizations even though structural fit affects performance in both periods. Hence there may arise, with some frequency, findings of a greater effect of structure on performance in earlier than later periods. These may each be interpreted by institutionalists as proof of a late adoption effect of mimetic isomorphism, but this will be false.

Institutionalists would need to show that any such late adoption effects are not caused by underlying differences in proportions of misfitted organizations, resulting in turn from competitive effects. However, at present, institutional research seems disinclined to empirically study effectiveness, fit, competitive pressure and the like, so it cannot rule out this alternative explanation of late adoption. In contrast, Armour and Teece (1978) and other economists or structural contingency theorists, could invoke in support of their argument evidence that the fit between strategy and structure affects performance (Donaldson, 1987; Hamilton and Shergill, 1992) and that low financial performance triggers structural adaptation (Ezzamel and Hilton, 1980; Hill and Pickering, 1986; Donaldson, 1987). Thus, at present, the balance of evidence favours the economic explanation of the findings of Armour and Teece (1978) rather than the institutional reinterpretation of the findings. The study by Armour and Teece (1978) should *not* be coded as support for the late adoption, mimetic isomorphism thesis.

None of the studies of the late adoption of organizational structure (Tolbert and Zucker, 1983; Rumelt, 1974; Armour and Teece, 1978) confirms that it is caused by mimetic isomorphism. In all three studies the late adoptions are consistent with structural adaptations to enhance the effectiveness of the organization and, by implication, are consistent with rational management.

Tradition Institutional theory is used also in the study by Eisenhardt (1988) of the different pay systems used by various retail stores. Therein the institutional contribution is the finding that the reason why shoe stores, in contrast to stores that sell other things, pay their sales employees low base salaries and high rates of commission is because they have previously paid them in that way (Eisenhardt, 1988). Such an invocation of traditions is hardly very illuminating. It is not an explanation, but rather a description through time, i.e., the dependent variable at one time is being 'explained' by itself at an earlier time (see Powell, 1991). A real theory explains the dependent variable by a cause, i.e., an independent variable which is not itself just the dependent variable.

Mimicry Fligstein (1985) offers a sociological analysis of the causes of adoption of the multidivisional structure by corporations. His theoretical discussion draws heavily on institutional theory (DiMaggio and Powell, 1983) and also on other theories and it sees interpretations of organizational events as being rational as generally problematic (Fligstein, 1985: 381n, 389).

Fligstein (1985: 387) finds evidence that firms are more likely to adopt the multidivisional structure as they diversify, as Chandler (1962) held, but also that the firms were more likely to divisionalize if the other firms in their industry had already done so, which he interprets as a mimetic effect. However, Fligstein also writes that firms were more likely to divisionalize 'when their competitors shifted structures' (388). If competitors adopt a divisional structure which is appropriate, they will achieve superior performance relative to a focal organization which has diversified and not yet divisionalized (as we discussed earlier; Armour and Teece, 1978). The structurally based superior performance of the divisionalized competitors will lower the performance of the more disorganized, focal, functionally organized corporation by taking away sales and profits. Thus the focal organization will be in strategy–structure misfit and suffer depressed performance, the combination of circumstances which leads to structural adjustment to regain fit by divisionalization (Donaldson, 1987). Thus industry effects should be seen as competitor effects which prompt structural adaptation by making the environment of the organization less benign, i.e., reducing organizational slack. The focal firm is not engaging in irrational mimicry but is motivated by functionalist considerations.

Even if the industry effect is not wholly due to competition, copying other organizations may be due to more than mimicry. Fligstein (1985: 380) writes:

The MDF [multidivisional form] spreads to various organizations as a response to other firms' behavior. The examples of successful firms such as Du Pont or General Motors provided the role models for other firms. The MDF has also become the accepted form for large firms. Business schools have taught the MDF as an important organizational tool, and managers have come to implement it.

Mimicking the structure of successful firms can be adaptive, functional and rational. This would be a case of functional adaptation based on vicarious learning, that is drawing on the experience of a company outside the focal organization. If managers learn such information in business schools this also is adaptive, as long as the divisional structure is presented as only being appropriate in certain situations such as diversification, rather than as being universally optimal. Surely most business schools, in fact, draw on discussions of divisionalization such as that in Chandler (1962), and teach about this structure within a contingency framework. Thus educated, professional managers would not see the divisional form as the *only* useful structure and would see divisionalization as appropriate contingently not universally. Professionalization of management increases awareness of different structures (functional, divisional, matrix, etc.) rather than inducing belief 'in one best way'. Thus managerial education and professionalization would not form the basis for adoption of the divisional form willy-nilly, out of obeisance to a single organizational form.

Again, the statement that the multidimensional form 'has also become the accepted form for large firms' is true after the event, when almost all large US firms have this structure. But this hardly explains how this came about, for in 1939, almost all (92 per cent) corporations did not have the multidivisional structure (Fligstein, 1985) and so this was not the accepted structure for large corporations in earlier periods. Early adoption was not based on mimicry or conformity to the majority, for the majority were not organized multidivisionally.

The mimicry argument produces the intended inference that functionally structured firms mimic divisional firms, *only* if one holds that divisional firms are more successful on average than functional firms. Thus attending to the successfulness of others would lead functional firms to copy divisional firms and divisional firms not to copy functional firms on average. The Chandlerian argument would provide such a premise, for the adoption of divisional structures by diversified companies such as Du Pont and GM is held to be appropriate, and therefore contributes to their success. A functional firm which was undiversified and which nevertheless copied the divisional form from Du Pont or GM would be making an inappropriate structural change and would suffer performance decrease, and would also be treating divisionalization as a universal best form. Such a move could fairly be described by the rather pejorative term of mimicry. However, a firm which was diversified and saw restructuring from functional to divisional as appropriate would be making a correct choice, that is an adaptation, and one which implicitly treats structure as contingent upon strategy. This might be described as vicarious learning, that is, drawing on the demonstration of other firms, but would not be mimicry in the sense of mindless conformity. Divisionalization in such a firm would promote effectiveness and be rational, and the perceptions and beliefs of the management would equate with the objective realities.

In sum, none of the arguments about mimetic structural change which Fligstein (1985) makes stands. The structural changes are more accurately conceptualized under rational adaptation of structure to strategy. Thus the argument derived from the institutional school collapses and we are left with the structural adaptation to regain fit theory, though perhaps with the addition of some vicarious learning.

Fligstein (1990b) has latterly offered a book-length treatment of the development of the large US corporation. He retains in this later writing a sense that organizations are socially constructed by actors and that they are located within a field of organizations which watch each other for clues to successful practice. Further, there is the idea that the action of one organization on another, and of one actor on another member of the same organization, involves the exercise of power and control. There is use of ideas such as the concept of the control which is held by the organization and its managers, whereby the organization becomes dominant and shapes the field of organizations. However, despite references to ideological, political, perceptual and power types of factors in the theoretical interpretation, this is all *just* an interpretation since there is no measurement of how organizations or their members see each other or influence each other. The data are restricted to the structural type and achieved diversification of the corporation, and to the disciplinary background of the CEO. Thus neither Fligstein (1985) nor Fligstein (1990b) provides evidence that demonstrates the validity of institutional theory by showing unequivocally an effect of institutional factors upon organizational structure that is independent of structural contingency theory effects.

Fligstein (1985) agrees with structural contingency theory that strategy leads to structure (Chandler, 1962). However, Fligstein (1991) also offers an explanation of strategic diversification as less than fully rational, thereby indirectly casting doubt on the rationality of the resultant organizational structure. Fligstein (1991) argues in power-political terms that organizations are shaped by the interests and power of their managers and by the power of the state. Organizations therefore remain inert in their unchanging organizational fields until a shock induces crisis and change. New organizations which enter the field provide a challenge to the old order and by their success constitute new role models to be emulated by the older organizations in the organizational field. Thus the strategic diversification of a corporation is not caused from within by rational decision of its managers but from without through mimetic isomorphism.

Fligstein (1991) takes as an organizational field the largest hundred US corporations over the period 1919–79. The strategy of each corporation is classified, by the degree of diversification achieved, into product-dominant, product-related and product-unrelated, that is, into three categories of increasing diversification ('dominant', 'related' and 'unrelated', hereafter). Fligstein has data for each corporation at the start and end of each of six ten-year periods, which for simplicity we will call the twenties, thirties, etc. Fligstein (1991: 328) presents new evidence of mimetic isomorphism which he draws together in these terms: 'One consistent interpretation of these patterns is that rapidly growing firms entered organizational fields with product-related strategies. Once the advantage of these strategies became apparent, other firms diversified, particularly in the Depression and the following decade.' However, while the corporations entering the top hundred were more diversified than those in the top hundred, the newcomers were actually more likely to be dominant than related. In the twenties and thirties, the influx of diversified corporations is held to be upsetting the existing top hundred corporations (328). However, among the newcomers in the twenties twelve were dominant and nine related and in the thirties ten were dominant and only five were related. Thus among the corporations entering the top hundred in the twenties and thirties the typical organization was a dominant, i.e., the least diversified type. The 'norm' among newcomers was the same as among the existing top hundred – the undiversified dominant type. Thus if the success of the newcomers had influenced the existing corporations it would have caused the existing corporations to retain their dominant strategy and not to diversify.

Fligstein (1991: 328) also argues that the failure of those corporations which left the top hundred was connected with their not diversifying, thereby cementing the lesson for the remaining corporations of the desirability of diversifying. While leavers were less diversified and less liable to diversify than stayers, the norm among leavers and stayers was the same – for both, the typical corporation was a dominant, i.e., the least diversified type of corporation (for the first four decades) (329, 330). Therefore the leavers as a group were not deviant from the norm of the stayers. Leavers did not provide an object lesson in the perils of breaking the norm of the stayers that initiated strategic change among the top hundred.

The newcomers' level of diversification at the time they entered the top hundred increased through the fifties and sixties, with the typical newcomer being related diversified, so that diversification was their norm in this era. If the increase in diversification among the existing top hundred had been caused by emulation of these more diversified newcomers, then this process would have caused the rate of diversifying to have increased over time among the top hundred, or at the least to have remained at its initial level. However, the rate of diversifying from dominant to related strategies among the existing, stable top hundred members peaks in the fifties at 38 per cent (of the dominant corporations) and declines thereafter to 26 per cent in the sixties and to 10 per cent in the seventies. Among dominant corporations, their rate of diversifying is declining during these thirty years, contrary to the norm among newcomers. Thus the later decades display behaviour which is opposite to that which would be expected from the mimetic isomorphism model.

Fligstein (1991: 320) also argues that the Depression provided a shock, as in a period of general economic decline, only diversification could provide a corporation with growth. This is the reason that '[t]he Depression era was the first major shift toward diversification in the largest firms' (326) rather than the twenties. However, the rate of diversifying from dominant to related was not really higher in the Depression era, the thirties, than it had been in the twenties. Among the total sample, the rate of diversifying was 8 per cent in the twenties and also 8 per cent in the thirties, i.e., the same. And among the stayers sub-sample it was 3 per cent in the twenties and 4 per cent in the thirties, only slightly more; while among the newcomers it was 31 per cent in the twenties and 29 per cent in the thirties, i.e., slightly less (329, table 13.2). The Depression did not provide the shock which shattered the status quo and initiated diversification.

Fligstein (1991: 322) refers also to a falling-off of the acquisitive, unrelated type of diversification and explains it by low returns, international competition forcing renewed cost concerns and the acquisition strategy moving outside the large corporations to raiders. These factors are different from the explanation offered by the theory of mimetic isomorphism and seem to connect more with economic theories of corporate behaviour (e.g., Rumelt, 1974; Jensen, 1989). Fligstein (1991) presents his analysis as showing how market organizations cannot be adequately explained by economic theories and require institutional theories, but here the institutional theory of mimetic isomorphism is forsaken for economic explanation. Moreover, the behaviour of the managers running these corporations is by implication more rational on this economic logic, driven by profit concerns and not any kind of blind mimicry.

The explanation in Fligstein (1991) of diversification by the theory of mimetic isomorphism seems less than secure. The study is at best only weak evidence for mimetic isomorphism. Strategic diversification in this study cannot be held to reflect an underlying institutional effect of the organizationally irrationalist or anti-management type.

Overall, the studies of organizations which have used the institutional theory of mimetic adoption (Rumelt, 1974; Tolbert and Zucker, 1983; Fligstein, 1985, 1991; Eisenhardt, 1988) have not produced convincing evidence that there is an effect of mimicry independent of contingency factors which directly cause organizational structure, apart from perhaps some 'effect' of tradition. There may be some vicarious learning from the success of other organizations, though this is difficult to disentangle from the effects of competition, but any such vicarious learning by organizations and managers is quite rational and compatible with functionalism.

Coercive isomorphism

Coercive isomorphism is studied in five empirical inquiries: Tolbert and Zucker (1983), Fligstein (1990b), Baron *et al.* (1986), Dobbin *et al.* (1988) and Orrù *et al.* (1991), and each will be reviewed in turn.

An empirical finding by Tolbert and Zucker (1983) is that in states where the state government legally required adoption, cities adopted the civil service regulations earlier than in states where there was no such legal requirement. This finding is consistent with a Weberian view that the legal order can induce compliance by its subject bodies. It does not support the cognitive institutional view of the social construction of reality type *à la* Berger and Luckmann (1966) which Tolbert and Zucker advocate: that norms alone, unrelated to legal compulsion or intrinsic need, will suffice to guarantee implementation.

Indeed, Zucker (1987: 444) subsequently writes that the explanation of organizational form by reference to state coercion is actually opposed to the explanation by cognitive elements and taken-for-granteds in institutional theory:

A third defining process, coercive, is central to state legitimation in the environment-as-institution approach, but it is explicitly considered deinstitutionalizing in the organization-as-institution approach, since any use of sanctions indicates that other attractive alternatives exist.

Thus if the state has to force people to adopt a particular form for their organization there must be other forms as possible alternatives known to the actors, and so the enforced form is not a taken-for-granted. Hence Zucker is acknowledging that explanations by reference to state coercion are evidence against the cognitive explanation of the Berger and Luckmann (1966) and Garfinkel (1967) type. The Tolbert and Zucker (1983) study supports coercive isomorphism but not the cognitive explanation of institutional effects.

Fligstein (1990b) provides an extensive documentation of the role of the state in the corporate economy, especially the influence of anti-trust regulations in shaping the degree and form of corporate diversification. Once again we see that the real meat of the institutional theory as empirically demonstrated, concerns the coercive role of the state on organizations. The more subjective aspects of institutional theory in the concept of control and like cognitive matters, are there only in the interpretation by Fligstein, rather than in the documented facts which pertain to the history of state regulation as contained in the public record. Hence the Fligstein study supports only the coercive isomorphism aspect of institutional theory. Fligstein argues that the state affects the degree of diversification used by corporations in their strategies. Since diversification strategy affects organizational structure (Chandler, 1962; Fligstein, 1985; Donaldson, 1987), this means that the state indirectly affects organizational structure via strategy.

However, there are some grounds for questioning the validity of the argument that the increasing diversification by US corporations from about 1940 was due to US governmental regulation (Fligstein, 1991: 321). Several countries other than the USA which are not usually credited with as strict an anti-trust regime as the USA have shown the same trend of increasing diversification among their large corporations post-1945, albeit with a time lag – France, Germany, Italy, Japan and the UK (Channon, 1973; Dyas and Thanheiser, 1976; Pavan, 1976; Suzuki, 1980). The importance of the US government in corporate diversification may be overstated by Fligstein (1990b, 1991) and so the degree of coercive isomorphism may be less than is presently supposed.

In a study entitled 'War and peace', Baron et al. (1986) examined changes in personnel administration in US industry during World War II. During wartime, governments in Western liberal democracies took extra powers (legitimated by the sense of national emergency) which reduced the autonomy of the private-sector, commercial corporations. The corporations changed their internal personnel administration so as to meet wartime conditions and these changes were required by the state. Baron et al. (1986) show that the new structures were not driven by contingency factors, i.e., by organizational size. These findings are interpreted as support for institutional theory. However, the findings of this study are only support for coercive isomorphism, especially in the sense of the power of the state over organizations.

In another study, Dobbin et al. (1988) also examine the case of personnel offices, indexed as the number of personnel function departments. These are affected by size, unionization and the government (Dobbin et al., 1988: 85). In terms of strength, size is strongest, (0.61), next is unionization, (0.36), and government (or 'publicness') is weakest at 0.18 (all standardized slope coefficients). Thus the contingency factor of size is over three times stronger than the institutional factor of the government. The results here differ from those of Baron et al. (1986) which showed that size had little correlation with the growth of the personnel function as a formal specialism in firms. Thus the results of the Baron et al. study about the failure of size to explain the growth of the personnel function may not indicate a general failure of the size variable on this topic nor of contingency theory more widely considered. The Dobbin et al. (1988) finding also supports the influence of the government on the organization, i.e., coercive isomorphism, and supports that aspect of the findings of Baron et al. (1986).

Dobbin et al. (1988) also studied the adoption by organizations of formal structural elements oriented to guaranteeing due process for their employees. Specifically, the elements were grievance procedures and affirmative action. The only institutional factor supported in their study is government and this only affects affirmative action, not grievance procedures. Moreover, the effect of government is weaker than the effect of size (Dobbin et al., 1988: 85). Averaging across the two indicators of the formalization of affirmative action, the effect of government is 0.40 which is lower than the effect of size of 0.59 (both in standardized slope coefficients) (85). Thus the effect of the institutional variable is substantial but secondary to the contingency variable of size. Hence the study supports an institutional effect separate from the contingency effect, but not such as to replace the contingency effect nor to overshadow it.

Dobbin et al. (1988) also theorized that the effect of the causal factors on grievance and affirmative action would be through the intervening variable of the existence of a personnel office. This would reflect the role of professionals in diffusing present fashions and conceptions of good practice between organizations through the professional network. However, the empirical results failed to find evidence that the existence of personnel offices intervened between size, unionization and governmental influence in their effects on either grievance or affirmative action – as Dobbin et al. (1988: 87) acknowledge. Thus institutional theory ideas about the role of professionals (i.e., normative isomorphism) are not supported. Only the coercive isomorphism idea in institutional theory is supported (DiMaggio and Powell, 1983).

The Dobbin et al. (1988) study shows that government affects organizations which are parts of the government or which are dependent upon the government. By the same token, it argues against the proposition that institutional phenomena occur equally in the private sector, for the study shows that the private organizations which had no connection with the government failed to adopt a formalized affirmative action approach, notwithstanding the commitment of the government to this approach. Thus the study is a demonstration that institutional theory is not a theory of organizations of every kind. The Dobbin et al. (1988) study shows that the institutional effect lacks generality because it consists of the power of the state and therefore applies mostly to organizations affected by the state. Private organizations such as firms which do not have the government as a client or regulator are freer of state power and so are less shaped by the state.

A further aspect of the theory in Dobbin et al. (1988) requires comment. The theory is very similar to the resource dependence theory of Pfeffer and Salancik (1978). Organizations exist in a political milieu. The organization adopts internal elements under the influence of more powerful organizations such as the government or out of a desire to receive governmental contracts. Indeed the empirical material in Dobbin *et al.* (1988) is strongly similar to the Pfeffer and Salancik (1978) analysis of how contractors to government comply with affirmative action requirements of the government (see chapter 5). Zucker (1987) admits that it is often difficult to distinguish between an institutional and a resource dependence theory explanation. Here both the phenomena and explanations appear similar across the two theories. It seems characteristic of institutionalism that such a glaring problem can exist and be acknowledged without any apparent resolution. Yet for a theory to be indistinguishable from another theory calls that first theory into question. If a theory is the same as an earlier theory then it makes no contribution. Moreover, if a theory is the same as another theory then it cannot be a separate, or a new, paradigm.

Use of institutionalism within cross-national research is displayed in the study by Orrù *et al.* (1991). They criticize the earlier institutional theory of Meyer and Scott (1983) (see pp. 103–4) which maintained that market-oriented organizations were less shaped by institutional and more by technical (i.e., contingency) factors. Orrù *et al.* (1991) present an analysis of market organizations in Japan, South Korea and Taiwan and argue that they are shaped institutionally. The organizations are shown to be isomorphic within each country and yet different between countries. This isomorphism is explained by the national peculiarities of each society, including the state, the property inheritance patterns, the strategies and the cultural definitions of legitimate organization. The object of study is not the enterprise but rather the group of enterprises which are key features of each country and which pattern in nationally distinctive ways. The case is well made for the distinctive nature of these business groups in each of the three countries and their homogeneity within each country. However, the explanation seems most clear-cut around factors such as the role of the state (e.g., the directive role in South Korea which funnels capital to the big enterprise groups) and the effect of family property inheritance in Taiwan (e.g., Chinese families divide the property among the sons, thus fragmenting the firm). The role of ideational factors such as concepts of legitimate authority and organization is asserted, but these factors remain shadowy with little detail offered.

The theory would suggest the need for anthropological and ethnographic sorts of evidence with qualitative data, linguistic meanings analysis and quotations from the actors themselves as to how they see their roles. However, almost no such material is offered and the main evidence is statistical data about cross-ownership patterns, asset size and the like. Much of this is the sort of data that an economist might present. Sources include the newspapers of the countries, marketing consultants and the China Credit Information Service (Orrù *et al.*, 1991: 389). The data used to support the institutional theory argument is not at all the sort of rich ethnography that the received stereotype of institutionalism as an insightful sociological analysis would lead one to expect. The sources are surely the media in which institutional theory would predict that the content would be as much myth as substance.

The selection of the business group rather than the individual constituent organization as the object of study is not a trivial matter. For individual organizations within those societies it is far less clear that there is isomorphism of their structures. In the case of Japan there are a number of studies which show that there is variation rather than isomorphism across firms in bureaucratization, differentiation, divisionalization and organicness (Marsh and Mannari, 1976, 1980; Suzuki, 1980; Azumi and McMillan, 1981; Kagono, 1981; Lincoln et al., 1981). Moreover, these studies show that the structural variations are accounted for by contingency factors (i.e., size, strategy, technology, etc.) in these Japanese organizations, similarly to the case of Western organizations. Thus the argument for institutional factors holds less at the individual organization than at the business group level. Overall, the study by Orrù et al. (1991) should be coded as showing an effect of nationality upon business groups but that the institutional effects are mainly coercive isomorphism, i.e., the power of the state and of the structure of capitalist property rights rather than more ideational factors of ideology, legitimacy, norms or beliefs.

In summary, the proposition which is supported by the five studies (Tolbert and Zucker, 1983; Fligstein, 1985, 1990b, 1991; Baron et al., 1986; Dobbin et al., 1988; Orrù et al., 1991) is that organizations are influenced in their internal structure by the state. The effect of the state on organizational structure is direct in three of the studies (Tolbert and Zucker, 1983; Baron et al., 1986; Dobbin et al., 1988), indirect (via strategy) in one study (Fligstein, 1990b) and apparently both direct and indirect in the other study (Orrù et al., 1991). Such influence may reflect coercion and legal compulsion, or may reflect the power of the state to reward with contracts, etc., or may be a more diffuse fear such as not wanting to offend a powerful body. But the sway of the state on its subject organizations refers only to the coercive isomorphism concept in institutional theory. This aspect receives support from these five empirical studies, but it is the only aspect of institutionalism that receives support. Moreover, of all the institutional research reviewed to this point in this chapter, coercive isomorphism is the only institutional-theoretical idea to receive unequivocal support.

Loose-coupling: theory and evidence

The loose-coupling version of institutional theory takes as its point of departure the open systems model of the organization (Meyer and Scott, 1983). Following previous organizational theory of the open system variety, the organization is seen as having an operating core where transformation of inputs into outputs takes place (Thompson, 1967). This core is organized to perform the actual work. Conventional organizational theory sees the operating core as controlled by a management hierarchy which is tightly coupled with the operating core. However, the present version of institutional theory consciously inverts this idea and speaks of a loose-coupling between operating core and organizational management hierarchy, so that the work organization is quite disconnected from the management organization. The management organization is primarily concerned with interfacing with the institutional environment. The environmental institutions hold norms and values about proper organization which constitute a set of expectations to which the organization seeks to conform in order to attain approval, legitimacy and support. Thus the management of the organization acts out a set of rituals of good organization and conformity, thereby creating myths about the nature of the organization which conform to wider institutional norms about what constitutes rationality.

It is a characteristic of modern society that the institutional order is a cognitive system and web of norms and values which define and legitimate the organizational sectoral systems and the occupational system of roles of 'doctor', 'nurse', 'primary school teacher', 'secondary school teacher' and so on (Meyer and Scott, 1983). These rationalizing ideologies may be in tension with the work actually done or how it is done. Thus the representation of the organization to the institutional environment may require that management creates a kind of facade structure of organization charts and documented programmes which do not accord with reality (Meyer and Scott, 1983). This management task can best be accomplished if the management level of the organization is only loosely connected with work organization at the operational level. This in turn allows the operating core to proceed with a degree of autonomy from the dictates of the institutional environment. Also, the loose-coupling facilitates the management level in representing the organization without the embarrassment of having to reconcile programmatic declarations with what is actually done, which often contradicts the official ideology. Moreover, in modern societies the rational myths held by the environmental institutions can be so difficult, inconsistent, and changeable, that the work of the operating core proceeds more smoothly unencumbered by these official pretensions. Likewise, given the inconsistent institutional expectations, the management level better represents the organization by making a set of partial and shifting representations to each different institutional body and this is assisted by not having to maintain consistency across external bodies or with the actuality of the core.

Consistent with their theory, Meyer and Scott (1983) argue that institutional effects on organizational structure are stronger in institutional organizations, whereas, in technical organizations, structures are more determined by task contingencies as a result of market pressures towards efficiency. Institutional organizations reflect the strong and difficult demands for conformity received by organizations in their societal sector, where operational efficiency is less important than meeting environmental expectations. Thus Meyer and Scott (1983) make a significant qualification about the domain of their theory that limits its generality. Nevertheless many organizations would be held by Meyer and Scott (1983) to fall within the category of institutional organizations and thereby be subjects of their loose-coupling version of institutional theory. This then is the loose-coupling institutional theory model of organizations advanced by Meyer, Scott and colleagues.

The writings of Meyer and Scott (1983), however, go considerably beyond this basic model and offer an extended body of theorizing. Much of the theorizing is at the level of the sector rather than the organization, i.e., the set of interconnected organizations which make up, say, the educational sector of society (Meyer, 1983). There is considerable complexity to the body of theory overall. Perhaps partly because of the supra-organizational focus and the complexity, this fuller institutional theory has not obviously been received into the organization theory literature, which tends to invoke the loose-coupling version of institutional theory only in its more basic form. Since our interest herein is on organizational theory and the ideas which are presently influencing it, it will be appropriate for us to focus upon the basic loose-coupling version of institutional theory, as it is this which has been received into the literature, and it is this which other organizational scholars usually mean by the loose-coupling version of institutional theory.

The kind of empirical evidence which is presented in Meyer and Scott (1983) are studies such as those showing that teachers interact little with the head-teacher, who has little control over what they teach, and so on. This is the empirical basis for the proposition that the operating core functions independently of management and thus the operating core is buffered from institutional processes. The isolated independence of the school-teacher in his or her classroom is one of the facts adduced repeatedly in Meyer and Scott (1983) as proof of institutional theory. Again much is made of the lack of inspection of teacher performance. Yet Meyer and Scott (1983) comment on their depiction, that the degree of independence enjoyed by teachers and school principals and their freedom from central administrative inspection, supervision and control is peculiar to the US school system and is not found in many other countries of the world where education is centrally controlled within the national hierarchical systems. By the admission of Meyer and

Scott (1983), the US school system is atypical of schools in modern societies. Thus the central and oft-repeated example of institutional theory is not even held by institutional theorists to apply to school systems in general. On the contrary, they point to the peculiar historical origins of the US school system as having grown from locally organized autonomous school systems supported by local interests, which only latterly and partially became integrated into an official system at state and federal levels (Meyer and Scott, 1983). Hence the US school system is too narrow an empirical foundation on which to erect the edifice of the loose-coupling institutional theory as a general theory of organizations.

Institutional norms

Meyer and Scott (1983) emphasize a study by Meyer *et al.* (1983). The argument here is that behaviour in the surveyed schools was generated from norms held in common across all those involved in the schools and thus reflected the institutional pressures:

agreements on the nature of the school system and the norms governing it are worked out at quite general collective levels (through political processes, the development of common symbols, occupational agreements). Each school and district – and each teacher, principal, and district officer – acquires an understanding of the educational process and division of labor, not from relating to others within the same organizational unit, but from participating in the same institutional environment, from sharing the same educational 'culture'. (Meyer *et al.*, 1983: 52)

The authors are at pains to display that the norms are institutional and are not organizational characteristics, in that they are *not* held in common by the teachers and principals in the same school. But this is a logically contradictory argument. If a norm is institutional and is held in common across all the members of an institution, then by definition the same norm must also be held in common across all the members of any one organization within that institution.

In fact, the results are consistent at the empirical level in that there is *lack* of consensus within each organization and also at the institutional level, i.e., across all the organizations. The survey asks respondents to state how far there are explicit school-wide policies in each of nine behavioural areas, e.g., type of curricular material to be used, instructional method or techniques teachers use, etc. Each respondent is asked to nominate for each behavioural area whether there is 'little or no policy', 'general guidelines only', or 'detailed explicit policy', i.e., which of three descriptions best characterize the situation. Consensus is then measured by seeing how far there is one category which receives a higher degree of endorsement than the others (Meyer *et al.*, 1983: 51). Complete consensus would be one category receiving 100 per cent endorsement and the other two categories receiving 0 per cent endorsement. Complete dissensus would be each category receiving equal shares, i.e., 33 per cent of the endorsements.

Only two out of the nine behavioural areas show much more than 50 per cent perception of the same level of existence of a policy by the school superintendents (Meyer *et al.*, 1983). (These two items are the existence of policies on written reports of student progress on grades and on identifying students with learning disabilities.) Mostly, these data show a lack of agreement among role-holders in the institutional system, with none of the seven remaining behavioural areas showing a majority of 50 per cent endorsing the same level of existence of a school-wide policy consistently across all the three hierarchical levels of superintendent, principal and teacher. Thus the talk of the existence of generalized institutional norms really holds only for two of the nine behavioural areas examined. There is evidence here of much disagreement over many of the nine behavioural areas of school life. Thus, in general, it might be truer to state of these data that there is consensus neither at organizational nor at institutional system level, and hence there is no contradiction – and neither is there support for institutional theory.

The only exceptions are the two items (student grades and learning disabilities) where there is a degree of institutional agreement within and between hierarchical levels. Moreover, these two items display low correlation among persons in the same organization, leading to the interpretation that there is consensus at the institutional level but not at the organizational level (Meyer *et al.*, 1983). Thus the claim that there is consensus at the institutional level but dissensus within the organizational levels rests on just two of the nine behavioural areas. These findings are interpreted as meaning that there is agreement within hierarchical rank but disagreement between hierarchical ranks. This is based on the low correlations between respondents within each organization.

The correlation within the organizational unit is measured as being that between the score of the superintendents and the average score of their subordinate principals. Being an average, this figure will vary less than the underlying variation of the set of principals who are subordinates of the one superintendent. The scores of superintendents will vary little because of their tendency to all be in the highest category (i.e., consensus within hierarchical level). Thus the two variables correlated together will each show rather limited variation and as a result the correlation will be attenuated and therefore low. Hence the low correlation here is partially artefactual and gives a misleading impression of dissensus within the organization.

The use of a correlation coefficient is not recommended when variation is limited in either variable, yet this condition obtains here. The point can be best understood by asking what would happen if there were perfect agreement on the item within and between hierarchical levels, e.g., all respondents endorsed the highest response level. With 100 per cent endorsement of one level of response, say the highest level, by both superintendents and principals, the covariance between their scores would be nil, and so the within-organization correlation between the scores of the superintendents and their subordinate principals would be zero. Thus the correlational analysis would lead to the conclusion that there was perfect agreement at the institutional level and, yet, zero agreement within each of the organizations which composes the institution. This is clearly a false conclusion and displays the inappropriateness of testing for organizational-level consensus in such data by the use of a correlation coefficient.

Thus the seemingly contradictory findings that, for two out of the nine items, there was consensus at the institutional level but not at the organizational level, is really just an outcome of inappropriate methodology. Even for these two items there really is no greater dissensus at the organizational level than at the institutional level. There is no empirical proof of the assertion that where institutional level agreement exists it is not based on agreement at the organizational level. Thus there is no real evidence of the institutional assertion that institutional norms exist at a level above and independent of norms at the organization level. This plank of the argument for institutional theory falls away. As we have seen, the study (Meyer *et al.*, 1983) provides little support for institutional norms; mostly it shows dissension and lack of norms, thus undermining institutional theory.

Another study of school districts in the San Francisco Bay area is reported by Meyer *et al.* (1978). Again they found that across numerous aspects there is much dissensus rather than consensus between district superintendents, school principals and teachers, and within each level also (e.g., among superintendents). Again, Meyer *et al.* (1978: 260) argue that the school system nevertheless coheres, reflecting the institutionalization of the wider society.

This institutionalization is composed of the shared understandings held in common by all the educators. However, Meyer *et al.* (1978: 260) explain that the study failed to detect this sharing of views because 'we did not think to ask our respondents questions about the structural matters on which agreement is so high as to be taken for granted'. Again, Meyer *et al.* (1978: 261) write of the structure: 'And on these elements the level of consensus is so high – and so much taken for granted – that we as researchers did not think to inquire.' Thus despite the empirical data showing mainly dissensus, there is held to be actual consensus around the taken-for-granteds that are so general in the society that the researchers also take them for granted and hence the empirical study fails to test for them. This argument allows the existence of shared meanings to continue to be asserted notwithstanding the failure of the study to demonstrate them. This kind of non-testable, non-falsifiable claim has been criticized by philosophers of science, who argue that such arguments protect false theories against refutation and should therefore be seen as unscientific (Popper, 1945).

In sum, the study by Meyer *et al.* (1978) fails to show much evidence from the survey data of institutionalization; there is little agreement among the educators in this geographic area. Neither study of the school districts by Meyer *et al.* (1978, 1983) provides evidence in support of their theoretical claim that the schools and school districts are shaped by institutional norms. The claims for cognitive-type causes such as taken-for-granteds are not sustained.

Institutional causes of bureaucratization

There are several studies which examine the idea that internal organizational structure is shaped by external institutional complexity: Meyer *et al.* (1987b), Meyer *et al.* (1988) and Scott and Meyer (1988). These will be discussed in turn.

In a study of school districts in the USA, Meyer *et al.* (1987b) examined the numbers of administrative staff and administrative expenditures. They found that the proportions of administrators and of administrative expenditures relative to student numbers rose with the extent of government funding and with the fragmentation of the system. These increases were greater for federal funding, which tends to be complex and fragmented, than with state funding, which is more integrated in its approach to the schools. Meyer *et al.* also see the state funds as more legitimate than the federal and so requiring less administration within the schools. Overall, the study lends some support to the characterization by Meyer and Scott (1983) of the institutional environment of US schools as being complex and fragmented and as requiring more effort by school administrators to manage in consequence.

However, while the greater number of administrators is documented, there are no data presented on what these administrators are doing. Thus the assertions in the theoretical writings of Meyer and Scott (1983) about administrators manipulating the impression of schools held by governments by giving a false picture, remain conjectures.

In a paper on 'Bureaucratization without centralization', Meyer *et al.* (1988) continue their analysis of education in the USA. They argue that in the years 1940 to 1980, education continued to become more bureaucratized but that this was not the result of centralization. Instead of bureaucracy being produced by the federal government, it was produced by more general rationalizing tendencies in society which involved the professions, with any centralist element being at state government level. Their data consists mainly of demonstrations that school systems became larger and more consolidated, and gained more administrative staff, and that these trends were not effects of funding. The supposed causes of bureaucratization were not measured so remain a conjecture.

Granted that the bureaucratization has not been caused by the federal government, the argument that the changes in the school systems result more from centralization at state level, through each state exercising a role as 'sovereign' as it expands its 'own domination over the local scene' (Meyer et al., 1988: 164), speaks of a considerable role for government, albeit state not federal. Thus, once again, the empirical case, as interpreted by the authors, seems to show the power of the government, though with the qualification that in the federal US system this is at state level. Overall, the study supports the theory of coercive isomorphism, i.e., the power of the government, rather than the loose-coupling theory variant of institutionalism.

A comment is warranted about the kind of data used by Meyer et al. (1988). Their variables are the official statistics collected at national level based on returns submitted by each state (Meyer et al., 1988: 143). But surely these figures sent by the state to the national centre are exactly part of the formal organization which the loose-coupling institutional theory of Meyer and Scott holds to be rhetoric differing from reality. School and school district administrators are supposed to be fighting to appease the impossible demands of higher levels by generating an illusion of conformity to the ideology of rationality as presently in vogue. And this leads them to relentless camouflage which would be expected to extend to reports of the 'body count' which are being sent up the line, and to games with definitions of students, staff, schools, districts, etc. At the least one would expect that Meyer et al. would address this issue and explain the consistency between these data and their theory. Yet such a discussion is not offered by them. Thus we are left at something of a loss to understand how data of a type called into question by a theory can be used to test that theory.

General discussions of institutional analysis paint a picture of an approach which is sensitive and inspired by anthropological and ethnographical concerns for forming a rich description of life as it is lived and the meanings for the actors in their cultural, subjective world. One expects to find much use in institutional analyses of qualitative and in-depth field methods. However, in Meyer et al. (1988) the analysis is of official statistics of the number of students and schools, and amounts of funding monies and the like – all of which are archival in source, to wit, official figures. The analysis is to take these data and plot time series, calculate variation coefficients and perform multiple regressions. There is no qualitative evidence presented as primary research. This seems curious for an approach lauded as more sensitive. The talk about institutionalism as a richly sociological understanding of the cultural, normative and softer dimensions of social life seems to be overstated.

In a further empirical article, Scott and Meyer (1988) report evidence about the school system in the USA. Again they report that the growth of administrators of school districts is positively related to the complexity of the external environment in terms of fragmentation through a larger number of public programmes; and this holds after controlling for the contingency factors of size and internal complexity (Scott and Meyer, 1988: 145). Similarly, at the school level, the number of school administrators is positively related to the complexity of the external environment in terms both of fragmentation through number of public programmes and of lack of integration in the reporting requirements imposed by the external programmes (150). Thus at both district and school levels, fragmentation is associated with administrators. Further, goals of the schools are affected by the external environment, with vocationally oriented school goals being positively related to the number of funded public programmes (156). Moreover, public schools reported that they were more under the influence of external groups, including the government, than private schools, and were more likely to receive on-site inspections from an external organization (156). Thus the empirical evidence shows overall that the external environment, through fragmented programmes, is associated with more administrators, and that the greater magnitude of the external complexity in public compared with private schools is associated with more external inspection and influence and broader school goals. Scott and Meyer interpret this as the more fragmented, complex environment of public schools, relative to that of private schools, subjecting them to more external influence and probing, which leads the school systems to hire more administrators and forces them to adopt a less coherent set of goals as they struggle to fulfil so many programme and constituency objectives. These results are further interpreted as being consistent with the loose-coupling theory (157).

Scott and Meyer (1988) argue that the effect of external complexity on administrators is an institutional effect separate from contingency theory effects of size and internal complexity. They distinguish their own finding and theory from what they term 'conventional' organization theory. However, for the district level analysis, the magnitude of the effect of external complexity on administrators is the same as that of internal complexity (Scott and Meyer, 1988: 144). Also, the effect of size on administrators is considerably larger (144). The magnitude of the institutional effect is one-eighth the combined magnitude of the two contingency variables of size and internal complexity. Hence the institutional theory adds little to conventional organization theory in the explanation of the number of administrators at the district level.

At the school level, the magnitude of the effect of size on administrators is about the same as the magnitude of the combined effects of the two external complexity variables. Hence at the school level the institutional effects are equal to the contingency effect in magnitude. Also, the effect of size on administrators is considerably weaker than at the district level (Scott and Meyer, 1988). Moreover, the external programmes have a greater effect at school than at district level. External complexity works more on the school, and at district level administrators are overwhelmingly influenced by size. Hence the institutional variables work at school level, whereas district level is shaped much more by conventional contingency factors. It is not the case that the district, as the administrative level more remote from the operating units (i.e., the schools), is shaped more by institutional pressures, as might be expected if they were performing the role of buffer between the operating units and the powerful but difficult to satisfy funding bodies. Thus the expectation from institutional theory, that the administrative levels further from operations are more involved with ritual and symbol in appeasing the funding bodies, is not supported by the pattern of these findings. It is the district whose complement of administrators is shaped more by size and the school whose complement of administrators is more affected by institutional factors.

The existence of a number of external programmes in a school increases the administrative complexity of the school. Thus the association between programmes and administrators is made through the volume of administrative work, which is consistent with the theory of Blau (1970). Similarly, the lack of integration between programmes in their reporting requirements means that there is more administrative complexity and thus more administrators needed, again consistent with Blau. The contribution of Scott and Meyer (1988) is better seen as showing how the administrative complexity which generates administrators is increased by externally inspired programmes. Hence these findings can be interpreted as adding to previous contingency theory such as Blau's.

Turning to the issue of breadth of goals, the method of Scott and Meyer (1988) is to measure breadth of goals by the magnitude of endorsement of eight goals (vocational preparation, college preparation, etc.). The more that each of the eight different goals is endorsed by the schools, the greater the breadth of goals of that school type and thus the less coherent the goals of that school type, on the interpretation of Scott and Meyer. This notion of goal breadth can be tested more formally by calculating the mean endorsement of the eight different goals. For the secondary schools, the mean is 51 per cent for the public schools (Scott and Meyer, 1988). For the private Catholic schools the mean is 77 per cent and for the private secular schools it is 56 per cent. Thus both sorts of private schools, Catholic and secular, have a higher mean than the public schools. Goal breadth is higher in private than in public schools. Thus there is no basis for Scott and Meyer to interpret their data as showing that public schools have less coherent goals than private schools. The assertion about goal incoherence of public schools is not proven, and so the claimed connection with external environmental fragmentation is not substantiated.

The statement that public schools suffer goal incoherence connects the empirical study to the wider theory that public educational organizations exemplify loose-coupling (Scott and Meyer, 1988). Thus, showing that public schools are not really goal-incoherent places a question mark against the interpretation of this study in loose-coupling theory terms. Moreover, it is only the goal incoherence statements that provide any attempt to show that these organizations are beset by conflicting external pressures or that they respond by devious misrepresentation to the external organizations by facade structures unrelated to the actual operations. Indeed, whereas the institutional loose-coupling theory of Meyer and Scott (1983) is full of spicy imagery of ritual and conflict, the findings of Scott and Meyer (1988) are 'plain vanilla'. The study shows that having multiple externally sponsored programmes with diverse reporting requirements leads to more administrators to handle them, and that public schools are recipients of more such programmes and so are more inspected, more vocational and more influenced by external organizations, including the government. This is consistent with organizational managers getting on with the job in straightforward fashion and is no proof of deviousness, ritualism, symbolism or of operational ineffectiveness. Again one is struck by the contrast between the heady rhetoric of the theory statements and the prosaic nature of the empirical findings which are offered as support for those theory statements.

Overall, the more one looks into the findings of Scott and Meyer (1988) the less their pattern and meaning supports institutional theory and challenges conventional organization theory. Their findings seem rather to complement and extend contingency theory (Blau, 1970). Externally originating programmes and their reporting requirements add to the administrative complexity of the organization and increase the number of administrators required, particularly in the operating units of the organization (i.e., the schools). This usefully sheds light on a component of the administrative complexity and administrative workload of these organizations and traces it back to specific parts of the environment. But this is no more than the idea that the differentiation of the organization mirrors the differentiation of the environment and that organizational complexity reflects environmental complexity (Lawrence and Lorsch, 1967; Thompson, 1967). Thus the empirical phenomenon is explicable in the existing structural contingency theory, and so no new paradigm is required. The institutional theory about rationalizing ideologies, myth, ritual, and symbol over substance is intellectual baggage that is in no way supported by the evidence in Scott and Meyer (1988).

In summary, the loose-coupling institutional theory of Meyer and Scott (1983) is mostly not supported by the empirical research which they and their colleagues have conducted and which they adduce as evidence for their theory (Meyer *et al.*, 1978, 1983, 1987b, 1988; Scott and Meyer, 1988). Overall, despite numerous studies there is no evidence offered that organizations erect facade structures only loosely coupled to their operations in a vain effort to appease difficult and inconsistent demands of superordinate bodies. Nor is there any evidence of myth and ritual. The empirical literature fails to bear out the colourful claims of the theory of Meyer and Scott (1983).

The cognitive turn in institutional theory

Subsequently, DiMaggio and Powell (1991) have offered a major contemporary statement of institutional theory. This places greater emphasis on the cognitive mechanisms whereby institutions are created and sustained, such as certain organizational structures being taken for granted by the people building the organization so that alternative structures are not even considered. They argue the desirability of using this kind of microsociological causal idea to create a microfoundation on which institutional arguments may rest. There is much citation of Garfinkel (1967) and kindred ethnomethodologists and social constructionists.

It is not clear, however, that institutional theories all rest on these cognitive types of explanations, especially given the prominence in so much institutional empirical analysis of the coercive role of the state (Tolbert and Zucker, 1983; Baron *et al.*, 1986; Fligstein, 1990b). Again the cognitive type of explanation is only one of the many types of institutional explanation reviewed by Scott (1987) and excludes not only state coercion but also organizational compliance with the institutional preferences of banks or governments, or to win approval from professional or accrediting bodies. Some of this compliance is motivated by a calculation about benefits resulting from compliance. This involves organizational members consciously deciding to comply and so is not unconscious and taken for granted. Thus the statement by DiMaggio and Powell (1991) is not an accurate reflection of institutional theory as it is, but more a programmatic statement about what they might wish it to become.

Since the project of DiMaggio and Powell (1991) is a special one for institutional theory, this suggests that their statement marks something of a schism within the institutional school. Moreover, this schismatic tendency may be seen as part of a process of differentiation through developing a distinctive stance, whereby one set of institutional theorists marks themselves off from another set of institutional theorists. The career dynamics so typical of US organization theory may be at work here again. The irresistible push towards novelty and product differentiation produces not only fragmentation of the field into paradigms but fragmentation within the paradigm. Efforts towards an integrated theory of organizations are thus even more frustrated.

On the issue of microsociological explanations and microfoundations, Zucker (1987: 443) makes the point that real taken-for-granteds cannot by their nature be readily identified and tested by social analysts: 'Institutional theory is inherently difficult to explicate, because it taps taken-for-granted assumptions at the core of social action.' One might reasonably ask how institutional analysis can ever tap the real taken-for-granteds and thus the most powerful shapers of organizational form. Any idea about how an organization should be structured that a person can articulate and put into words to tell to a sociologist is not, or is no longer, taken-for-granted by that person, for the person is now conscious of the idea. This creates the doubt that the investigation has missed the actual taken-for-granteds which really are taken for granted by the person and so cannot be articulated by him or her because he or she really is not aware of them. Thus all explanations by reference to a taken-for-granted are potentially flawed by being at too superficial a level and thereby missing the real taken-for-granted. Therefore any empirical evidence adduced by institutional analysis is immediately called as suspect by the theory itself. Hence the theory can never logically be verified. Thus the concept of taken-for-granteds in institutional theory is similar in logic to that of unconscious motives in Freudian theory; both are incapable of empirical test and are therefore unscientific (Popper, 1945). Thus the new programme advocated by DiMaggio and Powell (1991) is problematic from the outset.

The art museums study

In the book by Powell and DiMaggio (1991) there is a chapter by DiMaggio which analyses the history of the art museum. This is a chapter in a section of the book devoted to empirical investigations of organizations using institutional theory. Apparently the chapter is original to the volume and so its inclusion is the more significant, for here we are to see the power of institutional theory in illuminating empirical materials.

DiMaggio (1991) charts the development of art museums in the USA over the period 1920–40. He brings out the influential roles of the museum workers profession and of philanthropic funding bodies, particularly the Carnegie Foundation. The chapter shows how the development of art museums was shaped by ideas about art museums held in the profession and in the Foundation. In particular, emphasis is given to two differing concepts of the proper role of the art museum current at the time in the museum workers profession. The first was of art museums as temples for the preservation and celebration of high art, preferably in neoclassical buildings of an austere and imposing nature. The second was of art for the masses, with museums reaching out through educational programmes, preferably housed in buildings like department stores and dispersed in a network of branches each in a busy shopping area. DiMaggio documents initiatives to assert the latter over the former, then dominant, model, the actors involved and the importance of both the profession and the Carnegie Foundation. As an historical analysis showing the role of ideas and of environing influences on organizations, the chapter is valuable.

In presenting his case history DiMaggio (1991) makes explicit that he challenges previous institutional theory analyses, revealing and making good their deficiencies. In particular, while accepting that the museums reflected ideas and norms in their environment, DiMaggio criticizes the tendency of institutional theory in the Tolbert and Zucker (1983) mould to see norms as reflecting shared consensus. In contrast, DiMaggio writes of a conflict of ideas going on in the organizational field around the individual museums, which, as he points out, negates the proposition that this is based upon a consensus. Similarly, whereas Tolbert and Zucker write of the increasing legitimacy of an organizational form as it spreads and becomes the generally accepted norm, DiMaggio points out that, in the case history of art museums, there was an increasing dissensus over time as the two differing models were articulated one against the other. It is worth quoting DiMaggio at length on these two points:

studies of institutional diffusion have emphasized that organizational forms become more legitimate as they spread, focusing on the form per se rather than on variation among organizations of a given form with respect to structure, programs, and missions. In the museum case, we observe a contradictory dynamic whereby the legitimation of the form empowered and authorized the museum *re*form movement, which offered *de*legitimating criticism of existing museums. In other words, institutionalization bears, if not the seeds of its own destruction, at least openings for substantial change (see also Brint and Karabel [1991]).

... institutional theorists have focused on the general and apolitical process whereby ideologies that are societal in reach shape the form of new organizations. In particular, Meyer, Boli, and Thomas [1987a] (see also Jepperson [1991] and Jepperson and Meyer [1991]) argue that organizational forms are shaped by a 'Western cultural account' requiring organizers to justify their actions on the basis of widely accepted rational myths of justice and progress. The museum case illustrates this point: the museum reform movement borrowed progressive ideology quite explicitly to justify itself in terms of the values of efficiency and democracy. Nonetheless, the case also demonstrates a rather wide scope for conflict over the practical implications of the 'Western cultural account', as museum reformers and traditionalists struggled over the programs that equity required and the goals in terms of which efficiency would be measured. Discourse about museums was full of often unreflective allusions to organizational models from other fields. But the choice of models – whether the museum was more appropriately likened to the library, the department store, or the symphony orchestra – was an object of fateful debate (see also Friedland and Alford [1991] on contending logics of action). (DiMaggio, 1991: 287, emphases as in original)

Thus the museum history shows, according to DiMaggio, 'delegitimating' tendencies. This might be termed a process of deinstitutionalization (Oliver, 1992). This in turn challenges the whole institutional theory of a normative framework which surrounds organizations and which causes them to be shaped according to taken-for-granted ways of thinking. In the museum case the very taken-for-grantedness of the traditional concept of the neoclassical temple of high art was called into question. Thus the case history by DiMaggio does not demonstrate the way normative, unreflective thought structures influence organizational forms.

Moreover, the art museum case history does not support the cognitive turn in institutional theory of which DiMaggio and Powell (1991) write at the opening of their volume. The museum history of DiMaggio (1991), on his own interpretation, calls into doubt the cognitive, taken-for-granted kind of institutional theory in the manner of Garfinkel (1967) and the like. Thus the supposedly illustrative example of an empirical analysis using institutional theory contradicts that theory. The fact that both the case history and the theory appear together in the same volume and are written by the same author shows a great weakness in the institutionalist theory position. The inconsistency between theory and case history is large, rendering the overall argument chaotic. That this can all flow from the pen of the same author, DiMaggio, reveals a quite disturbing elasticity of thought, raising doubts about the intellectual substance of the institutional theory movement. Thus the cognitive turn in institutional theory which DiMaggio and Powell (1991) propound does not survive even to the end of their volume. This shows again the doubtful quality of institutional theory. It may be too much to call this kind of vacillating argumentation a theory.

As quoted above, DiMaggio (1991: 287) includes in his criticisms of previous institutional theory a tendency to make an apolitical analysis. In the museum history, DiMaggio brings out the role of political factors. He points out that the traditional concept of museums as places of connoisseurship and high art for the pleasure of the cultivated few was consistent with the status aspirations of wealthy benefactors and of the museums' trustees. This in turn made museum managers dependent upon these social elites. In contrast, the mass education, populist mission for museums lent itself to support from government, which could provide more reliable budgets and free museum managers from dependency upon the social elite. This is seen as enabling museum managers to successfully attain the status of more autonomous professionals. In this way DiMaggio introduces a more power-political slant to the study, and he fleshes this out with an analysis of which ideas and which personalities were in control of the professional committees and the funding bodies. Such an analysis has many affinities with resource dependence theory (Pfeffer and Salancik, 1978). The museums need to acquire resources, while avoiding associated dependencies, so as to maintain their autonomy, and this has implications for managerial power and is accomplished by interorganizational action including the use of justificatory ideologies. While such a similarity to another modern organizational theory may be unsurprising given the empirical material, and may be applauded as eclecticism, it hardly reassures about the internal coherence or distinctive contribution of the institutional theory paradigm.

Synthesis with the population-ecology paradigm?

There is some sympathy among some institutional theorists with the idea of a rapprochement between institutional and population-ecology theories; this is, of course, to be welcomed as helping to reverse the trend towards fragmentation and paradigm isolationism in organization theory. Both institutionalists and population-ecologists have hailed as a step in the right direction the research project on Toronto voluntary social service organizations (VSSOs) by Singh, Tucker, House and colleagues (Powell and DiMaggio, 1991). In a series of papers they analyse the population using population-ecology theory and methods, together with institutional factors (e.g., Singh *et al.*, 1986). They show that, after controlling for population-ecology factors such as density, there are institutional effects. In particular, institutional factors affect organizational mortality, in that mortality is lower for organizations with greater legitimacy (as indexed by listing in the authoritative directory, tax deductibility status recognized by the government, and number of persons on the board of the organization) (Singh *et al.*, 1991: 398). This is interpreted in institutional theory fashion as being a sign of legitimation and support by powerful bodies in the institutional environment. However, these same indices could also be interpreted in structural contingency theory terms as task-related factors. For example, a listing in the *Community Directory of Metropolitan Toronto* may well help clients to find the VSSO and claim help, or could assist social workers refer people to the VSSO. These results cannot be held to demonstrate support for institutional effects against task contingency effects for these indices are ambiguous in their meaning.

Singh *et al.* (1991) also present evidence of institutional effects in the form of a dummy variable which dichotomizes between two periods: one in which the government encouraged and provided additional funds for certain social service organizations and a subsequent period of discouragement and reduced funds. This dummy affects organizational foundings, mortality and intra-organizational change (Singh *et al.*, 1991). However, the dummy variable measures the difference between a munificent and a stringent environment as discussed in resource dependence theory (Pfeffer and Salancik, 1978), so once again the distinctive contribution of institutional theory as against resource dependence theory is unclear.

In so far as there is any institutional effect to do with legitimacy, population-ecology theory already includes this factor along with the physical resources in the environment (Hannan and Freeman, 1989). Again the distinctively 'institutional' element is not clear here. The simple variables are of the type already found in population-ecology research (Hannan and Freeman, 1989). The extent of the new synthesis between population-ecology and institutional theories is not obvious here. Any institutional element seems to be, yet again, the power of the state and so would be classified as support for coercive isomorphism. Overall, the synthesis offered by Singh and his colleagues between population-ecology and institutional theories is anaemic, rather than full-blooded, and looks more like a minor extension to population-ecology work. At best for institutional theory, it provides one more piece of evidence for the power of the state, i.e., coercive isomorphism.

Nevertheless, the attempt to combine the institutional with other theoretical paradigms, such as population-ecology, in empirical work is to be applauded as a step towards integration.

The institutional theory programme

Desynthesis in organization theory

The major previous statement of a societally oriented theory of organizations was provided by Parsons (1961). In his theory, the organization was analysed into three levels: the technical, the managerial and the institutional. The technical level handled the actual work, the managerial level provided co-ordination, and the institutional level dealt with the problem of legitimating the organization to the rest of society in terms of the shared values in society. Thus the Parsonian model saw the organization as needing simultaneously to handle the transformation of inputs into outputs through actual work, *and* to legitimate itself to society. Management came between these two levels, co-ordinating the work and also co-ordinating the technical with the institutional levels. Institutional theory essentially takes this model and emphasizes the institutional component while downplaying the component concerned with task accomplishment. Thus in institutional theory, as the name implies, the institutional function is not just *a* function, but becomes *the* function whose logic governs all else. The technical level, with its own logic in which tasks are accomplished through work performed by an organization fashioned by the requirements of the task environment, falls away, and is relegated to the status of being the preceding structural contingency theory, against which institutional theory is constructed in deliberate opposition. The full force of this theoretical position is displayed in empirical work wherein the structural contingency theory explanation is rejected as part of showing support for the institutional theory (e.g., Tolbert and Zucker, 1983; Baron *et al.*, 1986).

Hence it is as if institutional theory works by taking the Parsonian model and then selectively emphasizing one part, the institutional level, at the expense of other parts, such as the technical level. There is the nuance that institutional theory, on occasion, emphasizes cognitive over normative elements and tries to distance itself from Parsons (DiMaggio and Powell, 1991), yet normative elements remain integral to institutional theory, as they must, given the centrality of legitimacy in the theory (Meyer and Scott, 1983; Zucker, 1987).

The Parsonian model included in embryo both the structural contingency (or open system) and institutional models, as the technical and institutional levels, respectively (subsequently developed by Thompson (1967)). Thus the model is already in a way a synthesis of these two theoretical ideas of organizational adaptation to the task and institutional environments, respectively. Hence the more complex Parsonian model has been replaced by a simpler one, and in the process the rich and multifaceted nature of organizations has been replaced by a starker and simplistic version. The replacement, at the level of *a priori* theory, of complexity by simplicity, constitutes regression rather than progress, for the framework necessary to capture all the dimensions of the fully functioning organization is being lost. Once again, we see how a modern American organization theory is constructed to be antithetical to structural contingency theory, a step which is the opposite of a move towards synthesis. The theorizing is not taking one theory and then adding another theory to make a fuller whole. It is a process of taking a synthesis and then discarding elements to produce a highly partial and one-sided view. This partial view is then offered as if it were a complete theory of organizations, adequate to capture a full understanding. Instead of moving towards synthesis, we see *desynthesis*.

The institutional theory has been constructed by breaking up the Parsonian synthesis, extracting the institutional level and elevating this to the status of a theory, in order to have a theory which is the antithesis of the structural contingency theory thesis. Thus the history of organization theory at the hands of the institutional theory literature is not the dialectical progression of thesis, antithesis, synthesis, but rather the dialectical degeneration of synthesis, thesis and antithesis. This constitutes a move away from integration towards disintegration and fragmentation. And the pattern of dialectical degeneration is symptomatic of a literature driven by the desire for increasing product differentiation through the search for antagonistic opposition.

The underlying thought structure which produces institutional theory frequently works by taking an existing idea and inverting it. Organizations were seen as integrated systems in which management was closely related to operations: institutional theory holds that management and operations are loosely coupled and must be so. Organizational management was seen as interfacing with the super-system and reporting up to it: institutional theory holds that management deliberately dissembles in its reports, producing an image of the organization widely at variance with operational reality. Organizational effectiveness was held to be raised if societal sectors moved towards more integrated overall organization: institutional theory holds that organizational effectiveness is assisted by operations working largely independently of the official management hierarchy whose intervention would otherwise hamper effectiveness of operations. Thus the institutional theory frequently develops by taking an existing idea and inverting it to argue that the opposite is really the case. This is a procedure virtually guaranteed to produce novelty. It also makes for provocative statements. Hence use of dialectical inversion means that the theory so produced will pass the test of being 'New, Innovative and Provocative'.

Further, since the existing ideas are often the establishment ideas such as official versions of reality or policies about what should be happening, when these ideas are inverted, the result is a theory which is counter-cultural in stance. This counter-cultural quality gives institutional theory a 'modern', sceptical quality, by the admission of its authors: 'more of a social scientific inclination to doubt' (Meyer, 1983: 262). In this way, the institutional theory is fashioned so as to be consistent with the climate which has existed within sociology in the past two decades: the mood of counter-culture, the self-consciously 'critical' approach.

Yet the dialectic of inversion is used so liberally by institutional theory that there is at times almost a quality of the jester or prankster about it. While this may be entertaining, it is less obvious that this is wholly warranted or that it leads to an analysis which is ultimately serious or socially responsible given the gravity of the subject matter: the education of children and the healing of the sick. The writing is at times reminiscent of that of other sociological pranksters such as Garfinkel (1967). Again, this speaks to the sense in which institutional theory is part of a wider movement in sociology in the seventies with all the attendant counter-cultural values, but raises doubts about whether it is really the stuff of organizational science.

Incoherence of theoretical arguments

Zucker entitles her 1987 review article 'Institutional theories of organization'. The use of the plural 'theories' rather than the singular 'theory' speaks to the diversity of theoretical ideas within the institutional movement. This diversity is great enough that there is a problem in the lack of any unified intellectual structure which could be called a theory. Institutional theory, as Scott (1987) brings out in his commentary, posits several mechanisms which influence organizations towards compliance with structural norms. Some of these are conformity induced by particular ways of thinking, the inability to structure in ways unthinkable. A second mechanism is conformity to ideas of good practice as set by professional groups, universities and other expert and legitimating authorities. Both of these mechanisms are neo-ideational in that they give primacy to ideas as moulding structures. Other mechanisms inducing conformity in organization structures are calculative inducements such as government funding or bank loans to the 'properly organized'. Again another mechanism inducing conformity is coercion, usually by the state via legal compulsion. Scott (1987) himself acknowledges the heterogeneity of these various explanations. Institutional theory is plainly not an integrated theory. There is no explicit central axiom from which all the different mechanisms of structural conformity are explicitly deduced.

Proponents of institutionalism would be liable to hail the diversity of theoretical arguments assembled under the label of institutionalism as a laudable richness. Yet the welter of mutually contradictory assertions and inconsistencies is troubling (see Davis and Powell, 1992: 359). For instance, DiMaggio and Powell (1983) made what has been hailed as a central contribution to institutional theory with their theory of institutional isomorphism, namely that organizations through conformity with institutional norms become more alike over time, converging on the normative model for their field. Later, however, Powell (1991: 195–7) talks at length about variations in organizational response to the institutional environment and criticizes the theory of increasing institutional isomorphism as too simplistic (197). Institutional theory holds that the institutional environment determines organizational structure, yet Powell explicitly revokes this idea and argues that organizations should not be seen as passive and that conflicting institutional expectations allow entrepreneurs to manoeuvre creatively. Meyer and Scott (1983) argued that institutional effects on organizations were stronger in institutional organizations, whereas technical organizations were more market-driven and so more shaped structurally by task contingencies. However, later theory statements explicitly dispute this restriction, arguing for more general institutional effects (DiMaggio and Powell, 1991; Powell, 1991). DiMaggio and Powell (1991) give prominence to taken-for-granteds, that is cognitive constrictions, as shaping organizations. Yet Powell (1991: 191, 194) refers to power elites buttressing institutions, to actors using institutionalized rules to further their own ends, to challenges to some occupational groups or professions, etc. These processes would all bring taken-for-granteds into consciousness through social confrontation or individual private calculation of interest and are therefore incompatible with taken-for-granteds determining organizational structure.

Again, a feature of much institutional writing is the insistence on describing itself as the 'new institutionalism' as distinct from the 'old institutionalism' of Selznick and his colleagues (DiMaggio and Powell, 1991: 12). But, in the same volume, Brint and Karabel (1991) expressly criticize the new institutionalism and call for renewed appreciation of the old institutionalism of Selznick and the like.

It is not unknown for theories to change over time and this is a way in which theories are refined and strengthened. However, in the case of institutional theory, the way that later statements contradict earlier theoretical formulations seems incoherent and it is difficult to discern evolution and progress.

Fligstein (1991) explicitly criticizes the emphasis on the normative aspects of institutionalism. He argues at length that the structural transformation of American industry can only be understood by an analysis of power at the levels of the organization, the organizational field and the state. Moreover, while Fligstein (1991: 315) grants a causal role to the cognitions held by the actors, he argues that such perceptions and beliefs are shaped by the interests and structural positions of the actors. Hence, while Fligstein's analysis is presented and accepted as institutionalism, it is actually quite critical of institutionalism, especially of the microsociological formulation in terms of taken-for-granteds (DiMaggio and Powell, 1991). Again Fligstein (1991) argues that the stability of organizations and of organizational fields which results from the power structures requires a shock to induce crisis in order to produce change in the organizations or organizational fields. This argument is similar to that of Chandler (1962) whose performance-oriented adaptive functionalism is held to be the naive, old paradigm which institutionalism transcends.

Brint and Karabel (1991: 342) summarize institutionalism in this way:

The studies that comprise the new institutionalism in organizational studies are brought together chiefly by a shared antagonism to the idea that efficiency and market competition are the driving forces behind all organizational change, and by a shared agreement that much organizational structure and change derives from efforts to create or conform to categories and practices that give classificatory meaning to the social world.

However, in the study that Brint and Karabel (1991) go on to present of the introduction of greater vocational orientation into American community colleges, a major factor which they identify is the change in the labour market. In the early 1970s the demand for college graduates weakened such that students in these two-year community colleges shifted from the traditional liberal arts towards more vocationally oriented courses. The college administrators had been advocating such a swing for decades but their students had resisted until the labour market started to bite (Brint and Karabel, 1991). This is the sort of explanation an economist might favour because of its reference to market forces. The efforts by the college administrators to construct an ideology of vocationalism are presented as having gone on for decades and largely been ineffectual at capturing the minds and hearts of the students. Other factors played a role, such as state support after 1970 of increasing vocationalism, the way California provided a role model emulated by other states and the way other existing colleges affected niche competition (Brint and Karabel, 1991). Once again there is some support here for the institutional effect of the state, but there is little support for the effect of cognitive classificatory categories. There is hardly any evidence here of the importance of normative institutional effects over against economic effects of market competition-based efficiency arguments. Thus the case history presented by Brint and Karabel contradicts their opening theory statement.

Again, Powell (1991) talks about institutional effects as being manifest in path-dependent developments, i.e., choices made at one point are shaped by choices made at an earlier time. Much of his discussion and exemplification here draws upon analyses by economic historians. It illuminates the role of factors such as 'scale economies', 'increasing returns', 'irreversibility of investment' and 'technological interrelatedness' (Powell, 1991: 193). Such standard economic concepts as used by economic historians are drawn upon by Powell, who thereby subscribes to efficiency and market competition-based explanations. This undercuts claims that institutional theory constitutes a distinctive theory which rejects economic theories and offers instead explanation by reference to cognitive categories or like institutional phenomena.

Galaskiewicz (1991) offers an institutional explanation of institution-building in Minneapolis. The interest is in community-oriented charitable contributions. Earlier these were informally organized by the local power elite through social pressure. As the industry of the city became absorbed into national corporations with professional managers, the capacity of the local capitalists to deliver was endangered at potential detriment to the city. More formal structures of community contributions by industry arose which compensated. This featured governmental support, professional organizers, educational programmes and sponsorship by the older elite. Overall, the theoretical argument seems akin to classical structural functionalism: valuable social supports which were once provided by informal, local social associations were replaced by more formalized bureaucratic, professionalized structures. Again the events seem to be consistent with structural contingency theory applied at the level of the city: the contingencies shaping the task of gathering community contributions changed and so the structural adaptation was bureaucratization. Thus it is hard to see that this empirical case study shows the superiority of institutionalism over contingency theory. Again the actions of the old elite behind the scenes in sponsoring a new structure and the programmes of education and seminars on contemporary problems are not obvious signs that the process worked through taken-for-granted cognitive categories; *prima facie* they are indicative of conscious, reflective decision-making accompanied by persuasion to overcome resistance. Thus what the specifically institutional elements are in this study is unclear. That this paper should be one of the five studies selected by Powell and DiMaggio (1991) to illustrate the empirical power of institutional theory raises yet again the issue that institutionalism is not in fact a well-worked-through structure of thought.

Thus many of the core ideas of institutional theory are contradicted within the body of institutional writings. Indeed many of these self-contradictions are found within the same volume (Powell and DiMaggio, 1991). Many of the contributions in that volume offer criticisms of fundamental aspects of institutionalism (Brint and Karabel, 1991; DiMaggio, 1991; DiMaggio and Powell, 1991; Fligstein, 1991; Jepperson, 1991; Powell, 1991; Zucker, 1991).

Two opposing theoretical ideas may be reconciled by locating them within a wider framework which specifies the conditions under which each lower-level idea holds. It is not clear from present institutional statements that they are offering such a higher-order model, the writing being more discursive (e.g., Powell, 1991). Institutionalism is overall an amorphous body of writing with some commonalities but lacks the formal structure of a coherent theory. Given the fissiparous tendencies of its adherents, a more integrated theory may never be forthcoming. Indeed the body of writings seems to display in miniature the restless striving for novelty through negation of the previous theory which we ascribe herein to the US organization theory scene in general.

The rejection of functionalism

The main commonality between the ideationalist and calculative–coercive aspects of institutional theory, is a rejection of an explanation of organization structure as being highly functional for operational effectiveness (apart from isolated cases such as Galaskiewicz, 1991). For institutionalists, structures are not functional and rational, they are arational and of dubious effectiveness, being based on narrow conventional ways of thinking, conservative establishment ideas (of the professions, etc.), the desire to attain funding, or outright state enforcement (Powell and DiMaggio, 1983). Institutional theorists hold that there is some rationality and functionality in organizations conforming structurally; this avoids confusion, makes them intelligible, makes them legitimate, gives them funding and avoids coercive state sanctions. However, this is at best a moderate and minimal level of functionality and effectiveness (Powell and DiMaggio, 1983). This is a far cry from the view of structural contingency theorists that organizations adapt their structure to attain structures which yield a high level of effectiveness (Woodward, 1965; Lawrence and Lorsch, 1967).

This quality of being antithetic to functionalism is part of the reason for the theory's popularity, despite its readily apparent lack of theoretical unity and its severe problems of empirical invalidity. In rejecting functionalism, institutional theory takes on a novelty value, the new, alternative paradigm quality which is highly valued in academic circles, especially in America. As importantly, it takes on a socially critical stance. It is anti the old social scientific establishment, by rejecting functionalism and structural contingency theory, and it is antithetic to suggestions that present organizational structures are effective and well fashioned or tending that way. This latter cannot fail to appeal to anyone of a radical or socially critical tendency. As well, there is considerable appeal in arguments that the present organization structures are limited and stunted in their variety through conformity of unthinking minds, unconscious biases, ideologies of professional bodies and requirements imposed by banks and by the state. These are themes to warm the heart of any social critic.

Moreover, institutional theorists constantly take the explanation of organization structure out from the organization and into the wider society. This is a programme liable to appeal to any sociologist. They are part of a wider movement in organization theory to 'bring sociology back in' by 'bringing the society back in'. Unfortunately the programme works by 'taking organizational analysis out' of organizational sociology, in that it leads to neglect of the empirical results of organizational research. Institutionalism seems able to overlook the way its own research results frequently fail to support the theory (as shown above). And the institutional literature seems often to overlook findings from other branches of the organizational structural research literature which show the functionality of organizational structures and the way they are shaped by contingencies.

Organizations are not slavish copies of the surrounding institutional system. The institutional theory is refuted by the fact that organizations in the same institutional setting show variations in structure which consequently cannot be explained by the institutional factors and which co-vary with the contingency factors, their real cause (Pugh and Hickson, 1976). For example, employment security organizations, despite similarity of tasks and common location within the government, display wide variations in organizational structure, such as number of hierarchical levels or number of divisions, which are strongly related to the internal organizational contingency factor of size (Blau and Schoenherr, 1971). Again, institutional theory, like population-ecology theory, is contradicted by the evidence that organizations adapt to the task contingency factors of size, strategy, task uncertainty and so on (see chapter 2). In contrast, the evidence advanced by institutional theorists to seek to demonstrate that organizations are structured out of conformity with institutional norms is weak. We reviewed herein numerous institutional studies and showed that the institutional interpretation of the data was questionable. Even a supporter of institutional theory such as Scott (1987) is moved to admit that some of the evidence adduced by institutional theory is weak and capable of other interpretations.

The mainstream institutional theory of organizations rests on the idea that institutions influence organizations to adopt certain structures and that the resultant structures add little or no operational effectiveness gains to the organization. This implies that the institutions with which organizations interact, such as governments, banks, professional bodies and trusts, have no interest in securing organizational effectiveness or possibly would wish to reduce it. This is assuredly an anti-functionalist theory of society. It runs counter also to liberal political and economic theories about the nature of societies such as America. The anti-functionalist societal theory is contrary also to Marx's theory of capitalism where the whole social system worked through remorseless competition to heighten organizational effectiveness in regard to raising the capabilities of business firms. While the theory of society in the institutional theory of organizations may seem at first glance to be a neutral and minimalist one, in fact it is a nihilistic view of society of a kind which few serious social thinkers have endorsed.

The contribution of institutional theory

In a number of cases where institutional theory has been tested in empirical research, the data fail to provide strong support for institutional theory as normally understood, that is, as a theory emphasizing myth and symbol. The main proposition to receive clear and unequivocal support is that organizations adopt internal structural elements if these elements are a result of the influence of the state. In the empirical cases, it is not established that these structural elements have no functional value nor that the structures are adopted only as a facade rather than a reality. Thus these empirical cases of structural adaptation through state pressure may well be cases of adaptation by the organization in a functionalist, Parsonian theoretical sense. Hence the only major valid new contribution from institutional research is coercive isomorphism. Knowledge that organizations adopt certain structural elements out of deference to the state, rather than by autonomous adaptation to the task environment, is valuable. However, this is all in keeping with Weber (1968) and with traditional Weberian organizational sociology. And since these state-imposed elements may have positive functions it is compatible with functionalism. It speaks of increasing rationality and efficiency in organizations in modern society and provides no support for the cynical or jokester view that organizations are the opposite of what they seem and that rationality in organizations is mythic. Likewise the statist theory of organizations, because of its Weberian roots, is not any kind of new paradigm rivalling pre-existing functionalist organization theory. Again, there is evidence that externally originating organizational programmes raise the administrative complexity of organizations and thus their administrative staffs. This adds to, and is subsumable under, the conventional, functionalist organization theory of Blau (1970), but it is not a new paradigm.

As a distinct paradigm of organizational structure, institutionalism is fatally flawed theoretically and empirically. It would best be used in future to round out structural contingency theory by adding knowledge about the influence on organizations of the state within the Weberian, functionalist paradigm.

Conclusions

In conclusion, institutional theory is a fairly complex body of theoretical writings which encompasses several mechanisms, through taken-for-granteds to norms to state coercion, whereby the internal structure of the organization becomes shaped by the institutional environment. Explanation of organizational structure by reference to taken-for-granteds is unsustained in the empirical literature and may well be unsustainable because of the impossibility of empirically accessing true taken-for-granteds. The idea that institutional norms cause organizational structures to become more like each other over time is also contradicted by the evidence which shows increasing variance across organizations. Rather, the evidence from the empirical studies mainly supports the much more limited proposition that some internal organizational structural elements are adopted because of pressure from the state. This is valuable, and is compatible with traditional functionalism, Weber and structural contingency theory explanations of organizational structure.

The emphasis on norms, myth and symbol for which institutional theory is best known and which figures prominently in statements of institutional theory is not justified by the research results. Likewise, the playful inversions and jokesterism of institutional theory *à la* Meyer, while in keeping with a certain mood in sociology in the seventies, is in no way sustained in the findings that organizations do what the state says.

The institutional theory of organizations is one of the most prominent examples of the present-day tendency in American organization theory to depict organizations as irrational and duplicitous, as composed of myths and symbols, and as creatures of the normative and cultural system of society. Yet these theoretical claims remain mainly as grandiloquent assertions and rhetoric, at variance with the findings of empirical research. Scott (1987) has written of the institutional theory of organization as being in its adolescence. It is unlikely to enter adulthood.

5   A critique of resource dependence theory

Resource dependence theory argues that in order to survive, the organization must acquire resources (Pfeffer and Salancik, 1978). The organization therefore depends on external organizations for resources. The dependence gives rise to control of the focal organization by the external organization. The resource dependence perspective also applies inside the organization. The resources provided by certain organizational members are more important than the resources provided by other members. The internal control over resources gives some organizational members more power over the organization than other members. Thus the resource dependence theory applies at two levels of analysis: extra-organizational and intra-organizational. Pfeffer and Salancik (1978) offer a multilevel general theory of potentially great significance.

A political paradigm

The argument of Pfeffer and Salancik's (1978) book might be construed as a quite mechanical theory. It states that interorganizational resource dependencies generate external controls by other organizations on the focal organization and also on the intra-organizational power arrangement. It further states that the external constraints and the internal power configuration condition the behaviour of the organization, leading to efforts to influence the environment in order to ameliorate external dependence and retain a degree of organizational autonomy. This would be a straightforward objectivist theory, and there are strong elements of this present in Pfeffer and Salancik's argument. However, while Pfeffer and Salancik constantly reiterate their theme that organizations are externally controlled and constrained, they also argue against simple mechanical causation.

Pfeffer and Salancik (1978) assert that subjective and ideological elements play a role at numerous points in the causal chain. Organizations react to the environment as they perceive it but this is affected by the nature of organizational information systems. Organizations lobby the government and other powerful external organizations and seek to reassure them that they are already acting in the public interest and so require less control, or to obtain regulations favourable to their interests. Organizational members with particular specialized competencies attempt to have the critical resources of the organization defined in such a way that their competencies are the most apposite and hence they become the most powerful members of the organization. These are but examples of a sub-theme repeated throughout the text, that since the processes are human ones, then perception, information, secrecy, argument, visibility, values, etc. are important elements. Thus there is a distinctly subjectivist sub-theme which intertwines with the objectivist sub-theme.

Likewise, while there is a definite determinism in the argument that the organization is externally controlled, the organization is seen not as passively accepting such control but as resisting and using numerous types of response including seeking to influence external organizations or to alter the environment. Also an element of discretion is seen as being available to organizational management in how it responds to environmental pressures, so Pfeffer and Salancik (1978) argue that their thesis is not completely deterministic but allows some room for managerial discretion, albeit limited.

Thus the thesis of Pfeffer and Salancik (1978) is at root a model of political struggle, that is, of different parties seeking to influence each other to their own advantage, both between one organization and another, and between one organizational member and another. In numerous places, Pfeffer and Salancik state that the most adequate model of organizations is that viewed in terms of political analysis as advanced by Zald (1970). Their work is in the tradition of the earlier work of Zald and others.

There is a strong tendency for Pfeffer and Salancik (1978) to distance their work from the organizational behaviour and organizational theory work which has gone before in organization studies. Repeatedly Pfeffer and Salancik castigate previous work as too internally focused and as having ignored the political dimension. Any prior work not within the stream of political analysis of organizations as represented by writers such as Zald and Perrow is heavily criticized. Thus Pfeffer and Salancik make clear that their approach is to be understood as being a radical break with previous traditions in organizational analysis. They seek to change the whole mind-frame with which analysts approach organizations in order that they will see the truth and not fall into intellectual error. Thus, while Pfeffer and Salancik do not invoke Kuhn, nevertheless they claim the status of a revolution in thought of the kind which would customarily be classified as a paradigm revolution (Kuhn, 1970).

The significance of the theory

The book opens with a forthright critique of the discipline of organizational behaviour as being excessively preoccupied with internal organizational causes of organizational performance, such as leadership and the like (Pfeffer and Salancik, 1978). It argues that such internal factors have little effect on organizational performance, which is mainly externally determined. This launches the volume into a lengthy discussion of how external organizations affect the focal organization and of how the focal organization can in turn affect these external organizations. Most of this discussion is of phenomena which may be classified as interorganizational: mergers, joint ventures, co-optation, lobbying, cartels, etc. Of the ten chapters in the book, six (3 to 8 inclusive) are about interorganizational matters. The internal organization is discussed only to a limited extent throughout the whole book, examples being how external organizations impose affirmative action programmes in focal organizations, how organizations sense their environment, and internal power arrangements, including executive succession. Thus the thesis seeks to illuminate some aspects of internal structure, but mainly as they relate to interorganizational linkages. There are grounds for coding Pfeffer and Salancik as being mainly a treatise in interorganization theory, in that most of what the theory seeks to explain is interorganizational (e.g., mergers, etc.).

This raises the issue of whether Pfeffer and Salancik (1978) should really be discussed as a contribution to organization theory. If organization theory is to be defined narrowly as a theory about internal organization then a work on interorganization theory is not obviously a contribution to organization theory. The case could be made that, while mainly interorganizational, the theory does explain certain aspects of internal organization by linking them to the interorganizational phenomena. For this reason Pfeffer and Salancik counts as a contribution to organization theory, even narrowly defined as the theory of internal organization. Further, organization theory today would be broadly defined to include interorganizational relations by many scholars (e.g., Donaldson, 1975; Scott, 1992). Moreover, the interorganizational phenomena (mergers, etc.) which are analysed by Pfeffer and Salancik are clearly of importance and of interest in their own right. In terms of management theory, the interorganizational phenomena which Pfeffer and Salancik analyse are of interest to managers and so their theory must count also as a contribution to management theory. Pfeffer and Salancik is therefore to be counted as a contribution to organization theory.

A more difficult issue is whether the theory of Pfeffer and Salancik (1978) is to be coded as a rival theory to prevailing theories of organization.

Regarding organization behaviour theory, Pfeffer and Salancik are highly critical of organizational behaviour theory with its internal organizational emphasis on leadership and motivation, etc. Yet Pfeffer and Salancik do not really offer a refutation of prevailing theories of internal organizational behaviour for they mostly ignore it, though there are exceptions such as their resource dependence theory of leadership. The overall tone is highly damning of the discipline of organizational behaviour, but a book which largely ignores a vast range of intra-organizational behaviour cannot be accepted as having offered any kind of convincing refutation of organizational behaviour theory.

Pfeffer and Salancik (1978) argue that interorganizational phenomena govern more of the variance in organizational performance than intra-organizational phenomena, but by their same argument most of that performance is locked in by external arrangements and the focal organization has limited discretion. Even if, to use the figures of Pfeffer and Salancik, internal organizational factors account for only about 10 per cent of organizational performance, with the rest being externally caused, it is still of interest scientifically to know which internal organizational variables affect performance and why. Moreover, for a manager in an industry, the issue is how to be more effective than the competitor organization, which is also locked in, through adopting the optimal internal organization in his or her organization. If organization A achieves 8 of the 10 per cent while its competitor, B, achieves only 4 of the 10 per cent, then A will win over B, if both A and B share a similar environment and therefore are similar in the environmentally caused portions of their performances. Hence the intra-organizational sources of performance variation are still important and merit analysis. Thus the purportedly damaging attack on the discipline of organizational behaviour by Pfeffer and Salancik is unproven.

Turning to organizational structural theory, again the relevance of the Pfeffer and Salancik (1978) thesis is only limited. Since there is little attention by them to internal organization, a wide range of aspects of organization structure is not addressed or treated in any depth: span of control, vertical differentiation, project teams, matrix structures, organic structures, internal co-ordination devices, etc. Thus the Pfeffer and Salancik thesis largely ignores many of the phenomena which have been included in organization theory and in particular in structural contingency theory (e.g., Woodward, 1965; Pugh et al., 1969b). There are exceptions in that Pfeffer and Salancik argue, contrary to the structural contingency theory of Blau (1970), that size is not the cause of structural differentiation, which they argue arises as a response to demands on the organization by different external interest groups. But in the main, most of the structural phenomena in pre-existing theories of organization structure are not addressed by Pfeffer and Salancik.

In contrast, many of the phenomena which they analyse are at the heart of strategy theory: diversification, vertical integration, mergers, joint ventures, etc. Thus the theory of Pfeffer and Salancik (1978) is more a theory of corporate strategy than of organization structure. Their work should be considered more as a contribution to corporate strategy and corporate policy than to organizational structural theory. This means that their focus is more on strategic aspects of management: creating alliances, public relations, lobbying the government, etc. These are important managerial tasks but ones which are mainly restricted to upper-level managers and their staff. Middle-level and operational management are largely ignored as are the details of their organization. This is part of the tendency of Pfeffer and Salancik to treat organizations as political actors rather than work organizations which accomplish a task.

The idea that organizations are externally controlled by their environments places Pfeffer and Salancik (1978) in the pre-existing tradition of sociological theories which see organizations as situationally determined by their environments. There is a continuity with the preceding models of organizations in their environments which include structural contingency and the associated systems theories (Emery, 1959; Lawrence and Lorsch, 1967). However, whereas structural contingency theory focuses on the organization adapting its structure to the environment and hence focuses on the influence of environment on the organization, resource dependence theory includes a lengthy analysis of the organization altering its environment through mergers, co-optation, lobbying the government, etc. This idea of the malleability of the environment in resource dependence theory means that it shows that the organization influences the environment. This reverses the causality of structural contingency theory. For this reason, resource dependence theory joined with other contributions (Child, 1972a; Perrow, 1979) in creating a climate of opinion which challenges the structural contingency theory that environment causes organization, by asserting that, on the contrary, the organization can causally affect the environment. Thus organizations were no longer seen as needing to adapt to their environments as they could adapt their environment to themselves. This helped to diminish the respect accorded to structural contingency theory. The programme of structural contingency theory, that of studying how organizations needed to adapt to their environments, became seen as flawed and old-fashioned. However, this rejection of structural contingency theory is premature.

It can simultaneously be true that organizations influence their environments and are influenced by their environments. There can be two-way causality. As long as the environment is not completely malleable and the organization all-powerful, which seems an extremely unlikely state of affairs, the organization will still, to some degree, need to adapt to its environment, including through change of its internal organizational structure. Therefore the programme of structural contingency theory continues as relevant and valid. Notwithstanding such logical compatibility, the question of organizational–environmental influences tends to be seen as an 'either–or', with evidence for organizational influence on the environment seen as somehow necessarily diminishing the validity or importance of environmental influence on the organization. Pfeffer and Salancik (1978) contributed to the popularity of such views by their aggressive denial of the importance of intra-organizational phenomena and their extended analysis of how organizations influence their environments. Thus it behoves us to examine this analysis closely. Much of their argumentation and evidence for the idea that organizations alter their environments turns out to be flawed. Hence it is necessary to critique the Pfeffer and Salancik thesis in order to regain space in organization theory for the programme that there is importance and validity in studying how organizations adapt internally to their environments, i.e., the research programmes of organizational behaviour theory and structural contingency theory. This is not to deny, however, that some organizations influence their environment.

Denial of rational instrumentality

The central idea of resource dependence theory is that organizations are to be analysed as political systems interacting with the environing organizations. Pfeffer and Salancik (1978) articulate their view and distinguish it quite explicitly from the view of organizations as rational instrumentalities. In the opening paragraph of their chapter 2, 'Organization and social context defined', Pfeffer and Salancik (1978: 23) write:

One view of organizations, probably the predominate one, conceives of organizations as rational instruments for achieving some goal or set of goals. Parsons (1956) distinguished organizations from other social collectivities by noting that organizations had some purpose or goal. Perrow (1970) has described organizations in terms of their predominate goal orientations, and the idea that organizations have goals or objectives is one of the most commonly found aspects of the definition of organizations (e.g., Zedeck and Blood, 1974). This goal-oriented or instrumental view of organizations implies that organizations are collections of individual efforts that come together to achieve something which might not otherwise be accomplished through individual action. Just as tools have increased in their complexity and effectiveness for achieving various forms of manual work, so organizations have grown larger and more complex and provide more effective means of accomplishing various social objectives.

Pfeffer and Salancik then continue:

The importance of goals as a defining characteristic of organizations has been criticized on several grounds (e.g., Pfeffer, 1977). We prefer to view organizations as coalitions (March, 1962; Cyert and March, 1963) altering their purposes and domains to accommodate new interests, sloughing off parts of themselves to avoid some interests, and when necessary, becoming involved in activities far afield from their stated central purposes. Organizations are social instruments of tremendous power and energy, and the critical issue becomes who will control this energy and for what purpose (Perrow, 1972).

This passage is interesting and revealing. Pfeffer and Salancik have invoked what they concede to be a major existing view of organizations, namely the view of them as rational instruments, and then rejected it, without giving any rational grounds for the rejection. The rejection of a preceding dominant view in any academic field is no small matter, and the convention in science is that such a rejection must be argued rationally, through reason and fact. Yet the book offers none. Instead the argument jumps to the declaration: 'We prefer to view organizations as coalitions.' But science does not run on mere personal preferences; rather, it attempts to attain objective knowledge through explicit, reasoned discourse.

The final sentence of this passage is also interesting: that the critical issue is who will control organizations. Why is this the crucial issue? For many organizational scholars there are other crucial issues, including which organizational structures will most enhance economic competitiveness, prosperity, innovativeness, safety and democracy. Again no reasons are offered for selecting control as the key issue; it is done in a bald stipulation. Further, the statement that who controls organizations and for what ends are the key issues, is a classic statement of the New Left using exactly their customary language. The suggestion that the work of Pfeffer and Salancik (1978) is influenced by radical sociology or is broadly of the New Left can be better appreciated by a consideration of some of their examples. On page 25 we read that 'one purpose of the United States government was to encourage the manufacture and transportation of narcotics for sale to its citizens' – namely, 'heroin' (Pfeffer and Salancik, 1978). Thus the background world-view behind resource dependence theory is the New Left counter-culture of the sixties.

Yet the statements that organizations are coalitions in no way precludes organizations being rational instruments. Organizations are created and sustained by coalitions in order to attain certain objectives. Pfeffer and Salancik draw on March and Simon (1958) to argue that organizations maintain the coalition in being by offering each member inducements to participate in the organization in return for the contribution made to the organization by the participant. Pfeffer and Salancik make the point that the inducements offered include a degree of influence upon the organization and its goals. All of this is part of the coalitional model of the organization and is sound. But what makes the behaviour of a participant a contribution is that it helps the organization to do its work and to attain organizational goals. Thus the concept of a contribution has no meaning outside of the framework of the organization as a system of activity to attain some goal, that is, the view of the organization as a rational instrument. Again, inducements for organizational members to participate and to keep the coalition alive often flow from the operation of the organization and the fact that the organization attains its goals.

For example, a worker in a motor company contributes by putting the wheels onto a car. The organization completes the assembly of the car and sells it to a customer, thereby making sales revenue and an operating profit (the organizational goals). The company pays some fraction of the sales revenue back to the worker as his pay which is a large part of his inducement to continue participating in the organizational coalition. The concept of an inducement remains mysterious without an understanding of how many inducements flow from the accomplishment of task purpose and the attainment of organizational goals. Organizations are not simply political systems in which actors influence each other. They are also technical systems which produce real goods and services. They can also be economic systems which have internal cash-flows, some of which are used as inducements. In fact a lot of the inducement offered in many organizations to many participants is money derived from sales. Many participants are probably like the car worker for whom money, rather than opportunity to influence the company, is the major inducement, leading them to continue participating in the motor company (Goldthorpe et al., 1968).

Thus Pfeffer and Salancik (1978) attend to the political dimension of organizational life and down-play the sense in which organizations are real systems of work and production and are economic entities. Yet there is nothing in the recognition of organizations as coalitions which requires that one deny that they are also rational instrumentalities. The two ideas are not inconsistent or antagonistic. Moreover, in reality, organizations are both coalitions and rational instrumentalities. Organizations might be defined as rational instrumental coalitions. The participants contribute towards the organization, offering various inputs, including, for employees, compliance with organizational authority, and collaborate to attain the organizational goal so that all share (to some degree) in the fruit of organizational goal-attainment. Such a view is not new, having been expounded by earlier organization theorists such as Simon (1965) and Blau (1964).

The resource dependence theory of Pfeffer and Salancik (1978) denies the rational instrumental aspect of organization and thereby collapses the view of organization into the unidimensional view of an organization as only a political system. This is a regressive simplification. It is buttressed by the repeated selection in their book, as examples, of organizational phenomena from organizations which are 'political' in the everyday meaning of that word and that would be seen as such by any lay person. This leads to a failure to confront the extent to which organizations are systems for achieving some task purpose, such as building a dam, assembling a car, refining oil, designing an aeroplane, installing a telephone system, cooking a hamburger, or educating a child. And this theoretical omission is achieved by selectively avoiding any extended consideration of work organization in the analysis and as examples, despite the fact that many organizations are work organizations.

The over-emphasis on politics

Pfeffer and Salancik (1978) offer vivid illustrative material. A feature of much of this material is that it is taken from the domain which would be labelled as 'politics' in the everyday sense of the word. A great many of the case histories involve the government or organizations interacting with the government.

Conventional sociological theory, such as in Parsons, would maintain that there is an arena of society devoted to political matters and referred to as 'politics' or 'the polity', wherein power, influence and interests are the key concepts. But there is also an arena of life devoted to getting things done, in the economy and in more routine public administration, and this is the arena in which most organizations and indeed almost all work organizations reside. In this arena the key concepts are narrow goals and instrumental actions, with work organizations primarily shaped by these considerations. Work organizations also play a role within the political system, such as when a corporation lobbies the government. However, this does not mean that the work organization has become a political organization in which political influence becomes the primary activity, with the corporation organized in order to maximize political influence at the expense of getting work done. General Motors may lobby the federal government. This will involve some senior managers and some staff units (e.g., corporate affairs). GM might seek to influence indirectly via political grass-roots and state governments and this would involve some political activity by managers at local plant levels, but this would be likely to be limited to some managers for some of their time. GM would continue building cars and trucks, designing them and marketing them, so the majority of managerial efforts would go to the instrumental functions of performing and managing these operational tasks.

Yet one would hardly know from reading Pfeffer and Salancik (1978) that a corporation such as GM conducted any significant activities outside of influencing the government or influencing suppliers or colluding with competitors. The view of organizations projected by Pfeffer and Salancik is of them being largely political animals. This seems to us to be a major deficiency. If Pfeffer and Salancik presented their work as an analysis of the political dimension of organizations it would be unexceptionable and a valuable contribution. But they advance their theory as a new, widely encompassing theory of organization which is to sweep all before it, especially pre-existing organizational behaviour and organization theories with their naive, narrow focus inside the organization. However, inside the organization is where the work gets done and the internal work is what a lot of management is about. The thesis of Pfeffer and Salancik is one-sided and therefore becomes a distorted view of organizations. We believe that it is to a considerable degree false, being based on an exaggeration of reality and a tendentious interpretation of empirical results. Moreover, it yields a remarkably cynical view of organizations and their managers.

In numerous places in Pfeffer and Salancik (1978), statistical findings are presented with an interpretation which fits the theory that the phenomena are political. For many of these findings far more innocent interpretations suggest themselves as being more likely. For example, in a section which argues that organizations seek to attain beneficial state regulation by co-opting powerful interest groups, we find results from a study of electricity utilities by Pfeffer (1974). He reports that the proportion of people with agricultural backgrounds on the boards of these utilities was greater for areas whose population was engaged heavily in agriculture, and that similarly the proportion of people with manufacturing backgrounds was greater for areas whose population was engaged heavily in manufacturing. Moreover, Pfeffer and Salancik (1978: 212) state that these people were selected for board membership as political representatives rather than as customers, for Pfeffer and Salancik show that the correlation between members with manufacturing backgrounds and the population in manu-facturing was higher than with the utility's revenue from industrial customers. However, an alternative, more innocent, explanation is that board members were not selected according to political interest. If the political interest model were true, then the correlation with customer revenue would be predominant, and this is not the case. On the contrary, the predominant correlation is between background of member and population of the state – in farming areas there are more farmers. This is readily explicable in that in farming communities the pool of people from whom to draw board members is composed mainly of farmers. Therefore on a purely random basis farmers would be more likely to become board members. Nothing conspiratorial or darkly political about this.

Critique of components of the theory

We will now consider several of the core arguments of the political model of organizations which are presented by Pfeffer and Salancik (1978) in advancing their resource dependence theory. They are: conflicting external demands; interorganizational dependence as leading to interorganizational influence relationships; the idea of the enacted environment; alteration by the organization of its environment; co-optation theory; the theory of intra-organizational power; managing through manipulation; their alternate explanation of an intra-organizational phenomenon previously explained by contingency theory (structural differentiation); and the role of managers in organizations. Each of these issues will be subject to critical scrutiny. We will show that each of the core components of resource dependence theory is flawed and accordingly that the case for organizations as primarily political creatures is not well made.

The evidence adduced by Pfeffer and Salancik (1978) in support of their theory falls into roughly four categories. The first category is composed of studies conducted by Pfeffer and Salancik, individually or together or with occasional collaborators, and which are reported in depth with tables of numerical results. The second category is also composed of studies by Pfeffer and Salancik but which, in this case, are reported more briefly without tables of results. The third category is composed of studies by researchers other than Pfeffer and Salancik and which vary in extent from brief reporting through to more detailed work with tables. In the fourth category are various case histories. It seems from the presentation that the empirical material which is seen by Pfeffer and Salancik as the most important scientific evidence for their theory is given the most detailed report complete with tables of results. Accordingly, our critical commentary will examine this evidence in most detail. We will argue that much of this numerical evidence fails to support their theory to the degree that they contend.

The conflicting external demands

A plank in the argument of the external control of organizations theory is that organizations are surrounded by multiple interest groups, each of which pressures the organizations to meet the interests of that particular group (Pfeffer and Salancik, 1978). Thus, considering the several outputs or consequences of the organization, each environing interest group values the outputs in a way peculiar to that interest group. Moreover, values not only differ between various interest groups but they are in *conflict*, with one interest group placing an opposite value on an organizational output to that placed on it by another interest group. Thus if the organization satisfies one environing interest group it makes another environing interest group more dissatisfied. Hence it is the presence of conflicting demands upon an organization which makes the issue of dealing with environmental demands so troublesome and makes running an organization so political.

Pfeffer and Salancik (1978: 27) state: 'There is some empirical evidence consistent with the position that organizations confront incompatible demands.' Their evidence is taken from a single study by Friedlander and Pickle (1968) that studied ninety-seven businesses. For each they identified seven interest groups (owners, employees, customers, suppliers, creditors, local community and federal government). For each interest group an assessment was made of how far the business satisfied that interest group. The degree of satisfaction experienced by one interest group was then correlated with the degree of satisfaction experienced by a second interest group. In this way the intercorrelation of satisfaction between all the interest groups was generated. In the summary of the chapter ('Organization and social context defined') Pfeffer and Salancik (1978: 37) state:

Organizational effectiveness is the assessment of the organization's output and activities by each of the various groups or participants. Since there are conflicting criteria, effectiveness is inevitably defined only with respect to the assessment of a particular group – what is effective for employees may be ineffective for owners, and what is effective for creditors may be ineffective for owners, and what is effective for creditors may be ineffective for customers . . .

The task of organizational management, as developed from this view of organizations, is the management of the coalition to ensure continued support and survival of the organization. This task, which is problematic because of the reality of conflicting and competing demands, is necessary because of the organization's interdependence with other participants and organizations outside of its boundaries

Yet the results from the Pickle and Friedlander (1967) study fail to show that there are conflicting demands between employees and owners (see table 5.1). A conflicting demand would be revealed by a large negative correlation between the satisfaction of one interest group and the satisfaction of another, but this is not found. The satisfactions with organizational outcomes of employees and owners are *positively* correlated, +0.25, and this is statistically significant – as Pfeffer and Salancik show in their table (1978: 28, table 2.1). Therefore the more the organization satisfies the employees the more it satisfies the owners, i.e., harmony of interests, not conflict. Similarly, satisfactions of creditors and customers are *positively* correlated, +0.23, and this is statistically significant. The satisfactions of creditors and owners with organizational outcomes are not correlated, which means that they are unrelated and are not inconsistent or in conflict with each other. Thus the results from the empirical study cited by Pfeffer and Salancik fail to support the conclusions which they draw.

Table 5.1. *Correlations of satisfactions of seven parties-at-interest for ninety-seven business firms*

	Community	Government	Customer	Supplier	Creditor	Employee
Owner	0.23*	−0.12	0.37**	0.14	0.00	0.25*
Community		0.16	0.04	0.16	0.14	0.22*
Government			−0.09	0.11	0.20*	−0.07
Customer				0.17	0.23*	0.23*
Supplier					0.08	0.17
Creditor						0.08

Note: Significance of difference from zero correlation: * $p < 0.05$; ** $p < 0.01$.
Source: Pfeffer and Salancik (1978: 28, table 2.1). Reprinted from Pickle and Friedlander (1967: 171, table 1).

The results of correlations between satisfactions with organizational outcomes of the different interest groups are mostly weakly positive. Pfeffer and Salancik (1978) state that the interests of certain groups will conflict, on occasion, based on the existence of some negative correlations in the correlation matrix. However, there are only three negative correlations out of twenty-one. The largest negative correlation is only − 0.12, and none of the negative correlations is statistically significant. Thus all three of the negative correlations have likely occurred by chance out of sampling error. This is the stuff of the evidence of conflicting demands. The average correlation between any two interest groups is + 0.13, that is, low but *positive*. The results mostly show that satisfaction of the interests of one group is either moderately positively related or unrelated to the satisfaction of the interests of other groups. This is an environment in which there is almost no conflict between external interest groups and in which managers of the organizations are free to attend to the demands of one interest group without endangering the relationship of the organization with other interest groups. Pfeffer and Salancik's (1978: 37) conclusion that organizations face an environment which is 'problematic because of the reality of conflicting and competing demands' is false and is contradicted by the evidence.

That Pfeffer and Salancik can offer such a summary is testament to the power of the radical sociological school of thought to see conflict everywhere and see all social phenomena, including organizations, as enmeshed in politics. Thus organization theory can become acceptable to sociology by reaffirming a cherished component of the sociological *Weltanschauung*. In so doing, organization theory also gains a heightened sense of drama, of human conflict and social struggle. However, all of this is attained by ignoring the evidence from the empirical study.

The dependence and influence relationship

Another key theoretical idea of Pfeffer and Salancik (1978) is that power arises out of interdependence. Party A has power over party B if B needs something from A and if B has nothing to give A in return. More exactly, power does not arise through interdependence if A places as much value on what B gives A as B places value on what A gives B, i.e., each party is equally dependent on the other. Power derives rather from asymmetric dependence (Pfeffer and Salancik, 1978: 52). The dependence of B on A is greater the more important to B is the thing which B receives from A and the fewer the alternative sources of supply to which B could turn. Pfeffer and Salancik (1978) add a number of other caveats to this exchange-power theory in order to yield a theory of interorganizational influence, of how one organization comes to have influence over another organization as a result of asymmetric dependence. Pfeffer and Salancik provide a number of illustrations of interorganizational influence, but the evidence from systematic empirical investigations is restricted to two studies, one by Pfeffer (1972a) and one by Salancik (1976).

The study by Pfeffer (1972a) draws on one by Aharoni (1971) of Israeli firms. Pfeffer's study investigated the willingness of firms in Israel to comply with a government programme to develop certain areas through having firms invest in them. Conceptually, greater willingness to invest was taken to be the degree of interorganizational influence of the government on the firm. Theoretically, the influence of the government on the firm was explained by the dependence of the firm on the government. The empirical results support the theory that greater dependence leads to more interorganizational influence upon the dependent organization. They show also that interorganizational influence of the government on the firm is lessened where the government is itself dependent on the firm, i.e., reciprocal dependencies cancel each other out, reducing interorganizational influence.

As Pfeffer and Salancik (1978: 56) note, the questions asked in the Israeli study are hypothetical, and there may also be some tendency for respondents to give a socially approved response, i.e., those companies which do a lot of business with government are likely to espouse a willingness to comply with the government and yet they may not do so in fact. Since the two variables are drawn from responses given by the same manager the results may be inflated by response consistency artefact, i.e., respondents who say their company is involved a lot with the government may be more likely to state that they would continue this involvement in a hypothetical situation. Thus some part of what are low correlations in the results of only + 0.2 or + 0.3 may be artefactual.

The second study, by Salancik (1976), avoids these problems by having variables not assessed by respondents and, in particular, by measuring degree of actual compliance with a governmental programme. This study is an investigation into the degree of compliance by US firms with the requirement of the US government that firms supplying defence equipment have affirmative action programmes for women. The study examined seventy-eight of the largest US defence contractors. For each firm the degree of its dependence on the government was measured, as the percentage of the firm's total sales that were to the government, and the degree of the government's dependence on the firm was measured, as the percentage of total defence expenditure made up by sales from that firm. The mode of analysis was to correlate percentage sales to the government, that is, dependence of firm on the government, with degree of compliance on affirmative action for women. This correlation is calculated separately for firms on which the government is dependent and for firms on which the government is not dependent. And there is a further moderator variable used, which is the size of the firm, on the proposition that larger firms are more visible than smaller firms and may be expected to have adopted affirmative action for women in response to pressures from groups other than the government (Pfeffer and Salancik 1978: 58). Hence Pfeffer and Salancik examine the correlation between percentage firm sales to government and compliance with affirmative action under four different conditions (see table 5.2). They conclude that the results support their theory (Pfeffer and Salancik, 1978: 59).

However, if one looks at the US defence contractor study, the results are quite different and do not support the theory that there is a general effect whereby dependence promotes interorganizational influence upon the dependent organizations (see table 5.2). The effect of dependence raising influence upon the dependent organization will be registered in the American defence contractors study by a positive correlation between the percentage of the firm's sales to government and the compliance by that firm with affirmative action. Such positive correlations are present for large firms, but not for small firms where the correlation is either virtually zero (+ 0.02) or is negative (− 0.67) (Pfeffer and Salancik, 1978: 59). Moreover, firms classified as small make up the majority of the cases studied – fully two-thirds (fifty-two out of seventy-eight firms). Most organizations in the study do not show any evidence of greater dependence on the government leading to greater compliance with the governmental affirmative action programme. For half of these smaller firms, that is, twenty-six firms or one-third of the total cases studied, greater dependence on the government leads

Table 5.2. *US defence contractors' responsiveness to inquiry about employment opportunities for women as a function of proportion of sales to the government, firm size and control of production*

Type of Firm	Correlation	Sample size
Large, visible firm, not controlling production of items	0.84**>	13
Large, visible firm, with control of production of items	0.46*	13
Small, less visible firm, not controlling production of items	0.02	26
Small, less visible firm, with control of production of items	−0.67**<	26

Notes: (1) Significance of difference from zero correlation: * $p < 0.05$; ** $p < 0.01$.
(2) > Correlation is significantly greater than + 0.02 correlation ($p < 0.002$).
    < Correlation is significantly less than + 0.02 correlation ($p < 0.01$).
Source: Pfeffer and Salancik (1978: 59, table 3.2).

to *less* compliance with affirmative action, to a striking degree as shown in a *negative* correlation of − 0.67.

The expected positive correlation between dependence and interorganizational influence was found in only one-third of the firms. The relationship was virtually zero in one-third of the firms and negative in the remaining third. The relationship is about as strongly negative in the last third of the cases as it is positive in the first third of the cases. There is no support in these results for a general relationship between dependence and interorganizational influence. Dependence appears to be a very volatile phenomenon whose effect on influence swings wildly from having a positive effect to a negative effect. Sometimes dependence causes compliance with the wishes of the organization depended upon, while at other times dependence causes non-compliance.

For small firms, the effect of dependence on compliance is nil or negative. Yet the firms which are coded as 'small' here are the smaller two-thirds of seventy-eight of 'the top 100 defense contractors' in the USA (Pfeffer and Salancik, 1978: 57). Such 'small' firms are really quite large and so would probably include many firms which would be classified as medium-sized in the USA or as large in many other countries. Therefore the overwhelming preponderance of most firms in other countries of the world would fall into the 'small' rather than the large category used here. In so far as this study can in any way be generalized to other firms, the implication is that almost all firms in the world would have a nil or negative relationship between dependence and interorganizational influence.

Moreover, the dependence–interorganizational influence relationship becomes negative in 'small' organizations which have dependence of the government on them. In such a situation of governmental dependence on the firm, the more dependent is the firm upon the government, the *less* the firm complies with the government. The two dependencies do not cancel each other out as resource dependence theory holds. On the contrary, these results show that the direction of the effect of dependence on influence is reversed when the opposite kind of dependence is present, so that dependence leads to counter-influence, i.e., doing the opposite of what the exchange partner wishes. Counter-influence is a phenomenon not even recognized in the conceptual framework of resource dependence theory. Little wonder, because the theoretical proposition would be that the more an organization depends on another organization the more it disobeys the other organization; the more I depend on you the more I disobey you. Such a phenomenon makes a mockery of the whole idea of resource dependence theory and exchange-based power. Yet, in the results of Pfeffer and Salancik (1978), for every firm which displayed behaviour consistent with the resource dependence theory there was another firm which displayed the opposite behaviour. This calls into question the fundamental ideas of resource dependence theory.

Thus the US defence contractor study refutes more than it confirms the dependence–influence theory (for two-thirds of organizations act contrary to the theory). The two studies taken together provide only limited support for the dependence–influence proposition. The results from the second (US) study mostly argue against a dependence–influence relationship of the sort theorized and suggest that any such relationship exists at the most in only a small fraction of the work organizations in the world. The results from the second study make it seem more likely that the results from the first (Israeli) study are due to artefacts. The findings from the systematic empirical studies reported by Pfeffer and Salancik (1978) fail to provide clear support for the dependence–influence theory and raise real doubts about the existence of a general positive relationship between dependence and influence of the sort the theory posits.

Enacting the environment

Pfeffer and Salancik (1978: 72) draw on the concept of the enacted environment from Weick (1969: 64) whom they quote as saying: 'the human *creates* the environment to which the system then adapts. The human actor does not *react* to an environment, he *enacts* it' (original emphasis). The argument is that sensing the environment involves that human process of attention which in turn involves mental imagery. Further, meanings are given by the beliefs of the human observer as they create a representation of the external world. This in turn implies that the image of the environment of an organization may differ from one person to another even though all are members of the same organization. All of this is true, and yet none of these perceptual phenomena means that the organization enacts, meaning 'creates', its own environment. The environment exists independently of whether or not the organization perceives it. Thus the organization does not create its environment, nor does the organization enact the environment in the sense that the environment exists because the organization acts it out or makes a representation of the environment.

The term 'enact' is unfortunate in that it is vague and can suggest a variety of meanings. The statement that the organization enacts the environment can be interpreted as meaning that the organization alters or shapes its environment. Organizations can do this: some organizations, some of the time, alter their environment through merger, lobbying the government, and so on. Pfeffer and Salancik (1978) make this argument that organizations alter their environment in the objectivist part of their theory. Thus there is some danger that the concept of the enacted environment becomes confused with the concept of the altered environment. This in turn would imply that the alteration of the environment by the organization hinges on the organization creating the right mental model of the environment – as if imagination were all that was required to change the world. Yet, in order to alter the environment, the organization has to perceive the present environment, imagine a different one and then do something that changes the actual environment towards the imagined one. This process involves perception and imagination but also efforts at change which may or may not be successful. The concept of enaction implies that all that is required is the imagined environment. Thus the concept of enactment introduces confusing language and an excessively subjectivist quality into resource dependence theory. However, the Weickian concept of the enacted environment sets up for Pfeffer and Salancik their extended analysis of influence on the environment by the organization.

Altering the environment

Pfeffer and Salancik (1978) have a chapter entitled 'Altering organizational interdependence'. Its argument follows from the central premise that the key problem for an organization is to manage its interdependencies with other organizations in order to maintain autonomy and to survive. Pfeffer and Salancik (1978: 113) go on to state that one way of dealing with interdependencies is to shift the organizational boundary through growth and merger and thereby to internalize what were previously problematic interdependencies. In particular, three different types of merger are distinguished: vertical integration which eliminates interdependencies of the type termed 'symbiotic' (i.e., input–output connections), horizontal expansion which eliminates competitive uncertainties by absorbing competitors with whom the focal organization is said to have a relationship of 'commensalistic interdependence' (e.g., competition for the same customer) and diversification which spreads the organization across several industries and thereby reduces the dependence of the organization on a dominant organization in any one industry. Each of these forms of merger reduces a troublesome degree of dependence of the focal organization on other organizations.

The emphasis is upon securing stability, freedom from dependence and freedom from uncertainty, and upon survival. Pfeffer and Salancik (1978) are at pains to distinguish these explanatory variables from explanations by reference to the search for increased profit or efficiency. While noting in passing (Pfeffer and Salancik, 1978: 115) that profit or efficiency explanations are not incompatible with dependence theory, nevertheless Pfeffer and Salancik go to considerable lengths to show that profit and efficiency are not the explanations of merger and growth. This implies that resource dependence theory is to be distinguished from arguments which explain organizational behaviour ultimately by performance. Consistent with their theme, Pfeffer and Salancik conclude their chapter with the explanation that growth is motivated not by profit but by the search for stability in order to maximize the likelihood of survival (137ff.). Thus the predilection of resource dependence theory for emphasizing the maintenance of organizational autonomy and organizational survival is manifest in the treatment of the alteration of organizational interdependence.

Pfeffer and Salancik (1978) review a large number of interorganizational co-ordination devices which they argue reduce competition and uncertainty for firms: mergers, joint ventures, co-optation through the board of directors, cartels, trade associations and government regulation. They show that the circumstances under which each of these different forms of interorganizational co-ordination arise are similar; in particular many of these devices arise where the concentration of the industry is at an intermediate level. The finding that intermediate concentration predicts many different interorganizational co-ordination devices shows a rather remarkable degree of generalization from one phenomenon to another. This could well be considered a major empirical achievement of Pfeffer and Salancik, and it is one of the major empirical discoveries in their work. However, a question arises provoked by the generality of the result.

If in the same situation any of these different co-ordination devices can arise and produce the same effects, are they perhaps alternatives for each other? And if they are alternatives, since they differ in costliness, would not organizations utilize some of these devices more than others? The expense and trouble of a merger is surely much greater than the cost and trouble of putting somebody onto the board of directors. This would suggest some sort of contingency model running across these different forms of inter-organizational co-ordination device specifying under which circumstances one rather than another would be used. Or again, if each interorganizational device is correlated with intermediate co-ordination, they may be correlated positively with each other; thus they may go together and may need to go together, that is, they may be complementary. Whether the different interorganizational devices are alternative or complementary or in some way both, these comments point to a curious theoretical lacuna in Pfeffer and Salancik (1978) in that having shown that different interorganizational devices arose in the same conditions they did not provide a theoretical rationale which arranged these different devices contingently or interactively.

The theoretical contradiction of interorganizational co-ordination devices   A mainstay of the empirical analysis by Pfeffer and Salancik (1978) is reference to various interorganizational co-ordination devices (ICDs). They show that ICDs are more prevalent among firms which are in industries at intermediate stages of concentration. In this intermediate concentration situation competitive uncertainty is at its highest. A firm will seek to avoid this by utilizing one or other ICD.

It must be pointed out that the motivational argument about firms seeking to reduce competitive uncertainty is wholly speculative and is simply an attribution. No direct evidence is produced that this is why firms involve themselves in ICDs.

Pfeffer and Salancik (1978) find that firms in industries of intermediate concentration become involved in many different kinds of ICD: mergers, joint ventures, interlocking directorships and recruitment of a chief executive from outside the company. Yet each of these ICDs itself involves an element of diminution of autonomy. The organization has to share power with the merger or joint venture partners, or take a representative of an outside organization onto its board or into its top management office as the CEO. As Pfeffer and Salancik put it (1978: 261): 'Ironically, to gain some control over the activities of another organization, the focal organization must surrender some of its own autonomy.' This is surely more than an irony, for it strikes at the heart of the whole logic of the resource dependence approach. It is inconsistent to argue that in order to protect their autonomy, organizations take steps which reduce their autonomy (see Davis and Powell, 1992: 325).

Mergers   Pfeffer and Salancik (1978) examine in turn each of the three kinds of merger (vertical, horizontal and diversification). They seek to show that these changes in the organizational boundary are caused by interdependencies and the uncertainties to which these interdependencies give rise. The empirical results provide evidence that organizational mergers are related to resource interdependencies. However, it is not clear that the empirical data patterns reflect the political processes of managing interdependencies which are so central to resource dependence theory.

In part, the issue hinges on the broad and vague meaning of interdependence. When Pfeffer and Salancik (1978) talk of interdependence and uncertainty they mean an asymmetric interdependence between the focal organization and another organization, so that the focal organization is net dependent on the other organization and is therefore liable to be compelled to comply with wishes of that organization, leading to a reduction of the autonomy of the focal organization. Yet the way resource interdependence is measured in the analysis of mergers is mostly not by an assessment of asymmetric dependence but by rather more prosaic variables which simply examine flows of goods between sectors of the economy, i.e., Leontieff-type input–output flows between industries (see Davis and Powell, 1992: 325). These analyses tell us nothing about asymmetric dependence between organizations or any interorganizational influence or political-type processes.

Pfeffer and Salancik (1978) show that mergers between firms in different industries are more likely the more those industries are related through the supply of inputs or outputs to each other, i.e., are vertically integrated. This does not prove that such mergers are made in order to eliminate asymmetric dependencies or to establish greater control over the environment. At least one of the partners to the merger may feel that it is now being more controlled by the erstwhile other firm and its managers. Mergers are surely a reduction in autonomy. Again, where two firms vertically integrate this may be for reasons of efficiency such as improving scheduling, dovetailing the two production processes more completely (Chandler, 1977) and so on, i.e., the result is not just reduced uncertainty but lower costs and greater profit. Thus the motives are economic not just power-political. There is nothing in the data of the mergers analysis, therefore, which requires an interpretation in terms of political-type resource dependence theory.

Turning to mergers within the same industry, under the heading of symbiotic interdependence, Pfeffer and Salancik (1978: 123) show that the number of firms in an industry which merge with other firms in the same industry is positively related to the proportion of within-the-industry transactions in which that industry engages. Thus the more an industry is self-sufficient in input–output terms then the more likely a firm is to merge with another firm in that industry. Again such interorganizational behaviour is quite consistent with a search for operating efficiencies and synergies and is not obviously produced by political-type reactions to asymmetric dependencies, which again are unmeasured. Once again, merging is as much a reduction in a firm's autonomy as it is an increase in freedom from interdependence. Such mergers within an industry are shown empirically to be more likely when an industry is less profitable and less concentrated. This seems quite consistent with the industrial organizational economics theory which notes that an industry moves over time from being fragmented and highly competitive to being a mature oligopoly, in part through merger, resulting in higher industry profitability.

Under the heading of competitive interdependence, Pfeffer and Salancik (1978: 124) argue that some mergers of firms within the same industry are to reduce competition and to reduce competitive uncertainty. They argue that uncertainty is greatest at intermediate levels of concentration, because firms are few enough to affect each other but too many for 'tacit coordination'. Pfeffer and Salancik (1978: 125) report graphing the proportion of within-industry mergers against concentration and finding an inverted U-shaped curve. However, anti-trust legal constraints discourage further concentration through merger where concentration is already high. Further, these mergers are not necessarily related to any political processes of responding to asymmetric dependencies, which again are not measured.

Turning to the third and final type of merger, diversification, Pfeffer and Salancik (1978: 126) theorize that 'diversification is a strategy used for avoiding constraining resource dependence'. They present evidence (129) from the study of Israeli managers that the more a firm sells to a customer at present, the less they would wish to sell in future, i.e., they would hope to free themselves from the dependence. Such a reduction in percentage sales to an established customer could be accomplished, assuming the firm did not wish to decrease sales volume, by increasing sales to additional, new customers, i.e., by diversification.

Yet the data from the Israeli manager study is analysed by Pfeffer and Salancik (1978) in a way which makes it virtually certain that the results will confirm the resource dependence theory. The analysis correlates the percentage of actual sales to each customer with the reduction desired in future to that customer, and finds a positive correlation. Yet there is an in-built positive correlation between the actual sales and the desired reduction in sales. The reduction in sales can only be large when the actual sales figure is large. When the actual sales figure is small, say 5 per cent, the maximum possible reduction can only be small (i.e., 5 per cent). The magnitude of the possible reduction is constrained by the actual sales. The positive correlation reported by Pfeffer and Salancik (1978: 129) would be expected because of the in-built tautology. Hence the empirical evidence connecting greater actual sales to a customer to a greater desire to reduce sales to that customer in future is flawed. Accordingly, the proposition that greater dependence on a customer leads to attempts to reduce that dependence cannot be seen as proven by the Israeli manager study.

Firms may seek to reduce the percentage of their sales to the government as Pfeffer and Salancik (1978: 130) state from studies of US corporations. They report literature showing that US defence contractors sought to diversify away from government sales as the Vietnam war ended and there was a down-turn in government procurement. But this could be nothing more than firms seeking to diversify away from a declining market. This would be a rational action for profit-maximizing firms and is not proof that firms seek to avoid dependence *per se*.

Even if subsequent research showed that firms do seek to reduce the proportion of their sales to existing customers, these results would seem to bear an economic explanation. Where the firm is one of many sellers to a single customer, monopsony prevails and the monopsonist (the customer) will drive down the price paid to the firms. Thus the firm will wish to avoid such monopsonistic markets and look for markets with few suppliers and many, fragmented customers because prices therein will be attractive to sellers. Hence one could see the relations between organization and environment as discussed in resource dependence theory as being driven by economics. The relations between organizations are economic exchanges that are mediated by markets and prices. The factors which are held in resource dependence theory to determine exchange imbalance – numbers of buyers and sellers – are precisely the factors which set the market price. Thus what are seen as exchange imbalances may often be market price effects. Where there are many suppliers and one customer, the price will be low and this in itself will cause the supplier to wish to stay away, rather than any move to avoid dependence. The firms respond to the price signals in their efforts to maximize profits. They are not seeking to minimize asymmetric dependencies nor to minimize interorganizational influence and maximize autonomy, but rather to maximize economic returns. Thus the Israeli firms want to sell less to the governmental agency that procures non-military supplies and to wholesalers, because both outlets represent concentrated customers and therefore poor prices. And the Israeli firms will be less concerned to reduce the percentage of their sales to the government defence department because there are presumably few suppliers of equipment which the government needs desperately and therefore prices will be good. Thus these data on diversification are consistent with resource dependence theory but the theory overlooks a major variable which mediates transactions between suppliers and customers – price.

It cannot be said too strongly that one of the defining characteristics of the advanced industrial society is that most transactions of goods and services are done in the money economy (Parsons, 1966). As Weber (1968) states, trade is increasingly conducted in modern society by transactions in which goods and services are sold for money. If a person receives goods and services and pays money in return equal to the value of goods and services (that is the market price), then the transaction is complete and there is no residual obligation to comply with some future request. This is one of the great beauties of market transactions and makes them impersonal, clear-cut and final.

The resource dependence theory with its emphasis on political-type striving for independence ignores the economic market processes which connect these organizations. In this way resource dependence theory becomes a strangely misleading theory for it fails to refer to a major set of interorganizational processes, namely the economy. Resource dependence theory produces an image of organizations as survival-seekers desperately manoeuvring in political fashion to control or be controlled, whereas in reality those organizations which are firms are seeking to maximize profit-to-risk and adjust their strategy according to the dictates of the law of supply and demand. Since most organizations are in fact firms (i.e., small businesses are very numerous) and firms adapt to exchange imbalances mainly through price rather than compliance, it follows that the theory that exchange imbalance causes interorganizational compliance is false for most organizations in most respects.

In their analysis of mergers, Pfeffer and Salancik (1978) review literature which shows that mergers are not particularly profitable and may even be followed by a decline in profitability. Such an analysis hinges on the issue of whether mergers are profitable for the merging firm relative to the profit that firm would otherwise have attained, i.e., the opportunity cost for that firm. For a firm in a declining industry whose profit was also declining, a merger would be sensible even if the profit of the firm declined after the merger, if the profit would have declined *more* without the merger.

Organizational growth   Pfeffer and Salancik (1978: 136ff.) discuss the vexed issue of managerial motivation for growth and conclude against the view that managers pursue organizational growth for its own sake. They conclude that managers, even where ownership and control are separated, are profit maximizers. (This marks a real divide between resource dependence theory and organizational economics, wherein managers are seen as seeking to maximize salaries and the like, possibly through sales growth, at the expense of profit and returns to owners.)

Pfeffer and Salancik (1978: 137ff.) examine the relationship between organizational growth and stability and conclude that, while organizational growth does not lead to profitability, it does lead to greater stability, i.e., lesser variance in profit. Thus Pfeffer and Salancik argue that firms are not profit maximizers but are survival-oriented. Yet less profit variance means, in financial economic terms, less risk. Low risk is positively valued by investors, so that an investor will accept a lower profit if the risk is also lower. The economic performance of a firm is not merely profit but is the profit-to-risk ratio. Thus if, through growth, a firm lowers the risk even without raising profitability, it has thereby raised its profit-to-risk ratio, and so it has raised its performance. Thus stability obtained through organizational growth should be seen not just as survival-seeking but rather as profit maximizing based in the economic concept of profit-to-risk.

Co-optation theory

Pfeffer and Salancik (1978, ch. 7) extend resource dependence theory to ways that the organization influences the environment so as to benefit the organization. One such process is co-optation. For a corporation, the board of directors is one mechanism whereby the organization controls the environment; it does this by co-opting powerful environing groups onto the board. There they will become involved in helping the organization by influencing their constituencies on the organization's behalf.

Pfeffer (1972b) shows that the percentage of inside directors on boards is lower among corporations with high leverage and a regulatory environment. Among the outsiders are attorneys at law, and their number on a board is greater when insiders are low and the corporation has high leverage and a regulatory environment – interpreted as reflecting that attorneys are used to help deal with debt financing and with regulatory bodies. Also, the proportion of board directors who are representatives of financial institutions is greater where debt is higher, and thus financial need is greater. Pfeffer shows that deviation by a corporation from optimal board composition, as given by the contingency factors (size, debt and regulation), is associated with lower financial performance for the corporation.

The central theoretical processes, namely that outside board members co-opt powerful external environmental bodies and in this way raise corporate financial performance, is wholly inferred (for a critique, see Mintzberg (1983: 87)). Whether or not the outsiders on the board are in fact drawn from powerful environment bodies or are in a position to influence those bodies, and whether they do so and are successful at making the competitive environment easier and more munificent for the focal organization – all of this remains unmeasured and therefore unverified.

If more regulated organizations have more outsiders this might be because, since they are more conscious of their public profile, such corporations seek to assure the public of their bona fides and sound governance by including on their boards more honourable citizens and representatives of various sections of the community than would a less regulated corporation. Such outsiders might not necessarily be related to the regulatory apparatus nor be in a position to influence that apparatus. Again, the presence of more representatives of financial institutions where the debt-to-equity ratio is greater, could indicate control by lending institutions, not their co-optation.

Central to the argument is that representatives of these powerful environing bodies, once seated on corporate boards, become co-opted and influence the environing bodies on behalf of the focal organization. This implies that membership of a board powerfully affects individuals so that they become highly committed to the focal organization, so highly committed that their allegiance is swayed to the point that they pursue the interests of the focal organization back in the organization which is their home base. In contrast, studies of boards show that, at most, boards meet a day or two per month (Korn/Ferry International, 1988). Outside board members are thus spending the overwhelming proportion of their time outside of the focal organization and its culture. Again, the studies of boards point away from the idea that outsiders are typically inside the corporate mind-set of the focal organization (Mace, 1971; Chitayat, 1985). If a person who has served for decades in a bank or government can so readily 'change their spots' by moving onto a corporate board then this would negate the idea that their home organizations really are powerful environmental influences on the focal organization. Thus the resource dependence theory of co-optation is self-contradictory.

The theory of co-optation holds that a mechanism whereby established corporations exercise control over the market is collusion with other firms through corporate interlocks, that is, through overlapping board memberships (Pfeffer and Salancik, 1978). A member of the board of directors of company A is also a member of the board of directors of company B. Such corporate interlocks have been repeatedly studied and the documentary evidence of their existence has been widely interpreted as evidence about one of the means whereby big business colludes to control the markets and to suppress competition. However, Zajac (1988) has challenged the methodology used in many empirical studies of corporate interlocks. By a re-analysis of one of the data-bases used to assert the corporate interlock thesis, Zajac (1988) shows that the overlapping directorships held between companies in the same industry are a small proportion of all the overlapping directorships and are at about the level expected on a random chance basis. Hence overlapping directorships do not occur in the way that would be expected on the theory that they were purposefully created for anti-competitive collusion. Overlapping directorships are a general phenomena arising from the need to fill boards from a limited pool of suitable people, and given that process, some overlapping directorships will occur on a chance basis between firms in the same industry; but these are chance events and a small minority of all overlapping directorships. Going further, Zajac (1988) demonstrates that when directorships overlap between two firms in the same industry, the firms are usually in fact from different sub-industries and are almost invariably not competitors with each other. Thus the overlapping directorships cannot be a channel whereby collusive control is exercised by the two firms over the same product-market as the firms are not in the same product-market. By basing his analysis on the very sort of data used to argue for the corporate interlock thesis Zajac (1988) damages the whole substance of that thesis.

Pfeffer and Salancik (1978) see interlocking directors as allowing the organizations to co-ordinate with each other thereby lessening competition and raising profit. However, they have no evidence that interlocking directors raise profit. The resource dependence theory of the co-optive functions of corporate boards of directors has been tested by Burt (1983). Burt sees no evidence in his study for concluding that corporate interlocks raise profit after other factors affecting profit have been controlled (Burt, 1983: 177, 188). Burt states: 'One policy implication of this study for directorate ties, in sum, is that such ties should be left alone' (189). Moreover, Burt points out, directorate ties between corporate competitors are illegal in the USA, thus further undercutting the likelihood that, in countries with such laws, directorate ties raise profit through anti-competitive collusion between corporations (188). Hence the study by Burt, which goes beyond that of Pfeffer and Salancik (1978) in empirically testing the relationship of corporate interlocks to purported profit outcomes, fails to support their theory. The co-optive functions imputed to directorate ties are not confirmed empirically.

The resource dependence theory of boards of directors is problematic. It sees boards as providing a way to co-ordinate two or more corporations including anti-competitive collusion to secure unfair profits (Pfeffer and Salancik, 1978). Boards performing an interorganizational collusion function are thereby transgressing societal norms about fair play and would also be breaking the law in countries such as the USA where anti-competitive collusion is illegal (Burt, 1983). Moreover, by achieving collusion through sharing directors, corporations are transgressing in a highly public manner, for the identity of directors are matters of public record and thus shared directors are easily found. In fact this very availability of the identities of directors has permitted academic researchers to study directorate ties or corporate interlocks. Thus shared directors between corporations can easily be revealed and the corporations publicly censured. Further, even if the two corporations share a director but make no anti-social or illegal use of that link, the mere existence of such a visible link will raise suspicions and may embroil the corporations in negative publicity. Hence shared directors between corporations threaten the legitimacy of those corporations. The resource dependence theory of boards of directors is implausible as well as being not empirically supported.

The theory of intra-organizational power

As befits a theory based on power and politics, the resource dependence theory of organizations theorizes power relationships not only between organizations but also within organizations. It holds that the power of one unit over another within an organization arises from asymmetry in exchanges (Pfeffer and Salancik, 1978: 27, 53).

Evidence about the nature of intra-organizational power comes from research by Astley and Zajac (1990). A tenet of the theory that intra-organizational power is emergent is that it arises from the bilateral relationship between sub-unit A and sub-unit B. A influences B and B influences A to a degree, and the power between A and B is the net result of the effect of A upon B and vice-versa. Thus the distribution of intra-organizational power arises as a consequence of the complex network of bilateral relationships between sub-units A and B, and B and C, and A and C, etc. However, Astley and Zajac (1990) show empirically that the bilateral relationships model of power has only weak ability to explain intra-organizational power. Power differences between sub-units are determined, in the empirical study of Astley and Zajac (1990), by the centrality of the sub-unit in the workflow of the organization. The more central is the sub-unit to the workflow of the organization the more power that sub-unit has over other sub-units. Allocation of power between sub-units in this way would aid the flow of work between them, as the central sub-units would be most critical to the workflow and would be where bottlenecks would otherwise occur. Such an allocation of intra-organizational power is rational and functional. Intra-organizational power is revealed as arising not in an emergent or informal way through political processes but through a rational structure governed by the needs of the organization and its formal system as a whole.

A further aspect of the theory of intra-organizational power advanced by Pfeffer and Salancik (1978) is the idea that the organizational unit which provides the organization with important resources is the most powerful. This builds upon and extends the work of Crozier (1964), Hickson *et al.* (1971) and Hinings *et al.* (1974). Also, Hambrick (1981) has shown that the importance of a resource is defined by the environment and by the strategy of the organization. This view of intra-organizational power is consistent with functionalism, for the organization is treating with most respect whichever internal unit most helps it attain the goals of the organization. Thus the model is of the system and its needs rather than of struggle between self-interested, individual actors, i.e., internal politics. Indeed the prior theory of Hickson *et al.* (1971) is in the functionalist tradition and has been criticized from the quarter of anti-functionalist, power-political theory (Clegg and Dunkerley, 1977). Thus this aspect of the intra-organizational power theory of Pfeffer and Salancik (1978) involves no necessary connection with the political model of organizations which has been the target of the critique herein. The argument that organizations value resources essential to them is unexceptionable and quite compatible with functionalism and structural contingency theory (Woodward, 1965). The leading contingency theorist Lawrence has constructed a formal theory which synthesizes contingency and resource dependence theory and this reflects the fundamental affinity of the ideas (Lawrence and Dyer, 1983).

Thus the intra-organizational power theory in resource dependence theory should not be seen as the result of an emergent political process and does not involve replacement of the functionalist by the political paradigm.

Managing through manipulation

In a chapter entitled 'Managing environmental demands' Pfeffer and Salancik (1978) argue that while external interest groups seek to extract compliance from the focal organization, the focal organization can avoid compliance and thereby lessen external control over itself. Pfeffer and Salancik enumerate several techniques for managing environmental demands so as to nullify them. These techniques include secrecy to prevent the external interest group from knowing whether compliance has been attained, balancing off conflicting demands, and having regulation or norms which restrict the power of external organizations.

In a way this whole section is curious because if external interest group demands on the focal organization can be nullified to a degree then organizations are not completely externally controlled. This sits oddly with the opening argument that it is an error to see organizational behaviour as originating within the organization as a result of discretion exercised by managers (Pfeffer and Salancik, 1978). If organizations can influence the environment then this must be done by their managers and so leadership and internal organization must be more important than Pfeffer and Salancik credit.

The argument that organizations can resist external control through secrecy leads Pfeffer and Salancik to the prescriptive advice that organizations should use secrecy and attempt to fool external groups. For example, consider the following:

In the balancing of demands of the various groups, nondisclosure of what each group is actually getting can be a strategy employed to lessen the demands of the other groups. A group's satisfaction is largely determined by its aspiration level; a group is satisfied relative to what it expects to get. Aspiration levels are affected both by what the group has obtained in the past and by what competing groups obtained. Thus, employees may be willing to forego pay increases when the company is near bankruptcy and suppliers, creditors, and owners are also suffering. If the employees found that the owners were really secretly profiting, they would be quite irate. It is in the organization's interests to make each group or organization feel it is getting relatively the best deal. Knowledge of what each group is getting is best kept secret. (Pfeffer and Salancik, 1978: 96)

Yet in industrial relations, if employees are asked to forego a pay increase because the firm is financially strapped, the first suspicion of many unionists would be that the firm is lying. Employees and their unions would require quite some evidence to be convinced that the firm was in fact on the rocks and that it was legitimate to ask employees to forego a pay increase. Thus the Pfeffer and Salancik (1978) prescriptive advice on industrial relations is a deception which is so crude as to be unlikely to work. We see the way 'politically insightful' analysis which leads to sharp tactics, leaves the organization worse off. Employees will be more likely to willingly bear sacrifices if they can see they are genuinely needed and if they have not been given cause to mistrust management through previous failed attempts at deception by management. Recall that Machiavelli was a failed politician.

Pfeffer and Salancik (1978) argue quite extensively that unwanted external demands on organizations can be effectively curtailed by various tactics. They give several examples including having a secretary shield the manager from unwanted visitors, scheduling meetings at inconvenient times, packing meetings with loyal supporters, and requiring complainants to use costly litigation. They even give as an example research-oriented university professors posting as student office hours times when students are in class or at lunch. But surely all of these devices are well understood by adults in our society as avoidance tricks. It is a commonplace of investigative journalists and social critics to point out that in theory dissatisfied clients of a government department will be quickly set to rights but that in reality they are given the good old bureaucratic run around. These kinds of attempt at deception are readily called for what they are in public debate about the unresponsiveness of organizations. Dissatisfaction met with camouflage only increases hostility and further increases distrust between the organization and its external groups, leading them to press their demands with redoubled vigour. Here we see a tendency common among political theorists from Machiavelli onwards, to prescribe political strategies which are so obvious, and which are so universally detested that they are in reality not that effective.

Pfeffer and Salancik (1978), like many other writers on organizational politics, may seem at first reading to be politically sophisticated about the real world, but when they offer this bag of tricks as effective, they reveal themselves as naive. There is an extensive literature on how these kinds of attempt at camouflage and manipulation become dysfunctional, rebounding on the perpetrators (Argyris, 1964).

Rivalling contingency theory – structural differentiation

Pfeffer and Salancik (1978: 273) offer an explanation of structural differentiation which they set against the explanation by size which is associated with Blau (1970). Pfeffer and Salancik argue that structural differentiation is the response of the organization to demands by external interest groups. A new organizational unit is created to deal with each external interest group. This protects organizational autonomy as long as the organizational unit copes with its dependencies on its own. As Pfeffer and Salancik state:

When interests are not tightly interconnected and there is no need for actions to be consistent with all interests simultaneously, then it is possible to satisfy conflicting demands by establishing subunits to cope with each interest. Consumers may demand better quality products and more control over product policies. In response, the organization may establish a consumer affairs department. Demands are registered and consumers or their organizations are provided with access and a feeling of participation. (273)

Later, Pfeffer and Salancik return to their example of the consumer affairs department:

if subunits are loosely coupled then most organizational practices will be buffered from changes created by any single subunit in response to interest group demands. The organization can thus make small accommodations to interest groups without redirecting the activities of the entire organization. A consumer affairs department can deal with complaints about the product with a letter and a free sample, but the production and development departments remain unaffected. (274)

The way of dealing with complaints described here may satisfy some complainants and may be deemed to be an adequate way of dealing with complaints but it is only adequate in the sense of a minimum standard to get by. This approach is clearly not fixing the problem which would involve affecting the inner workings of the production department. Thus the response described here by Pfeffer and Salancik (1978) to complaints is ineffectual. And it is certainly completely the opposite of sound, conscientious quality management which would use complaints to diagnose faults and then prevent them occurring again. The customer complaint example is highly cynical. It illustrates again the problems which ensue once one adopts the view that 'it's all politics' and that management is all about massaging perceptions rather than actually organizing a work organization to perform high quality work.

The customer demand for quality products has ramifications for the quality of work done in the production department and for the quality of the components procured by the purchasing department. Since work organizations have, by their very nature, lots of tight-coupling between customers, production and procurement departments, no strategy which seeks to create separate departments for dealing with complaining customers in isolation from the rest of the organization will be viable. There is no loose-coupling in these examples on which such a strategy could be built. Pfeffer and Salancik (1978) invoke the Weickian concept of 'loose-coupling' but it misleads rather than informs their analysis. Loose-coupling is not just a state of mind. In many work organizations, task interdependencies mean that coupling is tight. Thus the theory of Pfeffer and Salancik on structural differentiation fails to persuade. It does not provide a valid explanation of structural differentiation that is a viable alternative to that conventionally provided in organization theory by the size-based theory of Blau (1970), which is well supported in empirical research (Blau, 1972; Child, 1973a).

The role of managers

In their opening discussion of organizational management, Pfeffer and Salancik (1978: 16) paint a highly novel picture of the role of managers. Given that organizations are mainly externally controlled, managers achieve little. But people like to feel that someone is in control even if nobody is really. Therefore a myth is created that managers of the organization are in control even though they are not really. The managers are rewarded when things go well and punished when they go badly, but either way, the managers deserve neither fate as organizational performance is not their doing. The manager is thus a 'scapegoat' and a 'symbol' (16). However, the symbolic role of management is unproven by Pfeffer and Salancik. Their analyses typically consist of showing that organizations take certain sort of actions quite predictably as a result of certain sorts of external pressures.

Pfeffer and Salancik (1978) also see the managers as dealing with dependencies by attending to and weighing different environmental demands in order to craft the organization's response. Thus managers take actions but this is largely a 'responsive' role, in that rather than decide between several starkly different alternatives, managers process information about the environment and influence demands and so on, and then the right course of action becomes fairly self-apparent. The responsive role of manager is quite similar to the role of managers in structural contingency theory: managers move the organization into fit by adapting the structure to the new state of the contingencies (size, technology, etc.). In so doing, the managers attend to the environment, the organization and its problems and select an organization structure which is largely predetermined and predictable.

Pfeffer and Salancik (1978: 266) speak also of a third role: the discretionary role of management. This is where managers alter the environment through mergers and so on, rather than simply responding to the environment. In the event, Pfeffer and Salancik state that few organizations or their managers are involved in playing this kind of discretionary role:

The discretionary role is more fitting to some organizations than others. Only a few have enough resources and scale to attempt to alter their contexts in a significant fashion. For millions of small business organizations, voluntary associations and nonprofit organizations, such change of the environment is virtually out of the question. (267)

Thus the discretionary role is available mainly to large organizations. Only large organizations alter their environments significantly. This places a considerable domain limitation on the organizations to which the thesis of adaptation by environmental alteration is held to apply by Pfeffer and Salancik.

Conclusions

In conclusion, the heart of the resource dependence theory of Pfeffer and Salancik (1978) is a political analysis of organizations and the interactions between organizations. While organizations sometimes play a role in politics it is far from certain that political matters dominate issues of work performance and the attainment of goals by organizations. Much of the evidence adduced by Pfeffer and Salancik in support of the political model turns out to have other and quite innocent explanations. A pervasive weakness of much of their evidence is that it does not directly address political processes and these are simply attributions which leave the evidence open to other interpretations.

The fundamental model is one of power arising through exchange imbalance which creates asymmetric dependencies. Yet for organizations involved in the supply or receipt of goods and services in the market, the condition of asymmetric dependence corresponds to specific supply and demand conditions which determine prices that leave no residual compliance obligations between transacting parties.

The political model posits survival and autonomy as of primary importance for organizations. Yet organizations seek to do more than survive and some organizations thrive. For this reason, organizations do not place primacy on their autonomy and will involve themselves in dependence on other organizations. The very act of creating an organization by an entrepreneur involves him or her accepting a dependence on customers, employees and so on. Thus organizations and their builders do not act to maximize autonomy but rather surrender autonomy for other rewards such as profits.

Pfeffer and Salancik (1978) see that some large organizations handle dependence by altering their environment through mergers and other means of interorganizational co-ordination. However, they see this avenue as open to 'few' organizations. Moreover, the merger and other interorganizational co-ordination devices studied by Pfeffer and Salancik must reduce the autonomy of the focal organization. Hence it is self-contradictory to argue that organizations seeking to gain greater autonomy will do this by taking steps to reduce their autonomy.

Moreover, such interorganizational co-ordination involves organizational managers taking action to accomplish it. Therefore internal management processes and structures must contribute to organizational performance. This is a logical implication of the theory yet runs counter to the argument in resource dependence theory that critiques internal organizational causation of organizational performance.

By the sheer space given in Pfeffer and Salancik (1978) to various ways the organization can influence its environment, coupled with dubious theoretical concepts such as the enacted environment and co-optation, Pfeffer and Salancik have given currency to the idea that organizations typically have great leeway in influencing their environments. This in turn is widely taken as signifying that organizations therefore avoid adapting themselves to their environments. Such reasoning is fallacious since logically an organization can influence its environment while also being influenced by the environment. Moreover, studies reveal empirically that organizations are typically influenced by their environments (Burns and Stalker, 1961; Chandler, 1962, 1977; Lawrence and Lorsch, 1967; Blau and Schoenherr, 1971).

The political model leads to the idea that managing is the manipulation of surface impressions to soothe people (either inside or outside the organization) rather than doing any real work, and that no real work need be done to attain organizational viability. Hence the political analysis of organizations leads to a cynical view of organizations and their managers. It is unlikely that managers or other persons following any of the naive manipulative ruses described by Pfeffer and Salancik (1978) would escape challenge by those whom they would manipulate, and it is fairly certain that organizations run in this fashion would not be high performers.

The political analysis of organization is riven with theoretical inconsistencies and is largely bereft of compelling support from systematic empirical research. While organizations sometimes find themselves in the political realm such as when interacting with the government, no more than a fraction of organizational action takes place within the political realm, for most is in the realm of instrumental performance of work. Thus the political analysis is a highly exaggerated view of organizations and their managements. There may be some contribution to understanding of organization to be had from the political view, but the present indication is that it is minor. The greater benefit to our understanding of organizations is to be had from viewing them as rational instrumental collectivities. But there is the danger of this being eclipsed by the political analysis model. The political model is a highly coloured and over-dramatized view of organizations. Yet the political model of organizations is largely a drama constructed in the telling of the story. There is a low degree of correspondence between the political model and the empirical reality of organizations.

6   A critique of organizational economics

Introduction

Analytic frameworks derived from economics have grown in popularity in the field of organizational theory. In particular, agency theory (Jensen and Meckling, 1976) and transaction cost economics (Williamson, 1985) have arisen as major theoretical contributions and these collectively may be termed the organizational economics approach (Barney and Ouchi, 1986).

Organizational economics has arrived as a major framework in the field of organizational studies and management. A theorist of transaction cost economics, Professor Oliver Williamson, received the Irwin Award for Scholarly Contributions to Management at the 1988 Academy of Management National Meeting and, at the same meeting, Professor Gareth Jones received the prize for the best article in the *Academy of Management Journal*, for his empirical study in the transaction cost framework.

The arrival of a new theoretical paradigm in a field always raises important questions for that field. On this occasion this is reinforced by the fact that organizational economics consciously presents itself as being based upon a powerful, contiguous, established discipline, namely economics. Economists like to see their discipline as more rigorous, more scientific and more theoretically penetrating than other branches of social science such as psychology, sociology and management studies (see Swedberg, 1990). For example, Caves (1980: 88), an economist, critically reviews research into organizational strategy and structure conducted by scholars in business history, business policy and organizational behaviour and concludes that while:

economists have something to learn from this literature ... I shall not let professional modesty blur an important conclusion: well-trained professional economists could have carried out many of the research projects cited in this paper more proficiently than did their authors, who were less effectively equipped by their own disciplines.

Because of the superiority of the economics approach, the economist Hirshleifer (1986: 321) has predicted the takeover of the whole of social science:

As economics 'imperialistically' employs its tools of analysis over a wider range of social issues, it will *become* sociology and anthropology and political science. But correspondingly, as these other disciplines grow increasingly rigorous, they will not merely resemble, but will *be* economics. It is in this sense that 'economics' is taken here as broadly synonymous with 'social science'.

Proponents of organizational economics have not been slow to display the same hubris in dealing with the more conventional organization and management theory whose meagre efforts are now to be transcended by the theoretically and methodologically more powerful economic analysis (see Jensen, 1983). Hesterly *et al.* (1990: 403) write: 'We argue that OE [organizational economics] has already made an important . . . contribution to our understanding of the nature and purpose of organizations.' They go on to forecast (402, 416) that, as a result of organizational economics, the prediction of Hirshleifer (1986) will be realized in the field of organizations, namely that organization theory will *become* economics, as part of the development that Barney (1990: 389) terms 'economic imperialism'. One also notes with interest that the résumés of some aspiring Assistant Professors in the USA in the management and organization theory field now list membership of the American Economic Association.

Agency theory holds that organizations can be analysed in terms of a conflict of interest between principals and agents (Jensen and Meckling, 1976). Particularly in the large modern corporation, the principals of the organizations are the owners, the many outside shareholders, who own but delegate control to the executive managers who are their agents (Fama and Jensen, 1983). Managers have interests, according to agency theory, which diverge from those of the principals and so may use their discretion to maximize their interests at the expense of the interests of the principals – this is termed residual loss (Jensen and Meckling, 1976: 308). Such residual loss can be curbed to a degree through various devices such as monitoring and sanctioning, including control over executives by a non-executive board of directors (Fama and Jensen, 1983). Agency theory tends to see managers as ever ready to cheat the principals or owners unless constantly controlled in some way.

Transaction cost theory holds that market failure occurs such that the normal economic pressure on economic actors to perform effectively breaks down and has to be replaced by hierarchical controls. In the large corporation with a multi-level hierarchy, middle managers enjoy a degree of independence from top management and begin to subordinate the corporate goals of the maximization of profit and shareholder wealth in favour of their personal self-aggrandizement. The solution is to increase control on middle managers by holding them directly accountable for the profitability of their division as assessed by an investigatory control staff of head-office accountants and the like, that is, the M-form corporation

(Williamson, 1970, 1971, 1981, 1985). Again, market failure can occur in transactions where a supplier to a firm makes asset investments specific to that transaction, therefore transforming the exchange into bilateral monopoly away from market-determined prices. Haggling over price is liable to ensue and the avoidance of such transactions costs is attained by recourse to administration of both transacting parties through a common hierarchy. This is achieved by merger of the two firms through vertical integration (Williamson, 1975, 1981, 1985; Alchian and Woodward, 1988); thus the duplicity and untrustworthiness of the managers in the two firms is resolved by placing a common boss over them. (In certain situations transaction cost theory specifies the adoption of a third, or hybrid, governance form such as long-term contracting (Williamson, 1991).)

It should be noted that agency theory and transaction cost economics are not always identical in their views, for example Williamson (1983) offers a critique of Fama and Jensen (1983) (see also Williamson, 1988). However, for present purposes, such differences between agency and transaction cost theories will be ignored as largely irrelevant to a critical discussion of organizational economics from outside the paradigm; similarly, differences within each of agency theory (see Eisenhardt, 1989) and transaction cost economics will be mainly ignored for the same reason. Our concern is with the broad shape of organizational economics as it contrasts with structural contingency theory.

Both agency theory and transaction cost theory derive from economics. Barney and Ouchi (1986) use the term organizational economics to describe theoretical contributions to organization theory from economics. Agency theory and transaction cost theory are not the *only* contributions (Barney and Ouchi, 1986), but they are among the more influential formulations on organization theory to have arisen from economics to date. Accordingly, the term organizational economics will be used herein to refer to agency and transaction cost theories.

Both these theories see corporate managers as inherently untrustworthy. While some part of economic thought takes such a view, not all of economics does, and the intellectual connection with economics is less than completely secure. In view of these considerations a more accurate title for the two theories of agency and transaction cost theory, in regard to their theories of organizational management, might be the theory of managerial delinquency. However, since the organizational economics label is established in the literature, we shall use it herein (e.g., Hesterly *et al.*, 1990). But let us note in passing that the label is a rhetorical device, for it claims the support of economics for certain theories, though that foundation is in actuality less sure.

Critiques of organizational economics

Robins (1987) has provided a critical discussion of transaction cost theory. This is a rather heterogeneous and complex set of remarks. He states that economic theory cannot be used to generate deductions about individual firm behaviour in the manner of transaction cost theory. Robins argues against the use of transaction cost theory to construct causal, general propositions. He writes that this detracts from the primary thrust of institutionalism to offer an appreciation of the way in which specific historical structures shape economic behaviour. Again, he challenges the presumption of transaction cost theory that the market is the natural medium of transaction that pre-dates efforts to organize transactions within hierarchy. The nature of such societal economic organization is to be understood by reference to historically specific formations of social class and the like. How any such explanation can avoid causal propositions is unclear.

Robins (1987) nevertheless sees a useful role for transaction cost theory as part of a more cautious approach of analysing the specific forms of organization that arise in each environmental setting. Transaction cost theory provides the key mediation between the organization and its environment. Robins applauds the attempt to analyse organizations in terms of the inducements and contribution at the level of individual in the tradition of Simon (1957). He also sees transaction cost theory as the vehicle to integrate structural contingency theory with his larger explanatory effort (Robins, 1987). However, this idea is not fleshed out and difficulties remain as to how transaction cost theory is to assimilate inimical structural contingency ideas such as the organic organizational structure (see below). Thus while being critical of pivotal elements of transaction cost theory and its foundation in economics, Robins nevertheless concludes that it is central for the reintegration of organization theory and future research. However, the argument is overall rather vague. In contrast, we have no problem with the aspiration to general, causal relationships in transaction cost theory and our reservations differ.

Perrow (1986) has also offered a critique of agency theory. His critique centres on the acceptance of the status quo inherent in the concern for the benefit of the principal rather than the agent, i.e., the property owner over the employee (Perrow, 1986: 227). Perrow is critical also of what he sees as the denial of power and authority in organizations within the agency theory model of principals and agents freely entering into contracts with each other. These criticisms are consistent with the broad theme of his work and are essentially a critique from the New Left with its concern for exploitation of workers under capitalism.

Perrow (1986) has also offered a critique of transaction cost theory. This includes challenging the idea that vertical integration cuts costs. Perrow (1986: 241ff.) points out several costs that may rise as a result of two firms merging. However, some of these sources of cost increase such as inflexibility are not transaction costs arising from opportunism in price-setting, which is the focus of Williamson's theory. Again, Perrow includes increases in costs through blurring of incentives through the erstwhile owner-manager of the merged company becoming a salaried manager; this would seem to be an economic argument of the agency theory and market failure sort. Hence Perrow's critical comments here are in certain regards wide of the mark and self-defeating. His broader point is that vertical integration, merger and so on, are driven by search for profit often through market domination rather than through greater efficiencies or for public benefit. This, again, is consistent with his critique being one from the New Left position (see also Francis *et al.*, 1983; Dow, 1987).

In contrast, the critique in this chapter is consistent with our concern (Donaldson, 1985a), and with the general theme of this present volume, for defending the boundaries of an autonomous theory of management and organization which is not subservient to any, more traditional discipline (here economics) and which is prepared to acknowledge positive rather than just negative functions for managers. Earlier we debated the merits of organizational economics with one of its proponents (Barney, 1990; Donaldson, 1990a, b).

While there are some potential gains to be had from the rise of organizational economics for management studies, there are several difficulties inherent in such a venture. The growing influence of agency and transaction cost theory presents a number of problems for organization studies. There is a problem in the lack of relationship of organizational economics to pre-existing traditions of inquiry in management theory. There is a problem that organizational economics is a regressive simplification. There is a problem of the evaluative and ideological colouration of organizational economics. This in turn gives a harshly moralizing stance to organizational economics relative to practising managers and constitutes an impediment to future collaboration between management academics and managers. These are all problems created for management studies by taking on board organizational economics. The adoption of organizational economics by management academics is based in part on the notion that they are drawing thereby on the authority of the discipline of economics. Yet many of the ideas of organizational economics are themselves contested within economics and thus come with no general licence of accreditation by that discipline. Each of these difficulties will be reviewed in turn below. An examination of two applications of organizational economics theory will also be provided. A critique will be made of the organizational economics approach to organizational structure in the M-form thesis of divisionalization, an organizational economics theory that rivals the structural contingency theory view of divisionalization, and in corporate governance.

(As compared with our earlier critique of organizational economics (Donaldson, 1990a, b), herein we take the analysis somewhat deeper regarding methodological individualism, the narrow motivational model, the regressive simplification, the neglect of prior organizational research, the ideology and moralizing, the offensiveness of organizational economics and corporate governance. We also pursue other issues: the contrast with structural contingency theory, the likelihood of opportunism, the relationship with economics, alternative interpretations of agency theory and the M-form thesis.)

The human model

Organizational economics follows much of economic theory in that there is a central role given in the theory to explanation by recourse to the actions of individual actors, that is to 'rational economic man'. This is part of a wider intellectual programmatic within social science of methodological individualism, that is, explanation of phenomena by reference to the actions of individuals – even if the individuals are treated in a highly stylized fashion. Like much methodologically individualist theorizing, in organizational economics, as in much of economics, this produces an emphasis on the motivations of individuals as crucial explanatory elements. More specifically, the individual is seen to act in his or her own self-interest, consistent with being a rational economic 'man', and this leads to postulates of opportunism and guile in managerial behaviour. Thus, in contrast to more collectivity-level or structuralist models in organizational studies which speak of the organization as a collective entity pursuing the organizational goal (Parsons, 1961; Chandler, 1962), organizational economics disaggregates the organization into individuals, each of whom pursues his or her individual self-interest.

This allows the study of how far agents act differently from what their principals would wish (Jensen and Meckling, 1976) and middle managers act differently from the intentions for them of their senior managers (Williamson, 1985). In these ways managements fail to maximize returns to owners, and corporations fail to maximize organizational profitability, with management spending some part of the organizational wealth on itself, e.g., through indulging in leisure or luxurious perquisites. The lack of explanation of organizational action by reference to the individual actions of motivated individuals has been a persistent criticism of collectivity-level structuralist explanations such as those in structural contingency theory (Silverman, 1970; Child, 1972a; but see Donaldson, 1985a). The new individualism of organizational economics has the potential to make good some of these deficiencies (e.g., the M-form theory of Williamson, 1970).

What merits critical scrutiny here is the particular model of 'man' used in organizational economics, that is, of the managerial actor as self-interested and opportunistic. This raises problems of its validity, completeness and evaluative connotation.

Williamson (1985: 30) states: 'Transaction cost economics assumes that human agents are ... given to opportunism, which is a condition of self-interest seeking with guile.' However, Williamson also states that his axiom of opportunism does not mean that every person acts opportunistically, but rather that some people act opportunistically. Furthermore, since economic institutions cannot readily identify and screen out the opportunists, they have to be built on the presumption that opportunism is possible and protect themselves accordingly:

I do not insist that every individual is continuously or even largely given to opportunism. To the contrary, I merely assume that some individuals are opportunistic some of the time and that differential trustworthiness is rarely transparent *ex ante*. As a consequence, *ex ante* screening efforts are made and *ex post* safeguards are created. Otherwise, those who are least principled (most opportunistic) will be able to exploit egregiously those who are more principled. (64)

Thus there is no general presumption of opportunism, but opportunism is nevertheless sufficiently widespread and severe that institutions are crafted so as to allow for it (under conditions of transaction-specific assets and uncertainty). Opportunism then becomes the central assumption of institutions and an ever-present apprehension of actors as they face each other in the transactions that they anticipate:

human agents will not reliably self-enforce promises but will defect from the letter and the spirit of an agreement when it suits their purposes. That somewhat dismal view of human nature alerts contracting parties (and those who would study contracting practices) to be wary of the hazards. To be sure, suspicions and precautions can be and sometimes are taken to excess ... But a healthy regard for opportunism is essential to an understanding of the purposes served by complex modes of economic organization. (388)

Thus the possibility of opportunism becomes sufficiently probable that it is the pivotal tenet of the theory of the economic institutions of capitalism in Williamson: 'Governance structures that attenuate opportunism and otherwise infuse confidence are evidently needed' (63).

In this way opportunism becomes an assumption that is constantly repeated in the theory statements with little space devoted to other, more benign, views of human nature. For example:

absent the hazards of opportunism, the difficulties would vanish ... Given, however, ... the proclivity of human agents to make false and misleading (self-disbelieved) statements, the following hazards must be confronted: Joined as they are in a condition of bilateral monopoly, both buyer and seller are strategically situated to bargain over the disposition of any incremental gain whenever a proposal to adapt is made by the other party. Although both have a long-term interest in effecting adaptions of a joint profit-maximizing kind, each also has an interest in appropriating as much gain as he can on each occasion to adapt. (Williamson, 1985: 63)

Again:

the manager behaves myopically with respect to the enterprise. The object being to maximize immediate net receipts, labor costs will be saved by utilizing equipment intensively, and maintenance expense will be deferred to a successor management ... the manager of the ... division proceeds to run [the assets] into the ground and leaves the firm to invest his augmented net receipts elsewhere.

To be sure, there are checks against asset abuses of both kinds ... These, however, are imperfect. Some managers may shrug them off if the immediate gains are large enough and if they cannot be required to disgorge their ill-gotten gains. (Swiss bank accounts have attractive features in that respect.) (138)

Further again, in discussing the relationship between management and the board of directors:

But the principal function of the board remains that of providing governance structure protection for the stockholders. Management participation should not become so extensive as to upset that basic board purpose. Where it does, managerial discretion is apt, sooner or later, to manifest itself in self-dealing or subgoal pursuit. (317)

And in reviewing his theory in his conclusions:

As with economic models more generally, the human agents who populate transaction cost economics are highly calculative. That is plainly not an attractive or even an accurate view of human nature. Economics is thought to be a dismal science partly for that reason ... But one does not need to assert that the only reliable human motive is avarice to recognize that much of the success of economics in relation to the other social sciences occurs because calculativeness is presumed to be present in nontrivial degree.

As compared with orthodoxy [in economics], the human agents of transaction cost economics are both less and more calculative. They are less calculative in the capacity to receive, store, retrieve, and process information. They are more calculative in that they are given to opportunism. Taken together, that appears to correspond more closely with human nature as we know it. Still, it is plainly a narrow prescription. It makes little provision for attributes such as kindness, sympathy, solidarity, and the like. Indeed, to the extent that such factors are acknowledged, their costs, rather than their benefits, are emphasized . . . The human agents who populate the economic institutions of capitalism are lacking in compassion. (391)

This then is the view of human beings, and, more particularly, of those who manage the economic institutions of capitalism, as devious self-aggrandizers requiring discipline.

Similarly, Jensen and Meckling (1976) specify some of the ways in which agents can gain at cost to their principals. One such set of costs arises from the manager indulging in more non-pecuniary benefits:

such as the physical appointments of the office, the attractiveness of the secretarial staff, the level of employee discipline, the kind and amount of charitable contributions, personal relations ('love', 'respect', etc.) with employees, a larger than optimal computer to play with, purchase of production inputs from friends, etc. (Jensen and Meckling, 1976: 312)

However, they see a more important class of costs to principals (i.e., owners) in on-the-job leisure which is increasingly taken by the manager as his degree of ownership declines:

Indeed, it is likely that the most important conflict arises from the fact that as the manager's ownership claim falls, his incentive to devote significant effort to creative activities such as searching out new profitable ventures falls. He may in fact avoid such ventures simply because it requires too much trouble or effort on his part to manage or to learn about new technologies. Avoidance of these personal costs and the anxieties that go with them also represent a source of on the job utility to him and it can result in the value of the firm being substantially lower than it otherwise could be. (313)

Thus when managers (apparently solely male in organizational economics) act opportunistically it is by avoiding work or playing with their computer or having 'personal relations' with attractive secretarial staff. This is the imagery offered by organizational economics.

Regressive simplification

At every turn the organizational economic view of the managerial actor is very particular, being only one out of a range of possible models of human behaviour. It presumes that human behaviour is the result of rational calculation about self-interest (Jensen and Meckling, 1976; Williamson, 1985). Yet at least some human behaviour is not calculative and is produced by unconditional reflexes, conditioned reflexes and habit. Some human behaviour is emotional and not rational. It is affectively rational in the terminology of Weber's (1968) classic discussion (and Weber is a classic methodological individualist). Within the category of rational behaviour some behaviour is motivated by orientation, not to ends, but to means. People may force themselves to do a good job, not to obtain outcomes which benefit them, but because they feel that they must do a good job (compulsive behaviour) or they ought to do a good job (normatively governed behaviour). Or again they may do a good job without necessarily intending to do so because they just enjoy doing the job (intrinsic motivation) and so do it thoroughly and well (Herzberg, 1966). Further yet, within the category of rational interest-oriented actions there also exist actions oriented to further the interests of others (altruism) or the collective (collectivity-oriented) (Parsons, 1951). People working within organizations may suspend their own personal interests or preferences and act to the conscious detriment of their self-interest out of loyalty to an organization, belief in the moral rightness of its aims or deference to the legitimate authority of those who give them orders (Weber, 1968; Etzioni, 1975). There are thus many causes of human behaviour in addition to rational calculated self-interest. Like economics itself, organizational economics largely ignores these other causes of human behaviour and constructs its theories on a very narrow base.

The eminent economist Kenneth Arrow (1985: 50) has referred to the necessity of recognizing a broader range of human motives than those drawn upon in conventional agency theory:

A third limitation of the present models is the restricted reward or penalty system used. It is virtually always stated in terms of monetary payments, although the present literature has begun to go beyond this limit by considering the possibility of dismissal. Still further extensions are needed to capture some aspects of reality, for there is a whole world of rewards and penalties that take social rather than monetary forms. Professional responsibility is clearly enforced in good measure by systems of ethics, internalized during the education process and enforced in some measure by formal punishments and more broadly by reputations. Ultimately, of course, these social systems have economic consequences, but they are not the immediate ones of current principal–agent models.

Thus even an economist feels bound to comment that the motivational model used in agency theory is too narrow.

One frequently encountered line of defence against attacks on the naive simplicity of the axioms in organization economics is the same as that used against the same critique in economics. The defence is to invoke the classic statement by Milton Friedman (1953) that axioms in economics, as in science, are not to be judged by their realism but by their predictive power, that is, their ability to coherently allow deduction of empirically valid hypotheses. This instrumentalist or nominalist account of the role of theories in science has come under increasing criticism within the philosophy of science (Chalmers, 1982). In brief, if theories are just useful fictions and offer no insight into real underlying causal mechanisms then they offer prediction but not explanation. Moreover, a function of successful theories in much of natural science has been not only to provide an accurate calculating device which captures the mathematical relationship between presently studied variables, but also, by their realist postulates, to prompt further hypotheses and research which show these 'unnecessary' realist elements in the theory to be true. Thus the unreality of the fundamental postulates of organizational economics is a damaging argument against the approach, and means that there are limits on how far organizational economics can ever be more than a partial element in management theory. The issue cannot be dismissed by reference to outmoded views in the philosophy of science (see McCloskey, 1983).

In contrast, organizational behaviour and organization theory have drawn on complex, multifaceted models of human behaviour and actions which have been developed in psychology and sociology over the decades. Yet these models are eschewed in organizational economics, together with all of their supporting research. This seems intellectually regressive. Indeed on turning the pages of organizational economics, one finds oneself back in the world of McGregor's Theory X: people are selfish, lazy and cannot be trusted, and must be controlled through reward–punishment schedules if there is to be any organizational productivity (McGregor, 1960). Yet there is also in organizational psychology the opposite model of 'man', McGregor's Theory Y, which states that people are inherently capable of intrinsically motivated work, of self-management, co-operation and trustworthiness (McGregor, 1960). There is some empirical research evidence for Theory Y, as there is for Theory X (Miner, 1980). By around 1970 most students of organization behaviour took the view that both Theory X and Theory Y enjoyed some degree of validity and that a more adequate model would be some more complex synthesis of the two, governed by contingency factors (Schein, 1972). In contrast, organizational economics would collapse all of this back to the stark singular pole of Theory X. Again, within the topic area of interpersonal or group behaviour the move is intellectually regressive, based on discarding previous intellectual achievements (Argyris, 1964). This is not obvious progress.

Moreover, not only are there variations in the motivations of people inside organizations that condition their organizational behaviour, but these motives themselves are not fixed. Perrow (1986: 232) argues that whether human motivation is self-regarding (as in agency theory) or other-regarding (i.e., pro-social) is affected by the organization and its treatment of the individual. Similarly, Argyris (1964) has argued that placing controls on organizational members, in the sort of way specified in agency theory, can lower trust, provoke resentment and reduce the stage of personal development of the members, leading to more individualistic motivations and less trustworthy, less pro-organizational behaviour. Thus the motivation of the members is not simply an exogenous variable to which the organizational structure needs to be altered, but is endogenous to the system, being in part the result of the organizational structure (Perrow, 1986). Hence the control structures postulated by organizational economics to curb residual loss and opportunism may to a degree create residual loss and opportunism. In this way the negative view of managers might become self-fulfilling without reflecting the true human potential of managers. Thus motivations and opportunistic behaviours that justify control structures may not be inherent but may be outcomes of such structures.

The particular model of man and woman used in organizational economics therefore breaks with the pre-existing theories in organizational behaviour which encompassed both Theory X and Theory Y in eclectic models. Moreover, these sorts of organizational behaviour motivational models undergird organization theory and, more specifically, the structural contingency theory of organizations (see the following section). Hence, in rejecting any veracity in the Theory Y view of people and in opting for a starkly Theory X view, organizational economics is breaking also with the pre-existing research on organizational structure and thus with organization theory.

Difference between organizational economics and structural contingency theory

Structural contingency theory holds that under conditions of task certainty the mechanistic structure which features strong hierarchical control is appropriate (Burns and Stalker, 1961). However, under conditions of task uncertainty structural contingency theory holds that an organic structure is appropriate, featuring loose hierarchical controls, mutual adjustment and widespread use of discretion, initiative-taking and participation by employees lower in the hierarchy (Burns and Stalker, 1961). Moreover, these lower-level employees in organic structures are seen as having an overall view of the project as well as technical knowledge, which they use to further the attainment of the project goals, rather than just to exploit the organization; as well, they are motivated by a commitment to material progress and to the external technical community (Burns and Stalker, 1961). Given these motivations, and the impossibility of a hierarchical pre-specification of employee roles, task effectiveness is enhanced by freeing employees from hierarchical control and bureaucratic encumbrances, and encouraging them to use their initiative through a democratic type of culture and a collegial social structure in the organization. This theory that organic structures are required in conditions of task uncertainty is one of the earliest structural contingency theories (Burns and Stalker, 1961), and is probably the most widely received one. Yet it is quite antithetical to agency and transaction cost theories, which see organic structures as never appropriate.

Agency theory considers delegation should be minimized as it leads to abuse. It also sees uncertainty as leading to delegation and as making monitoring and sanctioning of the agent by the principal more difficult (Eisenhardt, 1989). Delegation is never a state to be encouraged to facilitate an employee's proclivity for self-direction. All such exercises of discretion are injurious to the principal because of the malevolent motivation of the agent in agency theory. Uncertainty does not allow a looser structure which challenges the employee to greater creativity and use of technical knowledge for the good of the organizational mission. Uncertainty is an unfortunate condition which forces deviation away from complete personal direction of every detail by the principal, and which requires the use of other, less direct controls to try to stem the residual losses, such as shifting from monitoring behaviour to monitoring outcomes (Ouchi, 1978). Whether the hierarchical controls are behaviour- or outcome-focused, direct or indirect, personal or impersonal bureaucratic, they are still hierarchical controls, that is, controls by the principals upon the agents. They are, thus, all varieties and degrees of the mechanistic organization. These controls are quite antithetical to the organic organization which is based upon self-reliance and giving leeway to the expression of pro-organizational initiative (Burns and Stalker, 1961). Thus agency theory rejects the idea that effective structures vary between mechanistic and organic depending upon the task-uncertainty contingency and instead holds that mechanistic structures are always appropriate.

Similar remarks apply to transaction cost theory. This theory holds that market failures require the adoption of hierarchical controls. The M-form thesis is that, in the large, U-form (i.e., functionally structured) organization, control loss occurs and middle managers self-aggrandize at the expense of the corporation; the solution is a multidivisional structure which holds middle managers accountable for profitability to the head office which can monitor more effectively because of separation from operational decision-making and a corporate staff of accountants, etc. (Williamson, 1970). Thus again delegation in the large corporation is seen as giving leeway to the managers to give vent to their inherently anti-organizational motivation and this must be curbed by increased accountability and monitoring, i.e., by increased use of formal, outcome-based inspection. The head office in the M-form is designed to police the divisions as a primary activity. Hence there is no element of the organic model either structurally or motivationally in the M-form model, which is the mechanistic model of organization.

Again, transaction cost theory holds that in conditions of bilateral monopoly, costly haggling over prices will ensue unless the two firms merge through vertical integration so that a common superordinate can govern the vertical interdependence relationship (Williamson, 1975). Thus under bilateral monopoly the managers in each firm will try to cheat the managers in the other firm and the solution is hierarchical imposition to settle matters through authoritative fiat. Hence the view is that managers are untrustworthy if left to themselves, and that, since the 'discipline' of the market fails in bilateral monopoly, recourse must be made to hierarchical discipline. The prescribed model is the mechanistic one in terms both of structure and also of the motivations of managers, i.e., being the opposite of benign self-regulation and spontaneous collaboration. Bilateral monopoly is viewed as leading to market failure for several reasons including the uncertainty of the situation which prevents detailed pre-specification by contract to forestall devious opportunism by the two parties. Thus uncertainty plays the role (along with other factors such as transaction-specific asset investment) of being a factor which prevents free-market transactions such as spot price dealings from governing the relationship, and leads to vertical integration as the appropriate governance mechanism. Hence uncertainty leads to the adoption of a mechanistic organization structure in transaction cost theory. This is the opposite of structural contingency theory where uncertainty in the situation leads to the replacement of the mechanistic by the organic organizational structure (Burns and Stalker, 1961). Thus transaction cost theory rejects the traditional structural contingency theory views about the organic structure.

Hence agency and transaction cost theories of organization hold views about organizational structure which are sharply different from structural contingency theory. Thus organizational economics marks a break with the pre-existing, prevailing theory of organizational structure, i.e., structural contingency theory. Thereby organizational economics is a major step toward fragmenting the field and to preventing an integrated coherent view of organizations being offered to students and managers by organization theory.

Neglect of prior contributions

Moreover, the rejection of structural contingency theory by organizational economics is mainly implicit rather than explicit. One might have expected that agency and transaction cost theorists would have advanced their tendentious views only after a review of existing theories of organizational structure such as structural contingency theory, carefully revealing flaws in existing views and providing a reasoned basis for their rejection. However, while there is some discussion of sociology and organizational sociology in Williamson (1985) (e.g., Dalton, Gouldner, Perrow, Etzioni and Granovetter), there is hardly any considered refutation in either agency or transaction cost theory of structural contingency theory research. Neither the seminal statement of agency theory (Jensen and Meckling, 1976) nor that of transaction cost theory (Williamson, 1985) cite any work by the leading organizational behavouralists: Argyris, Bandura, Locke, McGregor, Mitchell or Salancik; and neither do they cite any work by any of the leading structural contingency theorists: Burns, Child, Jay Galbraith, Hage or Woodward. The rejection of Theory Y and of structural contingency theory with its organic structure is not based on a careful review of the theories and supporting research evidence (such as was reviewed in chapter 2).

Williamson (1985: 268ff.) reviews some organizational behaviour research on participation and satisfaction. He rightly concludes that there is no general relationship between participation, job satisfaction and productivity and sees that those relationships are conditional upon circumstances (270). However, he is unable to identify what such factors might be and sees this as requiring research to examine the tasks being performed by the subjects (270). Organizational behaviour and structural contingency work has already identified several contingency factors that condition the relationships between participation, job satisfaction and performance. These include task uncertainty, job scope, the education and professional orientation of the employee and the strength of the growth need of the employee (Herzberg, 1966; Hage and Aiken, 1967; Hackman et al., 1975). Thus Williamson is anticipating the creation of a contingency approach to these aspects of organizational behaviour and structure whereas this already exists.

In advancing his theory of the M-form corporation Williamson (1985: 279ff.) draws upon the historical studies of Chandler (1962); however he makes a different interpretation from Chandler's. Williamson argues that the M-form corporation (i.e., the multidivisional structure with supervision of divisions by a corporate centre) arises because of the opportunism problems in large U-form (i.e., functionally structured) corporations by managers of the functional departments: 'the pursuit of subgoals by the functional parts (sales, engineering, production) was partly a manifestation of opportunism' (280). However, this is an interpretation by Williamson that goes beyond that made by Chandler, who sees the multidivisional structure as caused by the problems of managing complexity rather than deliberate self-dealing by managers in the functional departments. For Chandler the need to adopt the multidivisional structure in place of the functional structure arose from the increasing administrative complexity resulting from diversification into several increasingly less closely related product-markets, e.g., Du Pont diversified from explosives into chemicals and paint, etc. The Chandlerian thesis hinges upon the problems of co-ordinating a complex set of activities rather than upon a problematic of obtaining co-operation among a set of managers who are pursuing their self-interests against the corporate interest. Thus the assumption about human nature differs as between Chandler and Williamson. Williamson sees a dark side where another scholar more intimate with the empirical materials in question does not. While the assertion of a differing interpretation is integral to any theory, Williamson provides no explicit argumentation as to why his interpretation is more valid than that offered by Chandler. Moreover, the Williamson account overlooks the role of the contingency factor of strategy, i.e., diversification (see subsection headed 'Critique of the M-form thesis', pp. 194–8). Hence a prior theory of some sophistication is rendered simplistic and this involves neglecting a contingency theory argument.

The neglect of prior contributions is what makes organizational economics so different and more like economics in approach, but it is hardly intellectually defensible or rational. The essence of science is the assertion of new theory in full recognition of existing theory and based upon a demonstration of the superiority of the newer theory over the old, in terms of theoretical coherency or empirical validity. Organizational economics fails to proceed in this way and is therefore unscientific. Some may welcome organizational economics as contributing to the pluralism of organization theory, but it is not itself pluralistic for it fails to treat fully contributions from outside its own narrow horizon, especially from outside economics. Thus organizational economics is a radical break from both organizational behaviour and organizational structural theory, particularly structural contingency theory. Organizational economics censors the intellectual past of organization theory.

The ideological roots of organizational economics

The origins of the peculiar view of the manager taken by organizational economics lie in economics and in political economy. In political economy, human happiness is maximized by free economic interaction between property-owning individuals through the market using price mechanisms to mediate transactions. Incursions into the laissez-faire, economic order through state regulation, state bureaucracy or collectivization of ownership are anathema (Smith, 1937; Anderson and Tollison, 1982; see also Jensen and Meckling, 1979). While economists vary in the strength of these beliefs, organizational economics includes some who hold these views in strong form. For instance, in 1983 Jensen and Meckling wrote a pamphlet which sets forth their public policy concerns; they see government as increasingly encroaching on property rights and, as a result, reducing liberty and wealth:

As the rule-maker, government can and does frequently *revoke* rights, when it decrees that henceforth it will not be legal for individuals to use their property or to enter into contracts in ways which heretofore had been sanctioned. When the government decrees that new automobiles sold must meet certain safety, anti-pollution, and fuel consumption requirements, they are revoking certain rights to use assets held in the name of the owners of firms, and the rights of consumers to purchase products without these devices ...

In the last decade in the United States we have witnessed a major upsurge in the revocation of rights. Examples abound and we mention only a few to illustrate the form and scope of the problem ... [t]he provisions of the Occupational Safety and Health Act which limit the freedom of individuals to contract with employers to work under more hazardous conditions in return for higher pay ... [v]arious antidiscrimination programmes which limit the employment policies of organisations and require employers to discriminate against white males and in favour of blacks, Mexicans, Indians, females, the aged and so on.

All these rights have been revoked without compensation to any of the parties ... Revocation has not been treated as an eminent domain proceeding under which the state is required to compensate property owners. (Jensen and Meckling, 1983: 4–5, emphasis in original)

Property rights are so central to the scheme of Jensen and Meckling that they are equal to human rights: 'it is worth pointing out a clever fallacy: namely, the false distinction between so-called "human rights" and "property rights"' (8). Jensen and Meckling conclude their scenario of increasing government intervention in Hobbesian fashion: 'If our analysis of the way western political democracies function is correct, then there is little reason to believe that the trend toward "Leviathan" government will be arrested' (10).

When economists turn to the modern corporation they see a state in miniature with all its attendant problems. The economist's heroic role-model of the small-scale, owner-managed entrepreneurial firm has become a bureaucracy through growth and diffusion of ownership and is staffed by middle managers who blunt the natural direct control of the entrepreneur over labour and capital (Jensen and Meckling, 1976). The existence of a managerial hierarchy between labour and top management, and also of professional non-owning top management between the firm and widely diffused owners, are recipes for economic inefficiency, since the owners are no longer the controllers and so incentives are blurred (Fama and Jensen, 1983).

Non-owning managers, far from being skilled specialists in management, loyal to the organization, and dedicated to the best interests of the collective organization, including the suppliers of capital, such as owners, are a distinct new class with their own interests (Berle and Means, 1932). The managers are seen as seeking to minimize their productive efforts, to give the organization and its owners as little as possible and to extract the maximum returns from the organization in pay, perquisites and leisure (Jensen and Meckling, 1976). This is the nature of managerial shirk. By extension these managers will act opportunistically *vis-à-vis* their fellow managers in other corporations, e.g., by seeking to set inequitable prices to organizations with which they are involved in long-term relationships as suppliers or customers (Williamson, 1985). The solution to these problems of shirking managers and their guileful behaviour is to control them more through closer monitoring, stronger incentive systems and bonds, or to integrate vertically with suppliers or customers so that price negotiation across organizational boundaries is replaced by hierarchical authority (Jensen and Meckling, 1976; Williamson, 1985) or to impose other disciplines such as threat of takeover, debt or bank control (Fama and Jensen, 1983; Jensen, 1989; Aoki, 1990). To say the least, this is a highly damning picture of managers and their motivation. Yet this is the very stuff of this modern-day theory of management.

At recent meetings of the Academy of Management in the USA, speaker after speaker invokes agency theory, the problems of managerial shirking, opportunism and guile among managers, and the on-the-job leisure propensity of managers, and talks about the way managers squander shareholders' wealth in company aircraft for the exclusive use of executives. Much of this is received by the audience either as the appropriate modern, formal theory of management or with gleeful laughter as yet another managerial ploy is recounted. One listens to 'tests' of agency theory which involve asking MBA students how much they think that they would cheat their company if they were its executives (Kosnik and Bettenhausen, 1988). One asks oneself if this is really a group called the Academy of Management?

There is a disinclination by agency theorists to treat academics, such as themselves, as the perfidious agents of their own theories. One exception to this occurs in a conference collection from Harvard Business School. On page one of chapter one, we read an agency theory treatment of the relationship between the reader, as principal, and the authors of the book as agents:

In writing this overview, we are acting as your agents. On behalf of our principal (you, the reader), we will try to offer an informative introduction to this volume ...

As is often the case in agency relationships, we the agents are closer to the subject than you the principal. But it is your interest that should be served. Can you be confident that we will inform you in the best possible manner? Not necessarily . . . there is some natural divergence of interest between the agents (the volume editors) and the principal. Yet there is also reason for you to think that we would not purposely mislead you.

You may be reading this to determine whether you should buy the book. Might we as volume editors, eager to make a sale, assure you, an executive, that an examination of our book can boost your profits and improve your labor relations? Probably not. There are at least two inhibitions to such a subterfuge: the market and personal reputation.

Books of this sort are sold through outside reviews and word of mouth. A disingenuous opening might well prove counterproductive. More important, your editors would sacrifice a substantial portion of their academic reputations were they found to misrepresent in this way. Such a loss of reputation would in no way benefit the misled reader. But it represents a threat sufficient to keep the present agents true to their principals' interests. (Pratt and Zeckhauser, 1985: 1)

Thus the problem of agency for academics, once raised, is resolved immediately. Yet if all that is required for academics to act honestly is 'the market' and 'personal reputation', is this not equally true of managers? Surely professional managers are subject to 'outside reviews' (audits, consultants, seminars, newly hired colleagues, colleagues leaving for other firms, etc.) and 'word of mouth' (gossip, gossip columns in the business press, etc.); and surely managers also have a 'personal reputation' to safeguard in their relations with more senior managers, directors and owners. If these mechanisms of outside review, word of mouth and personal reputation are sufficient to eliminate the agency problem between academics and their readers so that the issue is of no practical account, why is there nevertheless a serious practical agency problem of managers in their relations with owners. If intangible processes such as outside reviews, word of mouth and reputation suffice to control academics, why in the case of managers is there the necessity for a complex machinery of governance, of incentives and control systems, of carefully crafted contracts, of optimal financial reward and debt funding provisions, in short the whole panoply of institutional arrangements which requires research by agency theorists. Why does the problem of agency for managers require a social scientific literature whereas the idea of an agency problem among academics is the stuff of light comedy, settled on the first page.

This illustrates the curious, or not so curious, asymmetry of agency theorists, for whom their own behaviour is off-limits. The only sense we can make of all this is that agency theorists are willing to ascribe to managers a greater level of mendacity and deviousness than agency theorists ascribe to themselves.

The moral condemnation of management

The question of the treatment to be accorded to organizational economics is a difficult one. The future fruitfulness of pursuing this model cannot be known *a priori* and this forbids premature rejection. Moreover, some managers clearly act opportunistically, guilefully, not to say immorally, some of the time in some situations, so there is some basis to the opportunistic model of the manager. This opportunistic behaviour clearly contributes in some degree to organization dysfunctionality, suboptimal goal attainment and reduction in shareholder wealth. Opportunism merits academic attention, but we must beware lest organization studies falls into certain traps.

The narrowness of the model of 'man' in organizational economics presents several difficulties. It is one thing to state that managers sometimes act opportunistically, and to treat this contingently, as behaviour to be explained by reference to situational circumstances, as well as to underlying drives and interests. It is quite another thing to state as an axiom that all managerial behaviour is opportunistic, or opportunistic unless rigorously bounded by incentives and bonds. The axiomatic formulation renders the theory too narrow a model of man and woman and too poorly grounded in empirical research. Moreover, to state axiomatically that managerial behaviour is opportunistic, guileful and shirking is a pungent moral condemnation. It is guilt by axiom.

For managerial audiences the stark axioms of organizational economics are likely to sound shrill and offensive. Many managers perceive themselves to be working long and hard to do a good job for their corporation and the community at large, shareholders included. For university academics to tell them they are all cheats and greedy idlers is liable to provoke outrage. Bad enough that as a manager, one has to be told that one has failed to implement the most effective modern management approaches. That can be morally excused as lack of knowledge by practitioners. The conventional view of the partnership between management and management academics is that management academics, through their research and teaching, would help practising managers to attain more effective practices. But now management academics, under the influence of organizational economics, are stating that managers do not intend to act decently and that managers intend to defraud their company and client companies. This is a far more serious, moralizing kind of criticism for managers to have to hear from academics. The reception is unlikely to be unproblematic.

This is not to advocate that management academics should be fawning sycophants of management, serving up a distorted, flattering view of management. As academics, the first obligation is to the truth. That involves recognition and broadcast of the fact that some managers, some of the time, act in ways that are lazy, opportunistic, deceitful, disloyal, immoral, illegal and so on, reflecting their narrow pursuit of self-interest. This behaviour requires theories, such as those of organizational economics, that provide explanations of these facts. However, since managerial behaviour is only sometimes opportunistic these theories at best provide partial elements for a theory of managerial behaviour. Opportunism will be a postulate at a lower level in the hierarchy of theory, with accompanying statements specifying the contingent circumstances in which opportunism will arise. Opportunism will not be the foundational axiom on which the whole system rests, as managerial behaviour is more complex and multi-faceted than this.

In the world of practical affairs, organizational economics faces the profession of management studies with severe community relations difficulties. Those academics seeking support from management, whether in the form of enrolments for executive programmes, research access or financial support, might encounter opposition to the degree that management schools come to be publicly perceived as closely identified with organizational economics. The Academy of Management launched a new journal, the *Academy of Management Executive* as a deliberate attempt to reach out to the American executive audience. One can imagine executive reactions as they read clearly presented, nicely formatted articles which report the latest new-paradigm research telling the managers that axiomatically they are all guilty of ripping off their organizations.

The relative offensiveness of theories

Thus, in our view, organizational economics contains a strongly negative view of managers as cheats and idlers and the like. This is far more negative than the view of managers in structural contingency theory, as guiding the organization into adaptation to its environment and to the contingencies with resultant gains in organizational performance. Organizational economics is unusual in the pungency of its evaluation of managers, being more negative than the newer sociological organizational paradigms, such as population-ecology, institutional and resource dependence theories, none of which posits the anti-organizational, managerial guile of organizational economics.

A manager hearing the negative evaluation of managers contained within organizational economics would be expected to have the normal human emotional responses. Such negative images of managers would provoke more offence in the manager than would more benign or neutral, that is less offensive, views of managers. A manager offended by a theory would be likely to show reactions such as defensiveness or hostility and to withhold co-operation from an academic teacher or researcher associated with such a theory.

Elsewhere we have referred to organizational economics as being a more offensive theory to managers than other theories of organizational structure (Donaldson, 1990a). Barney (1990: 387) disagreed and saw organizational economics theories as no more offensive than traditional management theories. We emphasized that this is ultimately an empirical matter whose validity or lack thereof is to be established through field testing (Donaldson, 1990b: 398). The results of such empirical study of the differential offensiveness of theories are as yet awaited. However, some intriguing, suggestive evidence comes from a field study by Jones (1987). (This is the article in the *Academy of Management Journal* for which Jones won a prize of the Academy of Management.) The article is entitled 'Organization–client transactions and organizational governance structures'. The article reports field data and interprets them in terms of organizational economics theory. The variables are fairly standard organizational-type variables of the kind used in previous research guided by earlier theories such as structural contingency theory, for example the formalization scale of Van de Ven and Ferry (1980) (see Jones, 1987: 209). The organizational economics aspect lies more in the interpretation placed on them after data collection, rather than in their being inherently organizational economics variables.

Jones (1987: 215) explains the reason for the lack of distinctively organizational economics data of opportunistic cheating, shirking, self-interested acting with guile, and the like:

My original research design included questions concerning the extent to which client-contact employees could act or were acting opportunistically towards clients; however, managers were unwilling to allow employees to answer such questions so I could not explore this issue.

Thus managers saw the questions about opportunism as unacceptable and would not permit the research to inquire into them, whereas the same managers were willing to have questions asked which related to transaction uncertainty and performance ambiguity, e.g., how frequently employees deal with customers, the average time taken to deal with customers, etc. The managers granted researchers access to gather conventional types of organizational data but not the new organizational economics data on opportunism. This is exactly what the proposition about the differential offensiveness of theories would predict, i.e., that organizational economics ideas about employees shirking opportunistically are so pungently negative in their moral evaluations that they will be more offensive than other organizational theory ideas and hence managers will be unwilling to offend their employees by having them surveyed in these terms. No sooner is there contact in the field between organizational economics theory and real managers than the unusual hostility of the organizational economics view of employees provokes a wary managerial reaction. The consequence is a breakdown in co-operation between managers and academic organization theory researchers. Thus the fieldwork access problems in the Jones (1987) empirical study tend to support the proposition that organizational econ-omics is a theory which is more offensive to managers than are other more conventional organizational structural theories such as structural con-tingency theory.

Superior economics of co-operation over opportunism

Hill (1990) argues against the Williamsonian view (Williamson, 1975, 1985) that opportunism will characterize economic transactions of a given type (transaction-specific investments, etc.). Hill points out that in this type of transaction there are superior returns to co-operation, whereas opportun-ism yields lower returns. Therefore, over time, opportunism is selected out in favour of co-operation. Moreover, a consideration of game theory, which models the bilateral monopoly situation at the heart of transaction cost theory, shows that the market selects in favour of the more successful strategy of co-operation and against opportunism. In the work of Axelrod (1984), the optimal strategy includes the elements of being 'nice', that is, not initiating opportunistic action, and being 'forgiving', in that once the other party reverts back to co-operation the focal party does so (Hill, 1990: 507). Thus the bias is towards co-operation. Hence the game theory literature that constitutes the leading edge of microanalytic research fails to support the opportunism principle of Williamson.

Transactions where the future is open and there is no fixed end-date known ahead of time to the players render opportunism counter-pro-ductive, yet this is the more usual situation in business (Hill, 1990). Again, any gains through opportunism in one relationship between the focal firm and another firm may be more than offset by the loss of reputation for fair dealing; firms in other relationships with the focal firm will move to safeguard themselves from the sort of opportunism they have witnessed by the focal firm in the former relationship, thereby imposing transaction costs (Hill, 1990). In these ways the normal, on-going business relationships between firms are unlikely to embrace opportunism as the long-run equilibrium condition.

Hill (1990: 512) concludes: 'the construction of a long-term relationship based around cooperation and trust is optimal'. It is significant that Hill reaches this conclusion, in conscious contradistinction to Williamson (1975, 1985), after an in-depth consideration of concepts such as opportunism, market equilibria and the prisoners' dilemma game – the very framework that organizational economics utilizes.

Organizational economics and economics

Let us now consider the extent to which organizational economics is firmly based upon the science of economics. We will here examine four issues in turn: the elimination of opportunism and residual loss by competition, the empirical validity of the Berle and Means thesis about the separation of ownership and control, the validity of agency theory models, and the validity of the Williamsonian theory of vertical integration and the degree to which it is underpinned by the classical transaction cost theory of Coase.

The elimination of opportunism by competition

Mainstream, neoclassical economics holds that competition induces profit maximization by firms. Nevertheless, agency and M-form theories hold that departures from profit maximization that benefit the managers at the expense of the shareholders occur in the large corporation (Jensen and Meckling, 1976; Williamson, 1985). Williamson (1964) argues that such opportunism can arise within large corporations because of the limited competition that they face. This opportunism is called managerial discretion, that is, diverting part of the profit into excessive managerial salaries and the like. He distinguishes between the 'competitive' and the 'monopolistic' sectors of the economy. In the competitive sector there is long-run profit maximization. In the monopolistic sector managers are able to divert some profits into discretionary expenditures (Williamson, 1964: 170).

This monopolistic sector 'represents somewhat less than one-third of the economic activity in the United States' and 'includes most of the highly visible industries (steel, electrical equipment, automobiles, cigarettes, and so forth)' (Williamson, 1964: 171). This statement usefully helps us to understand that the managerial discretion theory is intended to apply only to a minority part of the economy. Moreover, it makes more concrete the industries to which the theoretical model is held to apply.

Williamson (1964: 171) goes on to state that such monopolies tend to be temporary – a widespread view among professional economists. He explains that: 'In the very long run, of course, the special advantages that insulate a firm from the pressures of competition tend to be eroded and may fail to be replaced by others. Hence, discretion that exists in the short run may disappear as the time period is extended.' In an accompanying footnote he specifies that by the short run he means 'somewhat less than two years' (171n). He also states that 'I would suggest that ... the managerial discretion models or similar ... be used in the intermediate run in circumstances where competition in the product market is not typically severe' (171n). And he defines 'the intermediate run as two to five years' (171n). Thus the theory of managerial discretion which Williamson propounds is stated by him to hold only where competition is limited, a situation which lasts only for a maximum of about five years, because the insulation of a firm from competitive pressures tends to be eroded within that time.

By implication, a firm in the monopolistic sector and so subject to managerial discretion in 1964 would no longer be so by 1970. Managerial discretion is a temporary phenomenon, a short-run aberration before the remorseless processes of competition in the economy restore profit maximization. This formulation makes the theory of managerial discretion more acceptable to mainstream economics, but renders the theory trivial. There is no on-going managerial discretion among large corporations that lasts for decades, injuring corporate profits and shareholder returns in a persistent way. There is limited and doubtful need for the imposition of controls and sanctions on managers, such as M-form structures, independent boards of directors and the like, for within five years any managerial discretion existing in a corporation will be curbed by competition. Again, there is no basis for propagating theories that speak of widespread discretionary expenditures, residual losses and managerial self-aggrandizement, since markets self-correct to remove the room for such dysfunctions. The baleful view of managers that is constantly repeated in organizational economics is contradicted by one of its seminal statements (Williamson, 1964). This brings out the inherent tension between organizational economics, with its recurrent imagery of managerial maladministration, and the economic view that all firms are subject to market forces that invoke profit maximization.

This is not the place to consider the state of competition in economies such as that of the USA, but there are surely signs that competition is substantial and increasing in many of our economies. In fact, governments in several countries have been expressly following policies aimed at increasing the competitive pressures on their domestic corporations in order to foster corporate effectiveness and enhance the internal administration of business. These policies have included deregulation, lowering tariff protection, privatization, commercialization, break-up of large monopolies and so on. Increasing competition has been seen in service industries such as banking, insurance, telephones and airlines (Channon, 1978). It is widely remarked that international competition is increasing and some even speak of the present era as one of 'hypercompetition'. The motor industry in the USA has witnessed increasing competition, with large corporations such as General Motors losing domestic market share in the eighties to Japanese manufacturers. The US steel industry has been suffering some decline under international and domestic competition. Thus some of the US industries identified by Williamson (1964) in the sixties as 'monopolistic' appear to be less so today. This increasing trend towards competition in the economy renders managerial discretion increasingly less extensive – according to the theory itself. Thus a consideration of increasing competition in the economy places organizational economics within the larger framework of economics *per se* which tends to cast doubt on the validity of the organizational economics ideas.

The invalidity of Berle and Means

M-form and agency theories argue that problems of opportunism and residual loss, that is, managerial agents behaving less than optimally for their principals, the owners, occur most acutely in the modern, large corporation with its diffused ownership and consequent separation of management from control (e.g., Williamson, 1985: 299). The classic work here is the thesis by Berle and Means (1932), *The Modern Corporation and Private Property*. This is repeatedly invoked and cited by contemporary agency theory writers (e.g., Jensen and Meckling, 1976; Williamson, 1985; Eisenhardt, 1989). The nub of the argument by Berle and Means is that corporations controlled by managers rather than owners return less value to owners and consume more value in managerial benefits. However, Stigler and Friedland (1983) present an analysis of data, approximating the period in which Berle and Means were writing, on large US corporations, and show that there is no statistical evidence that the managerially controlled companies differ from the owner-controlled corporations on these crucial outcome variables. As Stigler and Friedland (1983: 259) conclude:

Our own statistical analyses, using only data and methods familiar to economists of the time, yield no clear evidence that the management-dominated corporations differed much from owner-dominated companies in practices of executive compensation or in the utilization of assets to produce profits.

Indeed Stigler and Friedland state that in contradistinction to the wide reception of *The Modern Corporation and Private Property* in popular and policy discussion circles: '[a] much more modest role must be assigned to the book if we look for its effects on professional economic analysis' (259). Given the absence of empirical evidence of the validity of the thesis, Stigler and Friedland state as their finale:

The main tradition of economic theory was perhaps instinctively recognizing these facts when it continued to work in complete disregard of *The Modern Corporation*. (259)

Thus the Berle and Means thesis is invalid and shunned by mainstream economics.

Such a rejection of the empirical basis of a classic foundational study is a highly damaging move against certain agency theory formulations. One would think that agency and transaction cost theorists who nevertheless wish to pursue the Berle and Means (1932) thesis would show why the thesis is still valid despite the seeming disconfirmation by Stigler and Friedland (1983). However, while organizational economists routinely invoke the thesis as part of their standard argument, and indeed continue to use exactly the Berle and Means phrase 'the modern corporation' (e.g., Williamson, 1985: 273), they often do so without explaining limitations in the critique by Stigler and Friedland or even citing this important critique (Williamson, 1985; Eisenhardt, 1989). Thus the claims to scientific rigour and analytic precision of organizational economics (especially compared with their more sociologically and psychologically oriented organizational studies colleagues) must be taken with a pinch of salt. Some might argue that this critique is simply unknown to many organizational economics writers, yet it was published in a special issue of the *Journal of Law and Economics*, in which is also found an article by Fama and Jensen (1983) which is frequently cited by organizational economics writers (e.g., Williamson, 1985). Moreover, Stigler, as a Professor in the Department of Economics of the University of Chicago, that citadel of the new, tough-minded, rigorous economics which organizational economists so applaud, was also prominent for winning a Nobel Prize in Economics.

The limited validity of agency theory models

Turning to the content of agency theory models, another Nobel Laureate, Kenneth Arrow (1985: 48) has commented upon the tenuous validity of present agency theory in that it frequently specifies incentive schedules which are more complex than those in the real world:

But it is perhaps more useful to consider the extent to which the principal–agent relation in actuality differs from that in the models developed to date. Most importantly, the theory tends to lead to very complex fee functions. It turns out to be difficult to establish even what would appear to be common-sense properties of monotonicity and the like. We do not find such complex relations in reality. Principal–agent theory gives a good reason for the existence of sharecrop contracts, but it is a very poor guide to their actual terms. Indeed, as John Stuart Mill pointed out long ago, the terms tend to be regulated by custom. They are remarkably uniform from farm to farm and from region to region. Principal–agent theory, in contrast, would suggest that the way the produce is divided between landlord and tenant would depend on the probability distribution of weather and other exogenous uncertainties and on the relation between effort and output, both of which certainly vary from one region to another; the latter has varied over time as well. Similarly, the coinsurance provisions in health insurance policies are much simpler than could possibly be accounted for by principal–agent theory.

In some cases where principal–agent theory seems clearly applicable, real-world practice is very different from the model. In many respects, the physician–patient relation exemplifies the principal–agent relation almost perfectly. The principal (the patient) is certainly unable to monitor the efforts of the agent (the physician). The relation between effort and outcome is random, but presumably there is some connection. Yet in practice the physician's fee schedule is in no way related to outcome. Liability for malpractice can be seen as a modification of the fee schedule in the direction indicated by principal–agent theory, but it is not applicable to what might be termed run-of-the-mill shirking, and it requires very special kinds of evidence. In general, indeed, compensation of professionals shows only a few traces of the complex fee schedules implied by theory.

Even in situations where compensation systems seem closer in form to the theoretical, there are significant differences. Consider the incentive compensation schemes for corporate executives. They invariably have a large discretionary component. What is the purpose of this? Why should the incentive payment not be based entirely on observable magnitudes, profits, rates of return, and the like?

Thus Arrow draws our attention to the validity problems in present agency theory models.

Problems with the Williamsonian theory of vertical integration

Another area of disjunction between organizational economics and its supposed foundation in economics lies in the topic of vertical integration. Williamson (1975, 1985) holds that where a company that is supplier to a client company makes an investment in an asset specific to that client under conditions of uncertainty and opportunism, the cost of transactions between the two companies is raised. The economically optimal policy is to merge the two companies through vertical integration in order to reduce the transaction costs. The transaction cost theory of Williamson, Barney and Ouchi and others is derived from the classic theory of the Nobel Laureate, Coase (1937). Williamson (1985: 3) acknowledges Coase as the originator of transaction cost theory. Yet subsequently, at a conference in 1987 on his work, Coase (1991) publicly repudiated the Williamson theory that transaction costs lead to vertical integration because of transaction-specific asset investment and the resulting problem of opportunism.

Coase (1991: 69) is scathing and satirical about the arguments put forth by Klein et al. (1978). After quoting Klein et al., Coase (1991: 69) comments of their theory:

As Mrs. Robinson has said on a similar occasion, we are not surprised to see the man produce the rabbit out of the hat if we've just watched him put it in. What readers were no doubt hoping to discover about the relation of the costs of contracting and of vertical integration appears as an assumption. Even so, the conclusion they draw from this assumption, if not in error, is, I believe, misleading.

Specifically, Coase doubts that the quasi-rents produced by transaction-specific asset investments raise the costs of contracting to the point where vertical integration is the more economical alternative (70). Coase argues that a transaction-specific asset investment can be made by a supplier without the supplier and the client firm merging. He explicitly rejects the exemplar often used by later transaction cost theorists (Klein *et al.*, 1978), the acquisition in 1926 of Fisher Body (a supplier) by General Motors (their client). Coase points out that a major supplier of car frames to General Motors, A.O. Smith, retained its independence for more than forty years, with their relationship governed by contracting not vertical integration (71). Coase quotes in support of his views Stigler (1951).

Similarly Coase (1991: 70) argues that the potential opportunism is held in check by fear of losing future business deals (through poor reputation). Therefore opportunism is curbed because it is unprofitable. Hence Coase rejects two of the central pillars of the theory of vertical integration offered by Williamson (1975) and Klein *et al.* (1978): transaction-specific asset investment and opportunism. As Coase (1991: 70, 71) makes clear, he rejected both these ideas in the early 1930s prior to writing his classic 1937 article on transaction costs.

Thus the two ideas of transaction-specific asset investment and opportunism, so central to Williamson, Klein *et al.*, Barney and Ouchi, Jones and others in the modern organizational economics literature, are denied as flawed by the originator of transaction cost theory, Coase. In particular, the concept of opportunism which is important for the organizational economics imagery of greedy managers and conflicts of interest is dismissed by Coase (1991). Hence the 'dark side' view of human nature that Williamson explicitly acknowledges about his writings is specific to his variant of transaction cost theory. He makes explicit that his view on opportunism as a cause of transactions costs is 'very different from that originally advanced by Coase ... [He] is ... silent on the contracting hazards and maladaptions on which I rely to explain nonstandard contracting' (Williamson, 1985: 78n). While opportunism is now a shared tenet of many contemporary organizational economists, the concept has no necessary connection with transaction cost theory, as it was rejected by Coase. The negative view of managers and business people in modern transaction cost theory is a new twist. In advancing this negative view, contemporary organizational economists cannot claim a basis in classical transaction cost theory or in the authority of Coase. (Other arguments against the transaction cost theory of vertical integration are made by the economists Evans and Grossman (1983).)

Our brief consideration of professional opinion within economics serves to illustrate that there is no unquestioned body of established economic knowledge forming a solid foundation on which organizational economics rests. Indeed the situation is the reverse, with economics calling into question organizational economics.

A positive role for management

Economic theory and the manager

Castanias and Helfat (1991) have examined the role of management from the viewpoint of economic theory. They note that prevailing economically oriented discussions in organization theory tend to take the agency theory view of managers as agents with interests in conflict with their principals, the owners of the corporation. However, going back to economic theory in the form of the theory of comparative advantage as embedded in critical resources leads Castanias and Helfat to challenge the equation of economics with agency theory. Value is produced in organizations by the creation of advantage through the bringing together of distinctive resources and skills in a unique competitive system. This feat is accomplished in practice by managers who themselves contribute an embedded part of the organizational skills. It follows that organizational managers are creators of value and make an essential and positive contribution to the organization. Thus economic logic, when applied to the issue of managers in corporate organizations, leads, in their view, not to agency theory but to the opposite, i.e., managers as valuable.

Agency theory and the positive contribution of management

Within agency theory, the logic of the principal–agent analysis can lead to the view of non-owning managers not as liabilities but rather as essential assets. The modern large corporation is a coalition composed of a set of diverse stakeholders including outside shareholders, suppliers, labour and management. Stakeholders such as suppliers need to be able to transact with the corporation in a way which allows the suppliers to make long-term commitments, such as investments in transaction-specific assets, knowing that the corporation will honour its long-term obligations made to the supplier. But the corporation is largely not made up of a person or entity which exists in any single or stable or enduring fashion. In particular, outside shareholders might sell out their ownership of the corporation tomorrow, so how can they make a credible commitment to a supplier for long-term supply? Executive management, however, is the nearest thing to the person of the corporation, giving life to the corporation as a stable, enduring, singular entity, which can make credible commitments to long-term suppliers (Coffee, 1986; Shleifer and Summers, 1988). Thus the existence of the corporation and the economic market exchanges in which it is involved is facilitated by the existence of corporate managers (Garvey and Gaston, 1991; Garvey and Swan, 1992). Moreover, for this to hold, managers need to have long prospects of employment with the company in a career, a deep commitment to the organization as an on-going project and most of their economic wealth tied up in their organization through organization-specific knowledge and through dependence upon a salary and a company pension. Thus in economic terms, the theory requires that the manager be entrenched and a salaried employee rather than an owner. If managers were owners then share price appreciation could make them wealthy and free them from continuing economic dependence and on-going service to the corporation, thereby robbing the corporation of stable management.

Thus in a more thoroughgoing agency theory analysis, the corporation and its shareholders are best served by having managers as agents whose interests are divorced from the outside shareholders as principals. In this more sophisticated version of agency theory there is a functional value to the separation of interests of agents and principals. Agents best serve principals in the long run by using their discretion to take actions which principals might not prefer in the short run. Whether this theory is truer or falser than the more conventional version of agency theory, the point is that agency theory logic does not lead inevitably to the proposition that managerial agents defraud their principals, the outside shareholders, unless curbed. This cheating view is but one of several which can be deduced ultimately from a principal–agent framework. Therefore the version of agency theory which is presently received in organization theory circles cannot claim primacy. The view of managers as dysfunctional shirkers is not the inevitable conclusion of exploring the theoretical insights available from approaching organizations through the principal–agent framework.

Applications of organizational economics

Critique of the M-form thesis

Williamson (1970, 1971, 1985) has advanced the M-form thesis to explain the adoption of the multidivisional structure by large corporations. Smaller corporations use a functional, that is, unitary or U-form organizational structure. As they grow in size this leads to taller hierarchies and more and larger departments. Top management no longer tightly controls the organization through direct supervision, in particular of the middle management. This leads to control loss and suboptimal corporate performance as middle managers indulge in empire-building and other forms of self-aggrandizement at cost to the corporation. Thus the U-form structure becomes dysfunctional with growth in organizational size. The solution is to adopt the M-form structure. This features multiple divisions each given autonomy but held accountable for its profitability. The corporate central office is not involved in divisional decisions and is therefore psychologically distant enough to be an independent judge of the performance of each division and its management. The top executives are assisted in this evaluating role by a central staff who monitor and investigate the divisions (e.g., accountants) (Williamson, 1970, 1985).

It is clearly sound to argue that as organizations grow in size they grow a taller hierarchy, more departments and larger average-sized departments; the research of Blau and his colleagues shows this (Blau, 1970, 1972; Blau and Schoenherr, 1971). And it is valid to see top management in larger organizations as having less direct control over the whole organization than top management in smaller organizations, in part because of the intermediate layers of the hierarchy; this is shown in the research of Pugh *et al.* (1969a, b) and others (Child, 1972b). However, the assertion by Williamson (1970) that his leads to loss of control by top management is arguable.

Other organization theorists point to another mode of control in large organizations, wherein direct, personal top management control is replaced by impersonal control through bureaucratic formalization, i.e., job descriptions, standard procedures, budgets, planning and requirements for periodic performance reporting on sales, costs and so on (Weber, 1968; Pugh *et al.*, 1969a, b; Blau and Schoenherr, 1971; Child, 1972b). Much of this activity is supervised by the administrative staff that grows in size as total personnel grows and assumes increasing power over the line management (Mintzberg, 1979). Williamson (1970) accepts this argument with reference to the corporate central staff, but fails to acknowledge that this staff monitoring and controlling role can be played at lower levels in the hierarchy, e.g., accounting and personnel staff in a plant who monitor local line management and enforce head-office policies, plans and procedures (i.e., 'staff and line' organization). A third mode of control by top management over the organization is via selection, promotion and reward systems applied throughout the hierarchy (Mintzberg, 1979). A fourth mode is by creation of a corporate culture of shared norms and beliefs (Deal and Kennedy, 1982). Thus any loss of control by top management due to declining direct, personal control as organizational size increases is to degrees offset by increasing use of the other three control modes (Child, 1972b; Mintzberg, 1979). Hence it is not self-apparent that growth in organizational size leads to increasing control loss, and empirical evidence would be required to substantiate the contention. The stark model of the organization used by the organizational economist – direct, personal control through hierarchy – fails to encompass all the control modes actually used in large organizations, by ignoring insights and evidence available from the organizational sociological literature.

Williamson (1970) holds that control loss leads in turn to self-aggrandizement by managers through empire-building and the like (i.e., residual loss in agency theory terms). Again this is not demonstrated empirically. On the contrary, Blau (1970, 1972) has argued on the basis of empirical research that growth in organizational size and hierarchy actually leads to economies of scale in administration. Blau shows that the proportions of managers and administrative staff decline as organizations grow in size, thus contradicting the assertion by Williamson that organizational growth leads to excessive personnel costs through empire-building.

Thus there are grounds for doubting that large organizational size necessarily leads to either control loss or residual loss, and empirical evidence is required before these aspects of the M-form thesis can be accepted.

The prediction from Williamson's theory is that organizations shift from U- to M-form (i.e., functional to multidivisional structure) as a result of increasing size. However, the contrary explanation offered by Chandler (1962) is that strategy (i.e., diversification) causes divisionalization, not to stem increasing managerial delinquency but because of effectiveness enhancements from better co-ordination of more complex operations (i.e., several different product-markets). The derived hypothesis from Chandler is that strategy, not size, is the cause of divisionalization.

The relative causal influences of size and strategy on divisionalization have been investigated empirically. Results have been mixed, varying from strategy but not size as a cause of divisionalization (Chenhall, 1979), strategy dominates over size (Donaldson, 1982b; Palmer et al., 1987), strategy and size are about equal causes (Grinyer et al., 1980: 198), strategy and size are both causes (Fligstein, 1985), to size is a greater cause than strategy (Khandwalla, 1977: 499, 664; Grinyer and Yasai-Ardekani, 1981). Donaldson (1982b) has criticized methodological weaknesses in studies that show size as a cause and Grinyer (1982) has replied on their behalf, leading in turn to further argumentation against size (Donaldson, 1986b, c). There is a considerable weight of empirical evidence and argument against size as a cause of divisionalization, and most particularly for strategy as a cause at least as important as size. Thus the theory of a size effect on divisionalization receives mixed support at best. Divisionalization is empirically at least as well explained by strategy, whose underlying theory is of managers benignly seeking greater effectiveness through better co-ordination of inherently co-operative managers, rather than managers as delinquents.

Any effect of size on divisionalization may be explained without recourse to Williamson's (1970) theory of managers as delinquents. Jaques (1976) has argued that as organizations grow in size their internal complexity becomes too great to be managed given the limits in the cognitive capacity of top managers, and so they need to be broken into smaller, more manageable units, i.e., divisions. Thus the theory of Jaques (1976) predicts that size causes divisionalization, not because of managerial delinquency, but because of requirements for effective co-ordination.

In summary, the Williamson M-form theory is debatable and lacking in empirical substantiation. It is based on an incomplete model of organizational control. It assumes rather than demonstrates managerial delinquency. The predicted relationship between size and divisionalization is somewhat uncertain empirically since there is a strong influence of strategy on divisionalization. The strategy effect requires no postulates of managerial delinquency to explain divisionalization. Any effect of size on divisionalization can also be explained without recourse to the postulate of managerial delinquency. The M-form theory of Williamson must at the present time be viewed with considerable caution (for other criticisms, see Hill, 1985a). Accordingly, the superiority of organizational economic explanations over earlier sociological or psychological or management theory explanations must, for the phenomenon of divisionalization, be held in doubt.

Williamson (1985: 284) seeks to buttress his argument through asserting the underlying coherence of the theory. In particular, he notes 'an isomorphism' in that the three structures he distinguishes for the modern corporation (U-form, H-form and M-form) can be assigned to the three nodes on a diagram (285, figure 11-2) that is pictorially identical to his diagram of the contracting schema that summarizes his transaction cost theory (33, figure 1-2). This is achieved by considering the distinction between general purpose technologies that use transaction-nonspecific assets and special purpose technologies that use transaction-specific assets (33) as equivalent to the distinction between centralization and decentralization, respectively (285).

This equivalence is asserted through terming centralization and decentralization as information processing technologies (Williamson, 1985: 284). However, such a statement seems tenuous at best for there is more to organizational structure than information processing: centralization involves the distribution of decision-making authority (Weber, 1968). Moreover, Williamson omits to explain why centralization implies transaction-nonspecific assets and decentralization implies transaction-specific assets. Transaction-specific assets occur in vertically integrated corporations; yet the study by Lorsch and Allen (1973) shows that these corporations are, as a result of their vertical integration, more centralized than non-vertically-integrated, diversified corporations which (according to Williamson) have fewer transaction-specific assets. Thus the identity postulated between transaction-specific assets and decentralization is uncertain. In the absence of any explicit argumentation the isomorphism claimed by Williamson fails and the exercise is no more than drawing one picture like another.

Corporate governance

Corporate governance has been the subject of theorizing both in agency theory and transaction cost theory, and so this is also a suitable topic to test the validity of organizational economics.

Corporate governance refers to the high-level authority system of an organization, including particularly the structure for the control of executive management, the board of directors (Tricker, 1984). The managerial hegemony thesis has argued that in the modern, large corporation with dispersed shareholders, the executive management have taken control and run the corporation in their own interests to the detriment of the outside shareholder owners (Berle and Means, 1932). Agency theory and transaction cost theory both take this idea as their starting-point in the analysis of corporate governance, and argue that the systems of corporate governance can to a degree protect the interests of outside shareholders. This protection is achieved by having persons who are not executives act as the directors and as the chairperson of the board of directors (Jensen and Meckling, 1976; Williamson, 1985). Thus the shareholders, as principals, are to be protected from loss through adverse actions by the managers, as agents, by control by an independent board of directors. Organizational economics holds that in the absence of a strong, independent board of directors, shareholders will suffer because executives will shirk, profits will be channelled into overly generous executive compensation, profitless growth and empire-building will be used to boost executive prestige and salary claims, risk-averse strategies to secure the jobs of executives will be favoured and other forms of executive self-aggrandizement will all lower shareholder returns. Organizational economics postulates that shareholder returns and organizational financial performance will be maximized where executive tendencies to self-aggrandizement are held in check by a board of directors which features a board chair and at least a majority of directors who are independent, non-executives. Thus in the topic of corporate governance, organizational economics offers some specific propositions which can be put to the empirical test.

The antithetic Theory Y, when applied in the area of corporate governance, argues that managers are motivated by achievement and responsibility (McClelland, 1961; Porter, 1964), and that organizational financial performance and shareholder wealth will be maximized by empowering managers to exercise unencumbered authority and responsibility through having executives compose a majority of the board of directors and through having the chief executive chair the board (Donaldson, 1990a; Donaldson and Davis, 1991).

The research shows that the agency theory of corporate governance is to a considerable degree empirically rejected by the evidence and that the opposite view receives considerable support. The conclusion that having a board composed predominantly of executives leads to higher corporate performance is obtained in more empirical studies than obtain the opposite (positive in: Vance, 1978; Kesner, 1987; Rechner and Dalton, 1988; Sullivan, 1988; nil effect in: Pearce, 1983; Chaganti et al., 1985; equivocal in Pearce and Zahra, 1992: 431; negative in: Baysinger and Butler, 1985; Ezzamel and Watson, 1993; for a review and discussion see Donaldson and Davis, 1994). Having the board of directors composed predominantly of corporate executives leads to greater corporate investment in R&D and to less corporate diversification – both outcomes which tend to assist greater corporate performance (Hill and Snell, 1988; Baysinger et al., 1991). Thus the evidence fails to support the agency theory view that a board composed of non-executives leads to greater corporate performance. Turning to the board chair, Rechner and Dalton (1991) show that having the board of directors chaired by a person who is independent of the executive management leads to higher performance than when the board is chaired by the top executive. Berg and Smith (1978: 35) report a similar result; however, their table shows the opposite (table A1), so their study must be coded as equivocal. Another study finds a nil effect (Chaganti et al., 1985). And a fourth study shows superior performance of boards with *executive* chairs (Donaldson and Davis, 1991). Thus the findings are mixed on the effect of an independent board chair on performance.

Overall the research fails to confirm the agency theory idea that an independent, non-executive-dominated board of directors is required in order to control executive management. The present examination of the agency theory of corporate governance cautions that it is by no means wholly empirically valid. The opposite theory, derived from Theory Y, receives more support overall.

The failure of agency theory to find consistently that more controls on managers produce superior results calls into question the whole assumption of agency theory that managers are lazy or devious defrauders of shareholder wealth. If managers were inherently like that then greater controls on them would improve corporate performance and shareholder wealth, but the evidence largely fails to support the proposition. The evidence rather more shows that managers perform better under self-regulation, which is consistent with the more benign view of managers. However, there is need for further research to examine more closely the underlying motivations operating in managers when they are involved in corporate governance.

Moreover, it may well be that managerial motivations are more complex than agency and transaction cost theories hold. Managerial motivation may be contingent on various factors that cause it to shift between self-aggrandizement and pro-organizational actions. It would be a task for future research to identify what such factors might be. One such might be whether the manager had a reasonable expectation of continuing employment or expected termination imminently through, say, hostile takeover (Kosnik, 1987; see Donaldson, 1990a). Any developments of this type would help to bring corporate governance more within a contingency theory approach.

Conclusions

The opportunistic model of 'man' underlying organizational economics is too narrow to serve as a valid rounded theory and ignores too much previous research. This constitutes a worrying regressive tendency. The vaunted economic credentials are not as compelling as might seem at first glance: key elements of the theory and empirical evidence of organizational economics have been called into question by professional economists, including eminent ones. The narrowness of organizational economics reflects more than the focus of a paradigm. It bears signs of the influence of an ideology. This accords no real positive role for managers or management.

That this *is* ideology is evident in the tendency of organizational economics to ignore uncomfortable theoretical reasoning and facts, and in the highly evaluative and harshly negative tone of a system of moral condemnation masquerading as science. The axiomatic view, endlessly repeated in these writings, of managers as shirking, lazy and greedily siphoning off corporate wealth, poses a considerable problem for an academic science of management which aims for truth and which requires collaboration with managers. There may be elements of truth in the organizational economics view but they would be best developed within contingency models in which opportunism, etc. is one type of behaviour among others, including the opposite type, i.e., benign, pro-organizational managerial behaviour. Such an approach would avoid the lop-sidedness and extremism inherent in pursuing the organizational economics agenda.

Thus our overall view rejects organizational economics as any more than a partial approach that may illuminate some aspects of management and organization. As *the* approach to, or *the* paradigm for the analysis of, organizational management it is seriously flawed. There are dangers in having this one view dominate the field of organization and management theory lest it eclipse other sound, moderate contributions that capture significant aspects of the reality of management organization, such as structural contingency theory. The best approach lies in the continued construction of contingency theories in which a variety of behaviours and structures are seen as appropriate depending on the situation.

7   Towards a unified theory of organizational structure

A strategy for integration

A concern of this volume is that the pluralistic profusion of theoretical paradigms in the USA frustrates the creation of an integrated organization theory. US organization theory is presently fragmented into several mutually antithetic theories relating to each other in the manner of separate paradigms. Clearly this is unfortunate since it prevents the topic of organizational structure from enjoying intellectual coherence. It also prevents organizational science from having a consistent model to offer students and managers.

In his 1992 Distinguished Speaker address to the Organization and Management Theory Division at the Academy of Management Annual Meeting, Professor Jeffrey Pfeffer took as his theme 'Barriers to the advance of organizational science: paradigm development as a dependent variable'. He analysed the implications for an academic field of having a paradigm, comparing across a number of academic disciplines. Professor Pfeffer argued that there were advantages for a field in possessing a unifying paradigm and disadvantages from the lack of such a unifying paradigm in organization studies (see Pfeffer 1993a, b). The suggestion of this volume is that, in the field of organizational structural studies, a unified paradigm is desirable and achievable.

We have critically evaluated the major, contemporary US organizational structural theory paradigms; how might they be integrated into a unified theory of organization structure? More specifically, is it possible to synthesize population-ecology theory, institutional theory, resource dependence theory and organizational economics? Can these newer paradigms be synthesized with the older paradigm of structural contingency theory?

Since the paradigms contain diametrically opposed theoretical statements there can be no complete integration of the diverse theories as they stand. The foregoing critical review has indicated certain strengths and weaknesses of each. It would hardly be desirable to retain all of the weaker elements of each theory; it would be desirable to draw selectively on each theory to build the synthesis. Moreover, because of the empirical validity of structural contingency theory such a synthesis would draw heavily on that theory. Structural contingency theory would be the base onto which elements of the other theories would be added.

The organization is seen as existing in an environment with which it is interdependent and with which it transacts as an open system (Emery and Trist, 1965). The organization also has a set of purposes or goals (Parsons, 1961). The environment and goals interact to produce the organizational strategy (Ansoff, 1968). The strategy and the environment produce the internal organizational characteristics of the size, range of products or services, task uncertainty, requirements for public accountability and other situational or contingent factors (Burns and Stalker, 1961; Pugh et al. 1969b). The organization adjusts its structure over time to move into a fit with these task contingencies (Chandler, 1962; Donaldson, 1987). There are fits between size, public accountability and bureaucratization, between diversification and divisional and matrix structures, and between uncertainty and organic structure, as will be discussed below.

Organizations need to obtain resources from the environment. This is an idea of resource dependence theory (Pfeffer and Salancik, 1978), though it is present also in the systems theory on which structural contingency theory drew (Emery and Trist, 1965), so its acceptance here is not particularly a drawing upon resource dependence theory. Resource dependence theory argues also that the critical resource needs of the organization affects the intra-organizational distribution of power (Pfeffer and Salancik, 1978). Again this was advanced previously in the strategic contingencies theory of intra-organizational power by structural contingency theorists (Crozier, 1964; Hickson et al., 1971), so its acceptance here is also not in itself an act of synthesis between paradigms. However, resource dependence theory has usefully extended this core insight to argue that other power phenomena such as executive succession are shaped by the critical resource needs of the organization (Pfeffer and Salancik, 1978). The integrated theory of organizational structure would include these ideas.

Institutional theory can contribute the proposition that some internal organizational structural elements arise not from the task environment but from the institutional environment, particularly from the state, which compels compliance (DiMaggio and Powell, 1983; Tolbert and Zucker, 1983). However, in keeping with functionalist theory, structural elements adopted by the organization are typically adaptive, being functional for either the organization or the society, and usually for both, as neither organization nor state are motivated to push for the adoption of structural elements which are not in keeping with their objectives (Parsons, 1961, 1966). Thus the adoption of organizational structural features is typically rational at the collective level.

Population-ecology contributes the theory of organizational foundings or births (Hannan and Freeman, 1989). Population-ecology offers explanations of the phenomenon of organizational foundings which structural contingency theory had not encompassed. The theory and empirical research of population-ecology illuminates the ecological factors which affect rates of organizational foundings, such as the density of the existing population of other organizations (Hannan and Freeman, 1989). Likewise, population-ecology theory reveals the influence of ecological factors upon the rate of organizational mortality or death (Hannan and Freeman, 1989). Population-ecology research corroborates this empirically and includes in its explanation the influence of factors which are of the institutionalist type, such as legitimation from external bodies. Since both population-ecology and institutional theories use the concept of external legitimation aiding organizational survival, this itself marks a point of synthesis between these two paradigms (Hannan and Freeman, 1989; Powell and DiMaggio, 1991). Population-ecology also explains mortality in terms of the intra-organizational factor of specialism–generalism and its fit to the rate of environmental change (Hannan and Freeman, 1989). This apart, however, population-ecology does not address internal organizational causes of survival and so these determinants of organizational mortality must come from elsewhere, mainly from misfit between organization and environment as specified in structural contingency and resource dependence theories (in the case of the latter, misfit between the internal power structure and the critical resource needs).

Organizational economics, in the sense used herein of agency theory and transaction cost economics, argues that members of organizations, including their managers, are untrustworthy and given to acting deviously in a way to cheat owners or other organizations with whom they have entered a long-range relationship (Jensen and Meckling, 1976; Williamson, 1985). This view does not seem accurately to describe organizational members who are involved in long-term relationships with owners and partner-organizations. Organizational economics likely holds valid in the domain of relations between the organization and certain customers, in those cases where the interpersonal contact is fleeting and is not repeated and so there is no on-going interaction which leads to a social bond and honourable behaviour between the parties. This is exemplified by a person buying insurance from an insurance company. This is the situation in which the distrusting propositions of organizational economics apply, and, indeed, this is where organizational economics concepts such as 'adverse selection' and 'moral hazard' originate (Alchian and Woodward, 1988). Thus organizational economics applies at the boundaries of organizations with persons with whom there is little or no continuing personal relationship formed, i.e., customers (but see p. 212).

An integrated explanatory model of organizational structure

We will now assemble these theoretical elements into a model to explain organizational structure. The life of an organization can be broken into three phases: founding, life and death. During its life the organization makes internal changes. The internal aspects of the organization may be classified into three categories: contingency factors, intra-organizational power and organizational structure. The contingency factors include the critical resources as defined by the environment and the organizational strategy. The organization is affected by three external sources of influence: ecological factors (competition, etc.), the state and customers. This schematic model is shown in figure 7.1.

Organizational founding is affected by ecological factors which influence the need for such an organization and the opportunities. These factors include the availability of resources in the environment, customers, suppliers and financial support (Hannan and Freeman, 1989). Environment supportiveness is in turn affected by competition which reflects the number of other competitor organizations in the environment of the organization (Hannan and Freeman, 1989). Organizational founding will also be more likely where that type of organization is better understood and seen as legitimated and this also is part of the ecology. Thus the rate of organizational foundings first increases with increasing density and then decreases with further increases in density, yielding a curvilinear effect of density on organizational foundings (Hannan and Freeman, 1989).

Once in existence the organization will adopt a set of roles with which to co-ordinate its members and it thereby gains an organizational structure. The organizational structure changes over the life of the organization in response to the contingency factors: organizational size, task uncertainty, strategy, parent organizational size, public accountability and critical resources (as shown in figure 7.1).

As the organization grows in size the hierarchy becomes taller and the structure becomes more differentiated horizontally with each role and each sub-unit becoming more specialized (Blau, 1970, 1972). With increasing size there is also the growth of administrative work, separate from task work yet promoting task efficiency. This is seen in the Aston programme studies where the number and range of administrative functions performed by administrative personnel, that is, staff specialists as opposed to line management, increases as organizational size increases (Pugh and Hickson, 1976; Pugh and Hinings, 1976). It is seen also in the study by Blau and Schoenherr (1971) where the number and range of administrative functional divisions increases with organizational size. These studies also show that administrative work becomes more specialized with increasing organi-

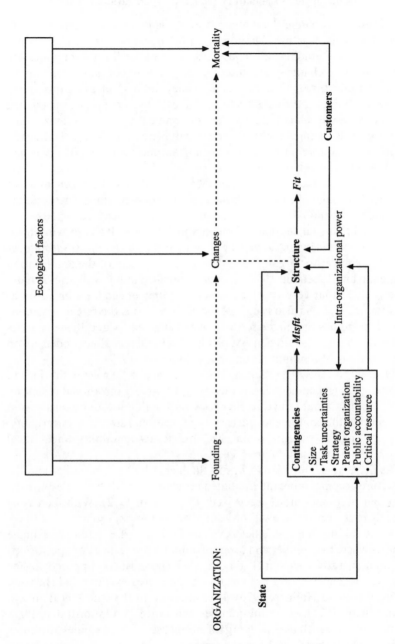

Fig. 7.1. An integrated explanatory model of organizational structure.

zational size, in that the administrative task is broken up into more specialized tasks of accounting, statistics, personnel, etc. as the number of administrators increases (Blau and Schoenherr, 1971; Pugh and Hickson, 1976; Pugh and Hinings, 1976). The growth in administrative specialization is based on the growth in the number of administrators as the organization grows in size (Blau and Schoenherr, 1971; Child, 1973b; Pugh and Hickson, 1976; Reimann, 1979).

The task and administrative work becomes more standardized and formalized with increase in organizational size; this is seen in both the Blau and Schoenherr (1971) and Aston programme studies (Child, 1973a; Pugh and Hickson, 1976; Pugh and Hinings, 1976).

There is also decentralization of decision-making authority with increase in organizational size (Child, 1973a; Pugh and Hickson, 1976; Pugh and Hinings, 1976). This reflects the need to delegate authority down the hierarchy as it lengthens with the increase in organizational size. The increasing burden of deciding about increasingly complex matters is spread among the growing ranks of middle managers. Such delegation brings decision-making closer to the work-face; it thereby reduces the communication distortions and delays that occur when decisions are taken several levels removed from the work-face.

The uncertainty of operations is increased by innovation in output or process. Uncertainty lowers the use of highly specialized task roles, standardization and formalization, since these bureaucratic mechanisms are too inflexible to cope with the variations in response that are required when novel problems are to be solved (Hage and Aiken, 1967). Greater uncertainty leads to more use of professionals, horizontal communications, participation, decentralized initiative-taking and teams focused on outputs (Burns and Stalker, 1961; Hage and Aiken, 1967; Van de Ven and Ferry, 1980). The organizational structure required for the management of innovation is identified in these terms in the distinction between mechanistic and organic structures (Burns and Stalker, 1961). There is evidence that structures which are more organic lead to, or are associated with, greater innovativeness in terms of the rate of increase in new organizational programmes (i.e., outputs) (Harvey, 1968; Hage and Dewar, 1973). Innovation increases the requirement for co-ordination across the functional elements involved in the product through interfunctional meetings, linking individuals, task forces and so on (Lawrence and Lorsch, 1967). Organizations that provide these structures to integrate their differentiated functional departments are more effective empirically (Lawrence and Lorsch, 1967).

Pursuing a diversification strategy leads to a shift from a centralized, functional structure to a more decentralized, multidivisional one, with the divisions being specialized by product or service (Chandler, 1962). Where distinct geographic areas are served then the divisions will be specialized by area (Stopford and Wells, 1972). Each division is autonomous in terms of operations and is assessed as a profit centre. The autonomy and profit assessment are facilitated by each division being a separate business not dependent upon the other divisions, thus each division can be operated independently and then evaluated independently. There is evidence that corporations whose organizational structures fit their strategies (e.g., a divisional structure with a diversified strategy) in consequence outperform those corporations whose organizational structures misfit their strategies (e.g., a functional structure with a diversified strategy) (Donaldson, 1987; Hamilton and Shergill, 1992; Hill et al., 1992).

Vertical integration between stages in production leads to reduced autonomy of product divisions and greater central staff in order to co-ordinate the flows of material between the divisions (Lorsch and Allen, 1973). The downstream divisions selling to the final customer can be assessed as profit centres; in contrast, the upstream divisions producing the raw materials need to be treated as cost centres, otherwise transfer-pricing problems result if both upstream and downstream divisions are evaluated as profit centres while involved in substantial trade with each other (Lorsch and Allen, 1973).

Where there is a medium degree of diversity by product or geographic area (or both) such that there are not self-sufficient divisions on either a product or area basis, then a matrix structure will be appropriate (Donaldson, 1985a; Egelhoff, 1988a, b). In a matrix structure a business unit reports to two bosses simultaneously such as the head of its product and the head of its geographic area. There is sufficient product diversity that a head is required for each product and there is also sufficient area diversity that a head is required for each area. Because of the lack of self-sufficient business units on either product or area, however, both sets of superior managers are required simultaneously, leading to both arms of the matrix. This is expressed by Davis and Lawrence (1977) as the contingency of 'dual focus' giving rise to matrix organizational structure.

Thus organizational structure as regards differentiation, bureaucratization and divisionalization is determined by the contingency factors of organizational size, task uncertainty and strategy (for further discussion see Donaldson, 1985a: ch. 14). These factors set the structure that is required for effective operations. Since organizational management wish to attain effectiveness the required structure becomes the actual structure. For instance, there is empirical evidence that organizations that diversify shift their structure from functional to divisional to regain fit (Donaldson, 1987).

Parent organizations influence the focal organization. The need to co-ordinate the focal organization with the parent organization reduces the autonomy of the focal organization and necessitates the adoption of reporting systems and other common procedures by the focal organization. The effect of the parent organization on the focal organization is greater for larger parent organizations (Pugh and Hickson, 1976). Size of parent organization is thus also a contingency factor of organizational structure.

Where an organization is part of the government or is under the government (i.e., is in the public sector) then the focal organization is under the control of the government as parent organization. There is a requirement that the focal organization be controlled quite closely to ensure the public accountability of public-sector organizations (Pugh and Hickson, 1976). Such public-sector organizations are subject to the authority of representatives of the public sitting on their governing boards and also in the parliaments to which the government itself reports. The power of the state in influencing public accountability is shown in figure 7.1 as the causal arrow leading from the state to the public accountability contingency.

A private-sector organization enjoys considerable delegation of authority from its board of directors to run itself mainly in the manner it thinks fit so long as it produces successful results such as profit. By contrast, the public-sector organization is scrutinized on a broader range of issues such as racial composition, the status given to women, the technology used (e.g., educational processes in schools and hospitals) and so on. Private-sector organizations are controlled mainly on ends (profits) and exercise discretion on means, whereas public-sector organizations are controlled on both ends and means (Mintzberg, 1979). Indeed public-sector organizations are controlled on whatever facets of their internal conduct the people's representatives care to question. In this way the will of the people is given effect in their public-sector organizations. The goal implicitly sought for such public-sector organizations is not just task accomplishment, that is, effective production of a good or service, but to be amenable to whatever other values the people choose, e.g., equal employment opportunity, no smoking at work, environmental friendliness, etc. This broadening of organizational goals and responsiveness to the public at large outside of the organization is captured in the contingency factor of public accountability.

There is also an effect of state power that forces organizations to adopt certain internal structural elements that are mandated by the state (shown by an arrow from the state to structure in figure 7.1). This is coercive isomorphism in institutional theory terms (DiMaggio and Powell, 1983). Whereas the contingency theory concept of public accountability refers to a general subordination of an organization which is in the public sector through its reduced autonomy in making its own decisions, coercive isomorphism refers to a mechanism whereby the organization makes specific compliance on issues directed by the state, e.g., equal employment opportunity or anti-pollution regulations (Tolbert and Zucker. 1983). Thus public accountability is a general control effected by centralizing power over the organization outside and above the organizational management, whereas coercive isomorphism is more targeted, influencing the specific content of a decision by mandating compliance to specific rules. Therefore the organizational structural variable affected differs, with public accountability affecting centralization of decision-making authority and coercive isomorphism affecting standardization, formalization and specialization, i.e., the content of organizational procedures, documents and specialized roles. An example is a requirement that a programme have a special office and personnel in the organization (Meyer and Scott, 1983). Moreover, coercive isomorphism applies not only to public-sector organizations but also to certain private-sector organizations that enter the purview of the government (Dobbin et al., 1988), i.e., the range of organizations affected by coercive isomorphism is broader than the range of organizations affected by public accountability. The effect of the state under coercive isomorphism is therefore distinguishable from that under public accountability both in the aspect of structure that is affected and in the types of organizations affected.

Where the ecological factors are benign then the organization is more likely to have the surplus resources needed to grow, diversify and expand geographically, thus changing the contingency factors and so producing a misfit with the existing organizational structure (Chandler, 1962; Pfeffer and Salancik, 1978). The organization then adapts its structure by moving from misfit with the contingency factor into a new fit (Chandler, 1962; Donaldson, 1987). Movement out of misfit is prompted by the adverse impact of misfit on organizational performance, e.g., low firm profitability (Chandler, 1962; Child, 1972a; Donaldson, 1987). Organizational performance is affected also by munificence of the environment in terms of resources, competition and so on (Hannan and Freeman, 1989). The state influences environmental munificence through government regulation and other policies (Hirsch, 1975; Pfeffer and Salancik, 1978). Thus the likelihood that an organization in fit will move into misfit and will then adopt a fitting organizational structure is affected by competition, resource abundance, state policy, etc. These ecological factors are causes of structure additional to the contingencies.

The organizational structure is affected by the internal organizational power distribution (Child, 1972a; Fligstein, 1985, 1990b). The powerful internal group is that which supplies the organization with the critical inputs that cannot be obtained from some other group (Hickson et al., 1971). The environment and the organizational strategy determine which input is most critical and thus which internal group is most powerful (Pfeffer and Salancik, 1978; Hambrick, 1981). This is shown, respectively, by the causal arrows from strategy and critical resource to intra-organizational power in figure 7.1. Moreover, the more powerful group also tends to provide the next CEO and thus shape the strategy, indirectly affecting thereby the internal power distribution (Pfeffer and Salancik, 1978). This is shown by the reverse arrow from intra-organizational power to strategy in figure 7.1. Further, organizational strategy leads to structure, so in shaping strategy the powerful group also indirectly affects structure; for instance, Fligstein (1991) shows that CEOs from sales–marketing backgrounds lead to the adoption of diversified strategies and Fligstein (1985) also shows that these corporations that have diversified their strategy then tend to adopt a divisionalized structure. There is also, of course, a direct effect of power on organizational structure, in that the structures are moulded by those most powerful within them. For example, Fligstein (1985) demonstrates that the CEO, presumably the most powerful executive, influences the organizational structure adopted, so that, for instance, CEOs from sales–marketing backgrounds lead to the adoption of the divisional structure whereas CEOs from manufacturing backgrounds lead to the retention of the functional structure (see also Pfeffer, 1981). The organizational structure is influenced also by the internal, administrative staff specialists (Child, 1973a) and their influence depends, in part, on the extent to which they can gain support from line management who are addressing major environmental challenges (Pettigrew, 1973, 1985).

Structural misfit lowers organizational performance (Khandwalla, 1973; Child, 1975; Donaldson, 1987; Hamilton and Shergill, 1992) as does competition and resource scarcity (Hirsch, 1975; Pfeffer and Salancik, 1978; Hamilton and Shergill, 1992). Each of these factors increases the likelihood of organizational mortality, i.e., disbanding. Organizational ecologists demonstrate that more crowded ecologies lead to organizational mortality, as the carrying capacity of the niche is approached or equalled, and this is taken to indicate the effect of increased competition (Hannan and Freeman, 1989; see also Barnett and Carroll, 1987; Barnett, 1990); thus the effect of density on the rate of organizational mortality is curvilinear, first decreasing with increasing density and then increasing. When these ecological factors occur together and simultaneously with intra-organizational misfit then the probability of organizational mortality is substantially increased.

The customer contact with the organization provides an interface at which problems of opportunism may occur because the contacts are limited and may lack the long-term, social nature which keeps both parties honest. The organization will seek to limit opportunism through customer selection and controls, but these efforts will not always be effective (Alchian and Woodward, 1988). If customers act opportunistically towards the organization to a substantial degree then organizational performance will be damaged. A large, sustained opportunistic loss, if the environment is not munificent, may lead to bankruptcy and disbanding of the organization. This is shown by the causal arrow from customers to mortality in figure 7.1. (Here we are bringing out the potential negative aspects of customers because that is the aspect featured in economic theories of adverse selection, etc. and the present model seeks to integrate such economic theories with other theories of organization structure. Customers of course also have a positive impact on the organization, purchasing output and providing revenue to enable organizational growth, etc.; in the present model these positive aspects are part of the ecological factors.)

Thus organizational mortality is determined by structural misfit, environmental stringency and customer opportunism.

In this way it is possible to bring together the different theories of organizational structure into a single model which captures some of the insights of each paradigm while providing a coherent view to explain organizational structure.

Other topics in organization theory

Thus far we have reviewed theories of the internal structure of an organization. However, the newer American paradigms have dealt not only in this but have also discussed other phenomena. Resource dependence theory and, to a lesser degree, population-ecology theory have discussed organizational strategy, such as diversification, mergers, joint ventures and cartels (Pfeffer and Salancik, 1978; Hannan and Freeman, 1989). Moreover, these and other phenomena include relations between organizations. Institutional theory also has contributed to the analysis of interorganizational relations (e.g., Orrù et al., 1991). The possibility exists that the newer paradigms will complement structural contingency theory by explaining phenomena which it does not explain, such as strategy and interorganizational relations. By making such a contribution a theoretical paradigm could contribute to organizational science even though it might contribute little or nothing to the explanation of internal organizational structure, for internal structure is only one dimension of organization.

Whether these newer theories do contribute, and by how much, to the explanation of the non-structural dimensions of organizations, such as strategy and interorganizational relations, is a large question which is beyond the scope of this volume wherein the focus is on organizational structure. Doubts have been expressed here as to whether some of the explanations of strategy and of interorganizational relations proffered by some of the newer paradigms are cogent and valid. Thus there is scope in the future for a continuing critical assessment of their claims to explain strategy, interorganizational relations and other dimensions of the organization that are additional to internal organizational structure. However, it is desirable to acknowledge the principle that even if a new theoretical paradigm does not supplement structural contingency theory, it may complement structural contingency theory by contributing to the explanation of dimensions of organizations other than internal structure, such as strategy and interorganizational relations.

Prospects for integration

The unified organizational structure theory offered here is an attempt at integration but is in a way a rather partial integration, being highly selective as to what role is given to those theories which are selected. This partiality is inevitable given that these theories are paradigms which therefore assert views of the world that are incompatible with each other. Thus any would-be integrator is bound to have to make choices between the paradigms. The unified theory here has drawn heavily upon structural contingency theory and has rejected those aspects of the other paradigms which are inimical to structural contingency theory. This is a conscious choice and yet one which is far from arbitrary. The discussion in this volume has shown that structural contingency theory is theoretically cogent and empirically valid, and more so than the antithetical theoretical paradigms.

In keeping with the concern for cumulation and for the building of an integrated science of organization structure which has underlain this volume, we have attempted to sketch here a unified theoretical framework for the explanation of organizational structure. Through its adoption the field of organizational structural analysis might regain the unity lost in the fragmentation caused by the rise of the several newer theory paradigms, and so a degree of theoretical unity could be restored. Such a development would allow the field of organizational structure to regain coherency and consistency at the theoretical level. However, this would occur only if the unified theory advanced herein was adopted generally by the organizational structural theory community. Yet some members of the community might disagree with the unified theory proposed here. Debate would be healthy and desirable and might lead to an improved formulation of an integrated theory, which would be no less desirable. A consensus around any unified theory would be a great improvement on the present scene.

It cannot be taken for granted that the unified theory proposed here, or any other unified theory, will attract sufficient consensus to quiet the present profusion of different and conflicting theories. The academic institutional system in the USA which so fragmented organizational structural theory in the seventies and which has produced a plethora of conflicting paradigms may continue, unabated, generating distinctiveness through product differentiation. Certainly a sceptic might express doubts about the likelihood that those originating novel paradigms are going to consent to merger into one consensual paradigm. Adherents of the newer paradigms may be quite out of sympathy with the unified theory offered here since it gives so much credence to structural contingency theory. However, a unified theory based around any one of the newer paradigms, population-ecology theory for example, is liable to fail to persuade the followers of each of the other newer paradigms, as well as those of structural contingency theory. The prospects may not be bright for an imminent reintegration of the currently competing paradigms into a unified theoretical framework. Nevertheless, such a unified theory is needed at the present time and it is the goal which all persons of good scientific conscience will wish to see achieved. Therefore, it is our scientific duty to offer such a unified framework to the field of organizational structural studies. We believe that in terms of theoretical cogency and empirical validity the case for reintegrating the field of organization structure around structural contingency theory, selectively supplemented and complemented by each of the other theories, is overwhelming.

It is possible therefore to abstract from the confusion of present sharply disjunctive paradigms in American organization theory, an integrated view of organizational structure which provides coherence and is empirically supported. Thus there is a consistent model which organizational structural theory can offer students and managers. In the topic of organizational structure there is a path through the contemporary version of the management theory jungle (Koontz, 1980). And there is no need for those treading that path to become cynical nor to despair.

8   A way forward for organizational structural theory

Our argument has been quite contrary to the trend in modern American organization theory. We have sought to argue against the view of the field as necessarily being a confusing profusion of paradigms. Our view is that the field of organization structure can be approached in a way which allows it to be rational and allows cumulation, continuity and moves towards an established science. Moreover, we reject also the view of organizations and their managers as lacking any collectivity-level rationality. We see organizations as making rational adaptive changes to their structures in order to promote greater effectiveness and greater capacity to perform their work task. And we see managers as the human actors who, in the main, obligingly work to bring about greater organizational effectiveness and enhanced attainment of the goals and interests of the organization as a whole.

This volume has considered each of the four newer paradigms – population-ecology, institutional, resource dependence and organizational economics theories. Each paradigm has been shown to have difficulties at both the theoretical and empirical level. There are problems in the internal logic of many of these theories producing difficulties in internal consistency and in intellectual coherency. There are problems also in their empirical base, with the theories either failing to adduce crucial empirical evidence in their own support or adducing unsatisfactory evidence. Thus in our view, the major newer paradigms recently introduced into American organization theory are severely flawed. There are some potentially positive features but these need to be carefully and selectively teased out of the wider theoretical statements in which they are encased. The previous chapter offered just such a synthesis around the core of structural contingency theory.

In contrast, structural contingency theory remains as a cogent body of theory which is intellectually sound and empirically valid, certainly more so than any of the would-be alternative theories of organization structure reviewed herein. Structural contingency theory enjoys considerable explanatory power. It explains the dynamic processes of organizational change and generalizes (Donaldson, 1982a, 1986a, 1987).

Confirmation of structural contingency theory has implications for the issues of rationality and the role of management in organizations. The model of the organization in structural contingency theory is of the organization as rationally adapting its organizational structure to changes in the contingencies in order to attain fit and performance. The research evidence supports the view that this is what indeed is happening in organizations over time. Thus organizational structures are confirmed to be rational and adaptive. Moreover, this is organizational rationality in that it is rational for the organization given its goals. Thus it is collectivity-level rationality rather than simply individual-level rationality whereby an individual organizational member attains personal goals at a cost to the wider organization.

By extension, the implied role of management is positive. The adaptation by the organization is carried out by managers in pursuit of the interests of the organization as a whole. Thus organizational managers are pro-organizational in their conduct rather than narrowly pursuing their self-interest to the detriment of the organizational collective. Hence managers make a positive contribution to the organization, and thereby to society, by steering the organization towards structures which are better fitting, thereby raising organizational effectiveness. Thus organizations are in matters of structure rational, and their managers contribute constructively to this state of affairs. Hence our inquiry leads us to reject the widespread tendency in the USA of late to deny organizational structural rationality and to paint management in a negative light.

Likewise it is possible in the topic area of organizational structure to proceed rationally and move towards the creation of a science of organizational structure, through processes of theoretical refinement, empirical testing and cumulation of later with earlier work. The collective efforts of many scholars over the past three decades can be brought together in a cumulating literature within structural contingency theory (see Gerwin, 1979; Donaldson, 1982a, 1986a, 1987; Miller, 1987).

Future research agenda

In an interview published in the *Organization and Management Theory Newsletter* (Pfeffer, 1993b: 5) Professor Pfeffer states: 'We're very trendy. We're very fashion conscious ... We need to be less trendy, less caught up with fads and fashions. We need to value the systematic collection of data on a number of issues much more highly than we do.' This is part of Pfeffer's argument that there would be advantages to organizational theory in having a paradigm that was followed rigorously so that the theory was developed to its full extent (see Pfeffer, 1993a, b). We agree that it is time for organizational theory to put away fads and fashions and to pursue more completely the research agenda of a theoretical paradigm.

Pfeffer (1993a) states that a field lacking a unifying paradigm will tend to be not only less productive but also politically weaker and likely to suffer, especially when resources become scarcer. He sees US business schools as undergoing a challenge that will accentuate internal political struggles so that organizational behaviour will increasingly suffer in competition with disciplines that possess a unified paradigm such as economics:

> It seems fair to forecast that contests for resources are likely to increase in universities and in schools of administration in the coming years. It also seems reasonable to suggest that the theoretical and methodological diversity and disagreements that characterize the study of organizations are disadvantages rather than advantages in this coming struggle. (Pfeffer, 1993a: 617)

Thus the present environment makes the adoption of a unified paradigm even more pressing. We hold that contingency theory, augmented in the manner outlined in the previous chapter, is the unifying paradigm for the study of organizational structure. Having sketched this theory in the previous chapter, the task here is to translate this approach into a research agenda.

The watchwords for the future research agenda are continuity and cumulation. We believe that structural contingency theory remains cogent as a general approach to organizational structural theory. Moreover, structural contingency theory enjoys a considerable degree of empirical validity, more so than is generally believed (see chapter 2; also Gerwin, 1979; Donaldson, 1982a, 1986a, 1987; Miller, 1987). The strength and potential of structural contingency theory argue that it should continue to be a focus for much work in organization studies, both in terms of theory-building and empirics. There remain many problem-situations in structural contingency theory which constitute anomalies or puzzles within the paradigm and which deserve attention. A concerted campaign of research pursuing those issues constitutes the best hope for students of organization to create a valid science of organizational structure which has implications for practice.

Key future research issues revolve around organizational effectiveness. Structural contingency theory postulates a fit between contingency and structural variables which leads to higher performance. This explains organizational structure and offers advice to managers. There has been considerable progress in the past thirty years in constructing models each of which relates a contingency variable to a structural variable or set of structural variables, and in the empirical validation of such models. However, much remains to be done.

One such model is the fit relationship between strategy and structure. The strategy–structure fit idea has been prominent in US business school curricula and textbooks. American contributions have been crucial, defining the seminal idea (Chandler 1962) and making early tests of the empirical validity of the strategy–structure fit idea (Rumelt, 1974). However, the results of the early tests were equivocal (Rumelt, 1974). While there has been quite a lot of research in the USA on the topic of divisionalization much of this has been concerned with the causes of divisionalization rather than the consequences for performance (Teece, 1980; Fligstein, 1985; Palmer et al., 1987; Mahajan et al., 1988). Similarly, empirical evidence (from the USA and the UK) that divisionalization leads to higher performance, although useful, leaves open the possibility that this is due to a superiority of the divisional structure *per se* rather than to the fit between strategic diversification and divisional structure (Armour and Teece, 1978; Ezzamel and Hilton, 1980; Teece, 1981; Hill, 1985b; Hoskisson and Galbraith, 1985; Hill and Pickering, 1986; Ezzamel and Watson, 1993). Again evidence that divisionalization is unrelated to the financial performance of firms is not evidence against the fit idea (Hitt and Ireland, 1985).

The crucial point for contingency theory is whether states of fit such as undiversified-with-functional structure and diversified-with-divisional structure have higher performance than states held to be misfits such as undiversified-with-divisional and diversified-with-functional structures. Some tests of these kinds of fit have not supported the fit model (Grinyer et al., 1980) or shown mixed findings (Hill, 1988). Steer and Cable (1978) offered a test of a fit model but unfortunately the operational definition of fit was unclear and so the theoretical meaning was ambiguous as to exactly which contingency factors constitute fit with divisionalization. Subsequently, a more formalized model of which strategies fit which structures has been constructed, and this has been validated on large US corporations (Donaldson, 1987). A further study of large corporations in New Zealand using a similar model and methods has also found support for the idea that there is a fit of strategy and structure which positively affects performance (Hamilton and Shergill, 1992). A study by Hill et al. (1992) also finds that strategy–structure fit affects performance. However, there is a need to test each component element of the strategy–structure fit models, such as in Donaldson (1987) and Hamilton and Shergill (1992), to ensure that each element is in fact a fit with a positive consequence for performance. There is also a need to check that such models do not reflect just the adverse impact on performance of one structure, that of the holding company, which would throw into doubt the wider notion of strategy–structure fit (Thompson, 1981; Hill, 1985b). As well, there is a need to identify any moderators such as organizational size. There is a requirement also to continue exploring alternative performance indicators, such as market rather than accounting measures (Buhner and Möller, 1985).

In the area of multinational corporate organization, British and American researchers have led the way (Stopford and Wells, 1972). Americans have continued to refine the contingency model of strategy–structure fit (Egelhoff, 1982, 1988a, b; Daniels et al., 1984, 1985; Ghoshal and Nohria, 1989). In both domestic and multinational cases there is scope for further refinement of the strategy–structure fit models and more work is needed to show its validity and generalizability.

Within the strategy–structure topic area, an important sub-set is the matrix structure. Since matrix structures have arisen more latterly than functional or multidivisional structures, they are still somewhat novel and there is some emphasis given to them in MBA courses and also in courses for practising managers. Both in public and private organizations, managers are increasingly grappling with the issue of whether they should have a matrix structure and how exactly it should be organized. This interest has been met by a literature on matrix structures, much of it of an instructional flavour and including various case studies (Corey and Star, 1971; Goggin, 1974; Davis and Lawrence, 1977; Knight, 1977). Various opinions about the suitability of matrix structures have been expressed, ranging from the idea that they are almost inevitable in multinational corporations (Galbraith and Kazanjian, 1988) through to the idea that the matrix is best avoided by organizations (Peters, 1979; Peters and Waterman, 1982). Contingency theories have been constructed which specify the conditions under which a matrix is appropriate (Davis and Lawrence, 1977; Kolodny, 1979; Child, 1984; Donaldson, 1985a, b; Egelhoff, 1988a) and the conditions under which each particular type of matrix structure is appropriate (Davis and Lawrence, 1977; Child, 1984; Donaldson, 1985a). However, there has been only a limited amount of empirical research to validate the relationships between contingencies, matrix structure and performance (Kingdon, 1973; Egelhoff, 1982; Joyce, 1986; Burns, 1989). There is a need for considerably more validation research on matrix structure, even to establish whether the additional complexity of the structure is worth the costs through increased benefits. And there is a need for research which empirically validates the contingency models of matrix structure and of the various types of matrix structure. Given the high degree of managerial interest in the topic of matrix structures and their prominence on the organizational change agendas of many organizations, there is a need for much more systematic research on this topic.

Similar remarks apply to another topic area in structural contingency theory, the fit between organizational size and bureaucratic structure. Theorists have argued that as organizations grow in size they must increase the bureaucratization of their structure in order to maintain fit and performance. Hence there is a whole series of points of fit constituting a progression whereby for each size there is a fitting optimal level of bureaucratic structure. Despite there having been an enormous amount of research investigating the connection between size and bureaucracy (for reviews, see Donaldson, 1986a; Miller, 1987), there are few studies which examine the idea of a size–bureaucracy fit which affects performance (Khandwalla, 1973; Child, 1975). In the research by Child (1975) the performance variable was measured prior to the bureaucratic structure variables, thereby raising the question of whether performance is a cause or an effect of fit. Thus existing studies in this area are to be seen as important first steps, but scientific exactitude requires that more methodologically refined studies be conducted in which there is less room for interpretation of causal meaning. There is clearly room for studies of size–bureaucracy fit in other organizations and settings in order to establish that the relationship enjoys general validity.

If we turn to one of the humblest and most basic issues in organizational structural theory, the span of control of a supervisor or manager, there is a need for further research. The span of control variable is basic in that it is a long-standing issue which was specifically identified by classical management theorists. They asserted a generally optimal span of six or seven (Urwick, 1956). It is basic also in that the span of control determines the optimal number of vertical levels in the hierarchy and also the degree of structural differentiation in the organization more generally (Blau and Schoenherr, 1971). Contingency theorists have argued that there is no universal optimal span of control and that the optimal span varies with contingency factors. A number of contingency factors have been identified and a weighting applied to them in an empirical exercise at one division of Lockheed Aerospace (Stieglitz, 1962; Barkdull, 1963). The resulting decision algorithm for prescribing optimal spans was used to reorganize that division. However, no systematic empirical validation of the algorithm against performance was made. Nor has there been subsequent validation despite the passage of decades and its continuing use in textbooks on organizational design (Child, 1984; Ford et al., 1988). Moreover, there is clearly considerable scope to include additional contingency factors and to examine whether the weightings used at Lockheed need to be adjusted for organizations of other types or in other situations, and if so by how much and according to what theoretically defined set of moderators.

The allied topic of the optimal number of levels in the hierarchy, and the optimal degree of vertical structural differentiation in general, deserves further empirical study. Blau (1970, 1972) has offered a highly general theory of how size leads to structural differentiation in order to raise performance. There has been a considerable amount of empirical research into the connection between size and vertical structural differentiation (Blau and Schoenherr, 1971; Hinings and Lee, 1971; Blau, 1972, 1973; Child, 1973a; Reimann, 1973, 1980; Donaldson and Warner, 1974; Blau *et al.*, 1976; Hinings *et al.*, 1976; Pugh and Hickson, 1976; Dewar and Hage, 1978; Agarwal, 1979; Beyer and Trice, 1979; Hickson *et al.*, 1979; Lenz, 1980; Van de Ven and Ferry, 1980; Ayoubi, 1981; Azumi and McMillan, 1981; Grinyer and Yasai-Ardekani, 1981; Lincoln *et al.*, 1981; Marsh and Mannari, 1981; Shenoy, 1981; Armandi, 1982; Conaty *et al.*, 1983). Nevertheless connections with performance have been far less frequently investigated. The study by Child (1975) failed to find a connection between the fit of size and hierarchical levels and performance. This paucity of performance-related research has prevented the creation of a validated organization design algorithm about the optimal degree of vertical differentiation for an organization as it grows in size.

Many researchers on size and vertical structural differentiation have been content to approach the performance issue indirectly, by studying the proportion of total employees who are managing and administering the organization (Donaldson and Caulfield, 1989). This follows the lead of Blau (1970) who argued that the administrative intensity, that is, the ratio of managers to workers, declines as size increases, thus yielding an increasing economy of scale in administration with size. Numerous studies – with varying results – have investigated whether or not the proportion of administrators declines with size (Lawler, 1947; Terrien and Mills, 1955; Haire, 1959; Anderson and Warkov, 1961; Lindenfeld, 1961; Draper and Strother, 1963; Haas *et al.*, 1963; Hawley *et al.*, 1965; Starbuck, 1965; Woodward, 1965; Blau *et al.*, 1966; Hickson *et al.*, 1969; Akers and Campbell, 1970; Zwerman, 1970; Blau and Schoenherr, 1971; Hinings and Lee, 1971; James, 1972; Blau, 1973; Child, 1973b; Goldman, 1973; Kasarda, 1974; Freeman and Hannan, 1975; Holdaway *et al.*, 1975; Blau *et al.*, 1976; Evers *et al.*, 1976; Reimann, 1979; Ford, 1980a; Van de Ven and Ferry, 1980; Ayoubi, 1981; Marsh and Mannari, 1981, 1989; Al-Jibouri, 1983; Routamaa, 1985; Cullen *et al.*, 1986). However, even where the proportion of administrators is found to decline with size this begs several questions.

In a large organization the managerial hierarchy is taller so there may be a smaller proportion of managers, but the average manager is paid more than in a small organization. Thus the question becomes whether or not managerial costs decline as size increases. This issue has not been investigated by Blau and his associates, nor by other researchers. Moreover, the real issue is not whether managerial costs decline with size but whether the costs of managers are out-weighed by the benefits they produce. This can be approached in part by asking whether output per manager rises as size increases. Blau and Schoenherr (1971) investigated this issue, but it has been virtually neglected by subsequent researchers. An exception is a study by Lioukas and Xerokostas (1982) which provides evidence that there are economies of scale in administration. But here again the work stops well short of specifying the optimal administrative intensity at each size level. There is a need to develop such a theoretical model and to validate it empirically. This would extend to an assessment of the administrative intensity which was optimal in terms of profit. Smith (1978) has examined empirically the relation between administrative intensity and profit. There is scope for much further work to identify the most profitable and efficacious levels of administrative intensity for an organization – for the organization and also for society.

Recently there has been a small upsurge in interest in studying the fit between organic structures and task uncertainty and its relationship to effectiveness. The theory builds upon the classic but non-quantitative study by Burns and Stalker (1961). Randolph and Dess (1984) have contributed a useful discussion of the need to study the effect on performance of the fit between environment, technology and organic structure in a multivariate framework. The work by Argote (1982), Alexander and Randolph (1985), Drazin and Van de Ven (1985) and Gresov (1989) builds on earlier work to produce quantitative, articulated models of the fit between organic structure and task uncertainty and other contingency variables, and fit is then related to quantitative variables of performance. This work is much needed and is a logical sequel to the original Burns and Stalker theory which has been widely received and repeatedly prescribed. Indeed the organic structure thesis is probably the most widely understood idea from within structural contingency theory. Thus the need for systematic modelling and empirical validation has been even more pressing in this topic area. Moreover, the organic structure fit model has been used as the exemplar in programmatic writing about the nature of fit–performance models by Van de Ven and Drazin (1985). However, the results to date of the newer wave of research into organic structure fit and performance have been mixed (Argote, 1982; Alexander and Randolph, 1985; Drazin and Van de Ven, 1985; Pennings, 1987; Gresov, 1989; Gresov et al., 1989). There is clearly scope for more work here and a careful examination of the detailed theoretical fit model, of the way performance is assessed and of the nature of the concept of fit.

It must count as an embarrassment to structural contingency theory that its best known specific theory of fit is at present in receipt of only partial empirical validation. There have been many studies of the relationships between task uncertainty and organic structure, and they tend overwhelmingly to support the positive relationship theorized by Burns and Stalker

(1961); for a review, see Gerwin (1979). But this begs the functionalist explanation of Burns and Stalker that the impact of fit on performance in turn causes the relationships between task uncertainty and organic structure. Thus there is scope for the fit–performance to be shown to hold generally across many types of organization and settings.

Nonetheless, the revival of interest in the eighties in researching the organic structure fit and its relation to performance is one of the most hopeful signs in American organization theory. It shows that at least in some quarters in contemporary American organization theory there is commitment to serious, long-range, cumulative knowledge development on topics which are of relevance to organizational managers, in that the organic structure thesis deals with how managers need to organize themselves and their subordinates in a day-by-day sense including detailed issues of job definition and interaction patterns. Moreover, the fact that Gresov could win the divisional award for the best paper based on a doctoral dissertation at the Academy of Management National Meeting in 1987 for his research on fit and have it published subsequently (in 1989) in the *Administrative Science Quarterly* is cause for hope.

The foregoing list of topic areas in organizational structural effectiveness is illustrative rather than exhaustive. It shows how topics first looked at decades ago, considered staple items in structural contingency theory, and which are standard elements in textbooks, nevertheless often have only a slim research basis of validated models of optimal structure. This is despite the fact that the total resources expended in American organization theory in the past thirty years – including research grants and research time of faculty and graduate students – must surely come to millions of dollars. Much remains to be done in this area despite three decades of research. What the topics considered here have in common is that they seek to relate organization structure to effectiveness. This is necessary for functionalist theoretical explanation, for management theory and for valid commentary on practice.

Thus far we have outlined some future research within the structural contingency theory programme. Since we hold that this theory remains central to the study of organizational structure it is appropriate that research in this tradition continue to be a mainstay of work on the topic of organizational structure. However, there may be additional insights to be had from the other theories – population-ecology theory, institutional theory, resource dependence theory and organizational economics. In the previous chapter we canvassed how these other theories might be added to structural contingency theory in order to create a more comprehensive theory of organizational structure. The task now is to sketch how this would translate into research.

Population-ecology can usefully contribute an analysis of organizational mortality (Hannan and Freeman, 1989). Structural contingency theory specifies states of misfit that lower performance and organizations often adapt their structures to regain fit and performance, as research has shown (see chapter 2). However, it is possible that some organizations may fail to make the adaptation and as a result suffer acutely poor performance and die (i.e., disband), for example, by going bankrupt. While population-ecology theory postulates such mortality from maladaptation, it needs to be shown empirically. Thus future studies of organizational mortality should include not only ecological variables that characterize the population, such as density and rate of prior mortality, but also intra-organizational variables, such as the degree of fit between the organizational structure and the contingency factors.

Population-ecology studies typically involve large numbers of organizations over long historical periods (Hannan and Freeman, 1989). Obtaining detailed data on the internal structure of every organization in the population would be difficult, expensive and probably infeasible. However, the important point is to obtain data on the organizations that disband, to test the proposition that they are more maladapted in some way than those organizations that remain in existence. For comparative purposes, a control group of continuing organizations, rather than the entire remaining population, may be studied for their intra-organizational characteristics, including degree of structural fit. By sampling both disbanding and continuing organizations and simply acquiring data on their intra-organizational characteristics the research project may be tractable. For similar reasons of data availability, the study of intra-organizational characteristics in organizational mortality may have to be restricted to the more recent period rather than the broad historical sweep attained in population-ecology studies. However, this would still yield knowledge that was valuable scientifically and practically.

Such research faces the complication that there are many intra-organizational characteristics apart from organizational structure that could potentially affect organizational mortality, e.g., technology, strategy, personnel, etc. The analysis would need to assess carefully these different possible causes of organizational mortality and this would increase the data required.

In addition to differential survival (i.e., mortality), ecological theory holds that populations are shaped by their newly born members being better fitted to their ecology than the members who die (Aldrich, 1979). This means that newly created organizations would differ from disbanding organizations in having a higher degree of fit between their internal organizational structure and their contingencies (through processes such as vicarious learning and random chance). This again is a testable proposition that requires empirical examination.

Together, differential survival and differential birth shape the population through the ecological mechanism of changing the membership of the population, as opposed to the structural contingency theory mechanism of change within a member. Is the distribution of organizational characteristics in a population shaped by membership change, as population-ecology theory holds, or is it wholly determined by the organizational adaptation process revealed in structural contingency theory research? If population adaptation through membership change occurs, does it account for a large or small proportion of population adaptation? This addresses the relative importance of population-ecology and contingency theories of organizational structure. If population-ecology were to be shown to explain a non-trivial amount of the structures of organizations, then its addition to structural contingency theory would be a significant contribution towards a comprehensive explanation of organizational structure.

It is also possible that such research would reveal that differential survival is more important in some settings than in others or for certain types of organization. Governmental organizations, and those in the public sector generally defined, are probably shielded from financial failure by government and public support, so that there may be less shaping of their population by differential survival. Accordingly, when adaptation takes place in such organizations, it may be primarily through internal adaptation by the individual, on-going organization. Similarly, the large corporation may enjoy lower mortality through size, wealth and market dominance, so that its population is relatively less affected by differential survival. On the other hand, the small firm, with its economic vulnerability and high failure rate may be a population shaped in higher degree by differential survival (Hannan and Freeman, 1989).

In these ways the study of organizational structure could be rendered more comprehensive and more sensitive to the conditions under which change in population membership shapes the distribution of structures in the organizational population.

If the research synthesis is to be extended further to incorporate institutional theory then we must consider the fit of the organization not only to task contingencies or the ecological environment, but also to the institutional environment, that is to the structure of norms, values and expectations which surround the organization (Meyer and Scott, 1983). Such pressures lead the organization to conform to the requirements of powerful external bodies such as the government, funding agencies and the professions (DiMaggio and Powell, 1983). Some part of the internal structure of the organization is shaped in conformity to these external expectations. Attempts to date to establish these institutional effects have not always been successful in all regards (see chapter 4) and there is a need to carefully distinguish institutional effects from the results of structural adaptation to task contingencies. The research reviewed herein mainly supports the power of the state to exact compliance from organizations (see chapter 4).

There is scope to extend the framework for explaining organizational structure through addition of the state-power variable, as was seen in the previous chapter. This may be developed further in future research as more aspects of internal organizational structure are shown to be affected by the state. Moreover, it is also possible that, over time, in some countries, the state may extend its influence over more organizations and more of their internal structures, so that future research may reveal more and more pervasive effects of the state. In other countries, however, the role of the state and its influence over organizations may diminish over time (e.g., Eastern Europe).

These organizational structural effects of powerful external bodies, such as the state or funding bodies, where compliance is achieved through legal compulsion or threat of loss of resources, are also subsumable under resource dependence theory. Thus continued successes in these kinds of explanation of organizational structure may be credited also to that theory and hailed as a point of synthesis between the resource dependence and institutional theories. Institutional theory is more distinguishable from resource dependence theory where the organization adopts a structural feature not out of overtly required compliance nor calculation of gain, but through more purely cognitive processes, such as institutionalized norms or taken-for-granteds (Zucker, 1977; Powell and DiMaggio, 1991). However, as we saw above (in chapter 4), attempts to date to establish such institutional effects in field studies of organizations have not been particularly successful. Future institutional researchers may tackle this issue with renewed vigour and may be able to substantiate their theoretical claim. However, until this is forthcoming, the institutional effects in organizational structural research will be confined largely to the effects of powerful external bodies such as the state.

Since the institutional effects on organizational structure are mainly limited to the power of external bodies such as the state or funding bodies that compel compliance and sanction non-compliance, it follows that their influence will tend to be restricted to visible aspects of organizational structure. Given that compliance is compelled by threat of sanction, the external body needs to be able to see whether the organization has or has not complied. Such aspects of organization that are visible to outside bodies include the identity of the CEO, the boards of directors, the proportion of employees of a certain gender or race, etc. In contrast, aspects of the organization applying to the internal operations are quite hidden from outside bodies, e.g., shopfloor organization, actual working relationships, influence between employees, etc. Institutional theory refers to this as the loose-coupling of organizations and stresses institutional moulding of the more visible aspects only (Meyer and Scott, 1983). Given this conceptual distinction there is ample scope for future researchers to identify which aspects of organizational structure are visible to each powerful outside body and then to ascertain whether or not they are moulded by that external body. This requires a programme of empirical research. Successes in this direction would provide the empirical support for the loose-coupling theory that is presently lacking (see chapter 4). The organizational structural aspects adopted at the behest of the powerful external bodies may have positive operational functions and so not be simply ritual – and this again is a matter for empirical demonstration.

Notwithstanding such scope for institutional explanation, the extent of institutional effects upon organizational structure is likely to be modest overall and localized to only the more visible aspects of organization. For large business corporations, with their complex internal operations dispersed down tall hierarchies and across numerous geographic sites, most of their organizational structure below the apex is probably little affected institutionally and much affected by the task contingencies, in order to operate effectively.

Resource dependence theory emphasizes the way organizations can improve their position by influencing other organizations, though admitting that this is limited to the few, larger organizations (Pfeffer and Salancik, 1978; see also chapter 5). This involves such organizations in interorganizational relationships, e.g., a large US motor corporation lobbying the federal government for protection against Japanese competitors.

This focuses attention on the parts of the organization that conduct such interorganizational relationships, e.g., the public relations department briefing lobbyists, the corporate affairs department dealing with government regulators, the corporate planning department identifying merger targets and dealing with consultants, the legal department negotiating the takeover and so on. In each case the issue is the organizational structure which that department or set of departments needs to adopt in order to perform effectively its task of influencing the environment. Contingency theory would hold that the departmental structure and interdepartmental co-ordinating devices will match the level of uncertainty stemming from the environmental body which it is seeking to influence (Lawrence and Lorsch, 1967; Thompson, 1967). This analysis has customarily been applied to line departments such as production, marketing and so on (Lawrence and Lorsch, 1967). There is a need to apply this analysis to corporate staff departments such as public relations and the like that have been neglected in previous structural contingency research. In this way resource dependence and structural contingency theory insights will be combined.

Agency theory, with its distrusting view of human nature, probably applies mostly to those persons in contact with the organization who are sufficiently remote to remain asocial, as we argued in the previous chapter. Customers purchasing insurance are the exemplars. Other types of customers and some temporary suppliers may be other cases. Here the organization has to deal with adverse selection and moral hazard. The organization has to anticipate that some among such customers will act opportunistically, concealing information and acting with guile. The organization will therefore modify its structure accordingly.

Those sections of the organization handling customers will include processes and structures that seek out information, require disclosure from customers, investigate the customer, acquire information from sources independent of the customer, maintain data on customers and so on. This will include standard procedures, use of forms, record-keeping, etc. Moreover, these elements will on occasion be structurally and culturally differentiated from other parts of the organization, that is, kept remote from the customer and separate from the organizational elements that are in contact with the customer. This is in part to allow the customer contact elements to develop rapport with the customer while the customer control elements remain distant and objective. For example, in insurance companies the customer interacts with a salesperson. The proposal is a written document that is sent to an organizationally separate department for assessment. In banks and commercial organizations customer contact functions are often organizationally separate from the department that assesses credit worthiness. At the extreme, the least 'customer-friendly' function, that of dealing with customers who have defaulted and owe a debt, is externalized to a debt collection agency that can meet recalcitrance with tactics that include hostility, leaving the main organization more 'customer-friendly' (Sutton, 1991).

Thus the contingency theory concepts of specialization and differentiation find new application here in the analysis of the organizational structures of functional departments and whole organizations often overlooked in the traditional structural contingency theory literature. In this way the insights from agency and structural contingency theories may be combined.

Agency theory and the associated M-form theory focus in the organization on opportunism by lower levels and how it may be curbed by higher levels in the hierarchy, through controls and central staff investigators, etc. While the theme of the need for hierarchical control is overdone in these theories there is nevertheless some opportunistic loss arising from actions of some employees. This in turn necessitates some elements of hierarchical control. This involves structures and processes of accountability, rules, standard procedures, centralized procurement, recording of transactions, financial book-keeping, budgets, authorization, audit and investigation by groups within and outside the organization.

The focus is upon accounting departments, audit departments and firms, procurement departments and the interactions of such units with those persons in the organization who are subject to their surveillance and controls (Caplan, 1971). The structures of these organizational departments and organizations require contingency analysis of how they fit to their particular tasks in order to function effectively. In addition to the usual structural elements, they may contain elements not found in more usual departments and which might appear unnecessary or dysfunctional until their special role is considered, e.g., requiring authorization from two separate officials, or requiring procurements to go to public tender, or sale of old equipment by public auction. Structures and processes that feature redundancy, duplication and double-checking in ways that would be considered wasteful in line operations are a common feature within these control departments and organizations. Once again, such accounting, procurement and central staff departments, and accounting and audit firms are typically neglected in structural contingency theory research and constitute a fertile area. In this way the insights of structural contingency theory may be combined with the agency and M-form theories.

Thus we see a number of topic areas for future organizational structural research wherein the concepts of structural contingency theory can be synthesized with concepts from population-ecology, institutional and resource dependence theories, as well as with organizational economics. This is likely to prove fruitful, injecting new life into structural contingency theory and also placing the newer theories on a more realistic footing. There are considerable opportunities to establish the empirical validity of select elements of the newer theories.

The most likely outcome will be that the newer theories will be shown to contribute to the explanation of organizational structure but only in limited and localized ways around the central core of structural contingency theory. Population-ecology may show how organizational structures are shaped in part by changes in population membership, though this is likely to any substantial degree only among small firms. Institutional theory may explain how certain aspects of organizational structure that are visible to outsiders may be moulded in conformity to the expectations of powerful outside bodies. These may well be the more ostensible, public features only, such as corporate governance and nature of employees. Resource dependence theory may explain the nature of certain interorganizational tasks in large organizations and thus the structures of the staff groups and upper management aspects which handle them. Organizational economics may explain the opportunistic nature of certain interactions between the organization and some outsiders and between the upper and lower levels within organizations on certain dimensions. These problems of opportunism craft the structures used for those staff groups and line management elements dealing with these outsiders or lower-level employees. In these ways, the contributions of the newer theories of organization to the explanation of organizational structure may be useful and distinctive yet limited and localized to particular organizations, particular parts of organizations and particular aspects of organizational structure. How far this is actually the case is a matter for future empirical research.

The core structural contingency theory remains an important approach for research into organizational structure. However, there is scope for improvement in it not just incrementally but more fundamentally. The notion of fit is not without problems. The mechanism of structural adaptation is under-explicated in structural contingency theory. The equilibrium focus illuminates but also conceals. And the whole mode of theorizing is perhaps too removed from economic concerns of cost–benefit. Again, organizational structural changes are by no means fully connected in prevailing theories of organization with movements in the economy. These and other issues constitute points of departure for fresh thinking about structural contingency theory. Thus structural contingency theory is far from a finished intellectual programme. There are exciting challenges ahead. Structural contingency theory continues to offer scope for creativity. Progress in organizational structural theory is to be made not by chasing the latest fashionable paradigms but by pursuing the structural contingency theory research agenda.

Epilogue: Some suggestions for change

In order for the foregoing research agenda to be fully implemented there need to be certain changes made. The primary change required in American organization theory is to move away from novelty towards validity.

With so many theories and paradigms on offer in the USA and with new ones coming along all the time, there is a danger that graduate students will not study or spend sufficient time on older theories such as structural contingency theory. This will be a particular problem where students are encouraged to concentrate only on the new. Comprehensive examinations of the field should ensure that the student has grasped the older as well as the newer theories and is sensitive to the fact that older theories can enjoy greater empirical support than newer ones. Recently there have been suggestions from Professor David Whetten of the University of Illinois and colleagues that special texts be produced for graduate students in organization theory which thoroughly present each of the theoretical paradigms and their attendant research together with the unresolved research questions. This would help to keep alive bodies of previous work and put them onto the research agendas of the next generation of organizational theory professionals.

Presently there are a number of centres for organizational research at US universities. Six of these universities have joined together in a Consortium of Centers for Organizational Research: Illinois, Michigan, Minnesota, Pennsylvania, Stanford and Texas. They hold joint workshops and there is an intention for movements of personnel between them. Such a link-up of major research centres is to be welcomed. It will be even more valuable if all of the best traditions of organizational research are represented therein rather than their having an exclusive focus on a few, perhaps more fashionable, theories. Accordingly, it is highly desirable that the particular predilections of any one centre are balanced by an alternative theoretical approach being taken in another centre. More specifically, there needs to be at least one participating centre in the consortium which specializes in the structural contingency theory approach. Graduate students and junior research workers could then circulate around the different centres as part of their preparation, being exposed to the best work of each theoretical school rather than, as at present, just to the favoured approach of wherever they happen to be. This circulation might be like that which occurred in Germany in earlier times.

Mone and McKinley (1993: 293) call for changes to the institutional structure of organizational research so that the negative effects of the uniqueness value are curbed:

We therefore recommend that organization studies develop publication outlets that encourage cumulative, integrative studies that seek to replicate and extend previous research findings. It may be useful to institutionalize the publication of empirical articles that are restricted to testing previously published theories rather than creating a unique theoretical base. It would then be more likely that well-crafted, integrated replications ... would be viewed as fitting commonly accepted norms.

We also suggest that journal editors make conscious, explicit efforts to encourage the reexamination of our extant knowledge base.

Mone and McKinley (1993: 294) call also for cumulative, integrative work to be rewarded and journal publication of such work would be a step in that direction.

There is a need for key journals in organization theory to value simply good work – be it novel or not. There are many unresolved questions in organization studies and there is thus need for plenty of work from theory construction, through empirical study, secondary analysis and meta-analytic review, to critical review. The key objective is to understand the organizational world more clearly, that is, to make a more valid analysis. Practical competencies like being able to offer advice on how to change the organizational world, or why not to change it, all flow from possessing valid knowledge. The main and distinctive contribution of the academic to the social discourse on organizations is to contribute to more understanding – that is to take us nearer to the truth (Donaldson, 1992).

Thus the task is to have editors of American journals change their values, to downgrade novelty and to upgrade validity. While key editorships are few, many respected academics sit on editorial boards and even more academics act as reviewers. These are all positions which are able to encourage a shift away from novelty towards validity, both in general policy and in acceptance of individual papers. If existing journals are unresponsive to the call, there is scope to establish new journals which will give greater value to solid, valid contributions than to ephemera.

We have sketched a number of changes that are needed in American organizational theory. If they were brought to pass they would greatly assist production of a research stream that would hasten the creation of a valid science of organizational structure.

References

Abernathy, W.J. and Utterback, J.M. (1978), Patterns of industrial innovation. *Technology Review*, 80: 40–7.

Agarwal, N.C. (1979), Nature of size–structure relationship: some further evidence. *Human Relations*, 326: 441–50.

Aharoni, Y. (1971), *The Israeli Manager*. Israeli Institute of Business Research, Tel Aviv University.

Akers, R. and Campbell, F.L. (1970), Size and the administrative component in occupational associations. *Pacific Sociological Review*, 13: 241–51.

Alchian, A.A. and Woodward, S. (1988), The firm is dead: long live the firm [Review of Oliver E. Williamson's *The Economic Institutions of Capitalism*]. *Journal of Economic Literature*, 26: 65–79.

Aldrich, Howard E. (1979), *Organizations and Environments*. Englewood Cliffs, N.J.: Prentice-Hall.

(1992) Incommensurable paradigms? Vital signs from three perspectives. In Michael Reed and Michael Hughes (eds.), *Rethinking Organization: New Directions in Organization Theory and Analysis*. London: Sage.

Aldrich, H., Staber, U., Zimmer, C. and Beggs, J. (1990), Minimalism and mortality: patterns of disbandings among American Trade Associations, 1900–1983. In J.V. Singh (ed.), *Organizational Evolution: New Directions*. Newbury Park, Calif.: Sage.

Alexander, Judith W. and Randolph, W. Alan (1985), The fit between technology and structure as a predictor of performance in nursing sub-units. *Academy of Management Journal*, 28: 844–59.

Al-Jibouri, Sadia Jabouri Joudi (1983), Size, technology, and organizational structure in the manufacturing industry of a developing country: Iraq. Unpublished doctoral dissertation, Mississippi State University.

Anderson, Gary M. and Tollison, Robert D. (1982), Adam Smith's analysis of joint-stock companies. *Journal of Political Economy*, 90: 1237–56.

Anderson, Theodore R. and Warkov, Seymour (1961), Organizational size and functional complexity: a study of administration in hospitals. *American Sociological Review*, 26: 23–8.

Ansoff, H. Igor (1968), *Corporate Strategy*. London: Penguin.

Aoki, Masahiko (1990), Toward an economic model of the Japanese firm. *Journal of Economic Literature*, 28: 1–27.

Argote, Linda (1982), Input uncertainty and organizational coordination in hospital emergency units. *Administrative Science Quarterly*, 27: 420–34.

233

Argyris, Chris (1964), *Integrating the Individual and the Organization.* New York: Wiley.

Armandi, B.R. (1982), Organizational size, structure and efficiency: a test of a Blau–Hage model. *American Journal of Economics and Sociology*, 41: 43–60.

Armour, Henry Ogden, and David J. Teece (1978), Organizational structure and economic performance: a test of the multidivisional hypothesis. *Bell Journal of Economics*, 9: 106–22.

Arrow, Kenneth J. (1985), The economics of agency. In John W. Pratt and Richard J. Zeckhauser (eds.), *Principals and Agents: The Structure of Business.* Boston, Mass.: Harvard Business School Press.

Astley, W.G. (1985a), Administrative science as socially constructed truth. *Administrative Science Quarterly*, 30: 497–513.

—— (1985b), Organizational size and bureaucratic structure. *Organization Studies*, 6: 201–28.

—— (1985c), The two ecologies: population and community perspectives on organizational evolution. *Administrative Science Quarterly*, 30: 224–41.

—— (1987), The community of organizations: an ecological perspective. In Samuel B. Bacharach and Nancy DiTomaso (eds.) (with C.J. Fombrun), *Research in the Sociology of Organizations*, vol. V. Greenwich, Conn.: JAI Press.

Astley, W.G. and Van de Ven, Andrew H. (1983), Central perspectives and debates in organization theory. *Administrative Science Quarterly*, 28: 245–73.

Astley, W.G. and Zajac, Edward J. (1990), Beyond dyadic exchange: functional interdependence and sub-unit power. *Organization Studies*, 11: 481–501.

Axelrod, R. (1984), *The Evolution of Cooperation.* New York: Basic Books.

Ayoubi, Z.M. (1981), Technology, size and organization structure in a developing country: Jordan. In D.J. Hickson and C.J. McMillan (eds.), *Organization and Nation: The Aston Programme IV.* Farnborough, Hants.: Gower.

Azumi, K. and McMillan C.J. (1981), Management strategy and organization structure: a Japanese comparative study. In D.J. Hickson and C.J. McMillan (eds.), *Organization and Nation: The Aston Programme IV.* Farnborough, Hants.: Gower.

Baran, Paul A. and Sweezy, P.M. (1968), *Monopoly Capital: An Essay on the American Economic and Social Order.* Harmondsworth: Penguin.

Barkdull, C.W. (1963), Span of control: a method of evaluation. *Michigan Business Review*, 15: 25–32.

Barnett, W.P. (1990), The organizational ecology of a technological system. *Administrative Science Quarterly*, 35: 31–60.

Barnett, W.P. and Amburgey T.L. (1990), Do larger organizations generate stronger competition? In J.V. Singh (ed.), *Organizational Evolution: New Directions.* Newbury Park, Calif.: Sage.

Barnett, W.P. and Carroll, G.R. (1987), Competition and mutualism among early telephone companies. *Administrative Science Quarterly*, 32: 400–21.

Barney, Jay B. (1990), The debate between traditional management theory and organizational economics: substantive differences or intergroup conflict? *Academy of Management Review*, 15: 382–93.

Barney, Jay B. and Ouchi, William G. (eds.) (1986), *Organizational Economics.* San Francisco: Jossey-Bass.

Baron, James P., Dobbin, Frank, and Devereaux Jennings, P. (1986), War and peace: the evolution of modern personnel administration in U.S. industry. *American Journal of Sociology*, 92: 250–83.

Baumol, William J., Panzar, J.C. and Willig, R.D. (1982), *Contestable Markets and the Theory of Industry Structure*. New York: Harcourt Brace Jovanovich.

Baysinger, Barry D. and Butler, Henry N. (1985), Corporate governance and the board of directors: performance effects of changes in board composition, *Journal of Law, Economics and Organization*, 1: 101–24.

Baysinger, B.D., Kosnik, R.T. and Turk, T.A. (1991), Effects of board and ownership structure on corporate R&D strategy. *Academy of Management Journal*, 34: 205–14.

Bedeian, A.G. and Zammuto, R.F. (1991), *Organization Theory and Design*. Chicago: The Dryden Press.

Benson, J. Kenneth (1977), Organisations: a dialectical view. *Administrative Science Quarterly*, 22: 1–21.

Berg, S.V. and Smith, S.K. (1978), CEO and board chairman: a quantitative study of dual vs. unitary board leadership. *Directors & Boards*, 3: 34–9.

Berger, Peter L. and Luckmann, T. (1966), *The Social Construction of Reality: A Treatise in the Sociology of Knowledge*. Garden City, N.Y.: Doubleday.

(1967), *The Social Construction of Reality: A Treatise in the Sociology of Knowledge*. London: Penguin.

Berle, Adolf, and Means, Gardiner (1932), *The Modern Corporation and Private Property*. New York: Macmillan.

Beyer, J.M. and Trice, H.M. (1979), A reexamination of the relations between size and various components of organizational complexity. *Administrative Science Quarterly*, 24: 48–64.

Blau, Peter M. (1964), *Exchange and Power in Social Life*. New York: Wiley.

(1970), A formal theory of differentiation in organizations. *American Sociological Review*, 35: 201–18.

(1972), Interdependence and hierarchy in organizations. *Social Science Research*, 1: 1–24.

(1973), *The Organization of Academic Work*. New York: Wiley.

Blau, Peter M. and Schoenherr, P.A. (1971), *The Structure of Organizations*. New York: Basic Books.

Blau, P.M., Heydebrand, W.V. and Stauffer, R.E. (1966), The structure of small bureaucracies. *American Sociological Review*, 31: 179–91.

Blau, Peter M., Falbe, Cecilia McHugh, McKinley, William, and Tracy, Phelps K. (1976), Technology and organization in manufacturing. *Administrative Science Quarterly*, 21: 21–40.

Bloom, A. (1987), *The Closing of the American Mind*. New York: Simon and Schuster.

Boorstin, Daniel J. (1983), *The Discoverers*. New York: Random House.

Bourgeois, L.J., III (1980), Strategy and environment: a conceptual integration. *Academy of Management Review*, 5: 25–39.

Brech, E.F.L. (1957), *Organisation: The Framework of Management*. London: Longmans, Green.

Brint, Steven, and Karabel, Jerome (1991), Institutional origins and transformations: the case of American community colleges. In Walter W. Powell and Paul J. DiMaggio (eds.), *The New Institutionalism in Organizational Analysis*.

Chicago: University of Chicago Press.

Buhner, R. and Möller, P. (1985), The information context of corporate disclosures of divisionalization decisions. *Journal of Management Studies*, 22: 309–26.

Burns, Lawton R. (1989), Matrix management in hospitals: testing theories of matrix structure and development. *Administrative Science Quarterly*, 34: 349–68.

Burns, Tom, and Stalker, G.M. (1961), *The Management of Innovation*. London: Tavistock.

Burrell, Gibson, and Morgan, Gareth (1979), *Sociological Paradigms and Organisational Analysis: Elements of the Sociology of Corporate Life*. London: Heinemann.

Burt, Ronald S. (1983), *Corporate Profits and Cooptation: Networks of Market Constraints and Directorate Ties in the American Economy*. New York: Academic Press.

Cable, John, and Dirrheimer, Manfred, J. (1983), Hierarchies and markets: an empirical test of the multidivisional hypothesis in West Germany. *International Journal of Industrial Organization*, 1: 43–62.

Cameron, K.S., Kim, M.U. and Whetten, D.A. (1987), Organizational effects of decline and turbulence. *Administrative Science Quarterly*, 32: 222–40.

Caplan, Edwin H. (1971), *Management Accounting and Behavioral Science*. Reading, Mass.: Addison-Wesley.

Carroll, Glenn R. (1985), Concentration and specialization: dynamics of niche width in populations of organizations. *American Journal of Sociology*, 90: 1262–83.

(ed.) (1988), *Ecological Models of Organizations*. Cambridge, Mass.: Ballinger.

Carroll, G.R. and Huo, Yangchung Paul (1986), Organizational task and institutional environments in ecological perspective: findings from the local newspaper industry. *American Journal of Sociology*, 91: 838–73.

Castanias, Richard P. and Helfat, Constance E. (1991), Managerial resources and rents. *Journal of Management*, 17: 155–71.

Caves, Richard E. (1980), Industrial organization, corporate strategy and structure, *Journal of Economic Literature*, 18: 64–92.

Chaganti, R.S., Mahajan V. and Sharma, S. (1985), Corporate board size, composition and corporate failures in retailing industry. *Journal of Management Studies*, 2: 400–16.

Chalmers, A.F. (1982), *What is this Thing called Science? An Assessment of the Nature and Status of Science and its Methods*, 2nd edn. St Lucia, Queensland: University of Queensland Press.

Chandler, Alfred D., Jr (1962), *Strategy and Structure: Chapters in the History of the American Industrial Enterprise*. Cambridge, Mass.: MIT Press.

(ed.) (1964), *Giant Enterprise: Ford, General Motors and the Automobile Industry: Sources and Readings*. Burlingame, N.Y.: Harcourt, Brace and World.

(1977), *The Visible Hand: The Managerial Revolution in American Business*. Cambridge, Mass.: Belknap Press.

(1980), The growth of the transnational industrial firm in the United States and the United Kingdom: a comparative analysis. *Economic History Review*, 33: 396–410.

(1982), The M-form: industrial groups, American style. *European Economic*

Review, 19: 3–23.

(1983), The place of the modern industrial enterprise in three economies. In Alice Teichova and P.L. Cottrell (eds.), *International Business and Central Europe, 1918–1939*. Leicester: Leicester University Press.

(1990), *Scale and Scope: The Dynamics of Industrial Capitalism*. Cambridge, Mass.: Belknap Press.

Channon, Derek F. (1973), *The Strategy and Structure of British Enterprise*. London: Macmillan.

(1978), *The Service Industries: Strategy Structure and Financial Performance*. London: Macmillan.

Chenhall, Robert H. (1979), Some elements of organizational control in Australian divisionalized firms. *Australian Journal of Management*, supplement to 4, 1 (April): 1–36.

Child, John (1969), *British Management Thought: A Critical Analysis*. London: Allen and Unwin.

(1972a), Organizational structure, environment and performance: the role of strategic choice. *Sociology*, 6: 1–22.

(1972b), Organization structure and strategies of control: a replication of the Aston Study. *Administrative Science Quarterly*, 17: 163–77.

(1973a), Predicting and understanding organization structure. *Administrative Science Quarterly*, 18: 168–85.

(1973b), Parkinson's progress: accounting for the number of specialists in organizations. *Administrative Science Quarterly*, 18: 328–48.

(1975), Managerial and organizational factors associated with company performance, part 2: a contingency analysis. *Journal of Management Studies*, 12: 12–27.

(1984), *Organization: A Guide to Problems and Practice*, 2nd edn. London: Harper and Row.

Chitayat, G. (1985), Working relationships between the Chairman of the Boards of Directors and the CEO. *Management International Review*, 25: 65–70.

Chomsky, Noam (1969), *American Power and the New Mandarins*. New York, Pantheon Books.

Christensen, C. Roland, Andrews, Kenneth R. and Bower, Joseph L. (1978), *Business Policy: Text and Cases*, 4th edn. Homewood, Ill.: Richard D. Irwin.

Clegg, Stewart, and Dunkerley, David (eds.) (1977), *Critical Issues in Organizations*. London: Routledge and Kegan Paul.

(1980), *Organization, Class and Control*. London: Routledge and Kegan Paul.

Coase, Ronald H. (1937), The nature of the firm. *Economica*, 4: 386–405.

(1991), The nature of the firm: influence. In O.E. Williamson and S.G. Winter (eds.), *The Nature of the Firm: Origins, Evolution, and Development*. New York: Oxford University Press.

Coffee, John C. (1986), Shareholders versus managers: the strain in the corporate web. *Michigan Law Review*, 85: 1–109.

Conaty, J., Mahmoudi, H. and Miller, G.A. (1983), Social structure and bureaucracy: a comparison of organizations in the United States and prerevolutionary Iran. *Organization Studies*, 4: 105–28.

Corey, Raymond, and Star, Steven H. (1971), *Organization Strategy: A Marketing Approach*. Boston, Mass.: Division of Research, Graduate School of Business

Administration, Harvard University.

Crozier, Michel (1964), *The Bureaucratic Phenomenon*. London: Tavistock.

Cullen, J.B., Anderson K.S. and Baker D.D. (1986), Blau's theory of structural differentiation revisited: a theory of structural change or scale. *Academy of Management Journal*, 29: 203–29.

Cyert, R.M. and March, J.G. (1963), *A Behavioral Theory of the Firm*. Englewood Cliffs, N.J.: Prentice-Hall.

Daft, Richard L. (1980), The evolution of organization analysis in ASQ, 1959–1979. *Administrative Science Quarterly*, 25: 623–36.

(1986), *Organization Theory and Design*, 2nd edn. St. Paul, Minn.: West.

Daft, Richard L. and Lengel R.H. (1984), Information richness: a new approach to managerial behavior and organization design. *Research in Organizational Behavior*, 6: 191–233.

Daft, R.L. and Lewin, A.Y. (1990), Can organization studies begin to break out of the normal science straitjacket? An editorial essay. *Organization Science*, 1: 1–9.

Daniels, John D., Pitts, Robert A. and Tretter, Marietta J. (1984), Strategy and structure in U.S. multinationals: an exploratory study. *Academy of Management Journal*, 7: 292–307.

(1985), Organizing for dual strategies of product diversity and international expansion. *Strategic Management Journal*, 6: 223–37.

Davis, Gerald F. and Powell, Walter W. (1992), Organization–environment relations. In Marvin Dunnette and Laetta M. Hough (eds.), *Handbook of Industrial and Organizational Psychology*, 2nd edn., vol. III. Palo Alto, Calif.: Consulting Psychologists Press.

Davis, M.S. (1971), That's interesting! Towards a phenomenology of sociology and a sociology of phenomenology. *Philosophy of the Social Sciences*, 1: 309–44.

Davis, Stanley M. (1972), Basic structures of multinational corporations. In Stanley M. Davis (ed.), *Managing and Organizing Multinational Corporations*. New York: Pergamon.

Davis, Stanley M. and Lawrence, Paul R. (1977), *Matrix*. Reading, Mass.: Addison-Wesley.

Dawson, S. (1980), Natural selection or political process: the dynamics of organisational change. *Personnel Review*, 9: 49–54.

de Tocqueville, Alexis (1945), *Democracy in America*. New York: Knopf.

Deal, T. and Kennedy, A.A. (1982), *Corporate Cultures: The Rites and Rituals of Corporate Life*. Reading, Mass.: Addison-Wesley.

Dess, Gregory G. and Beard, Donald W. (1984), Dimensions of organizational task environments. *Administrative Science Quarterly*, 29: 52–73.

Dewar, Robert, and Hage, Jerald (1978), Size, technology, complexity, and structural differentiation: toward a theoretical synthesis. *Administrative Science Quarterly*, 23: 111–36.

Dill, W.R. (1958), Environment as an influence on managerial autonomy. *Administrative Science Quarterly*, 2: 409–43.

DiMaggio, Paul J. (1991), Constructing an organizational field as a professional project: U.S. art museums, 1920–1940. In Walter W. Powell and Paul DiMaggio (eds.), *The New Institutionalism in Organizational Analysis*. Chicago: University of Chicago Press.

DiMaggio, Paul J. and Powell, Walter W. (1983), The iron cage revisited: institutional isomorphism and collective rationality in organization fields. *American Sociological Review*, 48: 147–60. Reprinted in Walter W. Powell and Paul DiMaggio (eds.), *The New Institutionalism in Organizational Analysis*. Chicago: University of Chicago Press, 1991.

(1991), Introduction. In Walter W. Powell and Paul DiMaggio (eds.), *The New Institutionalism in Organizational Analysis*. Chicago: University of Chicago Press.

Dobbin, Frank R., Edelman, Lauren, Meyer, John W., Scott, W. Richard, and Swidler, Ann (1988), The expansion of due process in organizations. In Lynne G. Zucker (ed.), *Institutional Patterns and Organizations: Culture and Environment*. Cambridge, Mass.: Ballinger.

Donaldson, Lex (1975), *Policy and the Polytechnics: Pluralistic Drift in Higher Education*. Farnborough, Hants.: Saxon House, D.C. Heath Ltd.

(1982a), Divisionalization and diversification: a longitudinal study. *Academy of Management Journal*, 25: 909–14.

(1982b), Divisionalization and size: a theoretical and empirical critique. *Organization Studies*, 3: 321–37.

(1985a), *In Defence of Organization Theory: A Reply to the Critics*. Cambridge: Cambridge University Press.

(1985b), Organization design and the life-cycles of products. *Journal of Management Studies*, 22: 25–37.

(1986a), Size and bureaucracy in East and West: a preliminary meta analysis. In S.R. Clegg, D. Dunphy and S.G. Redding (eds.), *The Enterprise and Management in East Asia*. Hong Kong: University of Hong Kong Press.

(1986b), Divisionalization and size: a reply to Grinyer. *Australian Journal of Management*, 11: 173–89.

(1986c), The interaction of size and diversification as a determinant of divisionalization – Grinyer revisited. *Organization Studies*, 7: 367–79.

(1987), Strategy and structural adjustment to regain fit and performance: in defence of contingency theory. *Journal of Management Studies*, 24: 1–24.

(1990a), The ethereal hand: organizational economics and management theory. *Academy of Management Review*, 15: 369–81.

(1990b), A rational basis for criticisms of organizational economics: a reply to Barney. *Academy of Management Review*, 15: 394–401.

(1992), The Weick stuff: managing beyond games. *Organization Science*, 3: 461–6.

Donaldson, Lex, and Caulfield, Clyde C. (1989), Economics of scale in public and private administration: is market discipline mythic? Working Paper, 89–003, Australian Graduate School of Management, University of New South Wales.

Donaldson, Lex, and Davis, James H. (1991), Stewardship theory or agency theory: CEO governance and shareholder returns. *Australian Journal of Management*, 16: 49–64.

(1994), Boards and company performance: research challenges the conventional wisdom. *Corporate Governance: An International Review*, 2:141–50.

Donaldson, Lex, and Warner, Malcolm (1974), Structure of organizations in occupational interest associations. *Human Relations*, 27: 721–38.

Dow, Gregory K. (1987), The function of authority on transaction cost economics. *Journal of Economic Behavior and Organization*, 8: 13–38.

Downey, H.K., Hellriegel, Donn, and Slocum, John (1975), Environmental uncertainty: the construct and its application. *Administrative Science Quarterly*, 20: 613–29.

Draper, Jean, and Strother, George B. (1963), Testing a model for organizational growth. *Human Organization*, 22: 180–94.

Drazin, Robert, and Van de Ven, Andrew H. (1985), Alternative forms of fit in contingency theory. *Administrative Science Quarterly*, 30: 514–39.

Duncan, Robert B. (1972), Characteristics of organizational environments and perceived environmental uncertainty. *Administrative Science Quarterly*, 17: 313–27.

Durkheim, Emile (1964), *The Division of Labor in Society*. New York: Free Press.

Dyas, Gareth P. and Thanheiser, Heinz T. (1976), *The Emerging European Enterprise: Strategy and Structure in French and German Industry*. London: Macmillan.

Eccles, Robert G. and Crane, Dwight B. (1988), *Doing Deals: Investment Banks at Work*. Boston, Mass.: Harvard Business School Press.

Egelhoff, William G. (1982), Strategy and structure in multinational corporations: an information-processing approach. *Administrative Science Quarterly*, 27: 435–58.

(1988a), *Organizing the Multinational Enterprise: An Information Processing Perspective*. Cambridge, Mass.: Ballinger.

(1988b), Strategy and structure in multinational corporations: a revision of the Stopford and Wells model. *Strategic Management Journal*, 9: 1–14.

Eisenhardt, Kathleen M. (1988), Agency and institutional-theory explanations: the case of retail sales compensation. *Academy of Management Journal*, 31: 488–511.

(1989), Agency theory: an assessment and review. *Academy of Management Review*, 14: 57–74.

Emery, Fred E. (1959), *Characteristics of Socio-Technical Systems*. London: Tavistock.

Emery, Fred E. and Trist, E.L. (1965), The causal texture of organisational environments. *Human Relations*, 18: 21–32.

Etzioni, Amitai (1975), *A Comparative Analysis of Complex Organizations: On Power, Involvement and their Correlates*, revised edn. New York: Free Press.

Evan, William M. (1966), The organization set: toward a theory of interorganizational relations. In James D. Thompson (ed.), *Approaches to Organizational Design*. Pittsburgh: University of Pittsburgh Press.

Evans, David S. and Grossman, Sanford J. (1983), Integration. In D.S. Evans (ed.), *Breaking up Bell: Essays in Industrial Organization*. New York: Elsevier.

Evers, F.T., Bohlen, J.M. and Warren, R.D. (1976), The relationships of selected size and structure indicators in economic organizations. *Administrative Science Quarterly*, 21: 326–42.

Ezzamel, M.A. and Hilton, K. (1980), Divisionalisation in British industry: a preliminary study. *Accounting and Business Research*, 10: 197–214.

Ezzamel, M.A. and Watson, R. (1993), Organizational form, ownership structure and corporate performance: a contextual empirical analysis of UK companies. *British Journal of Management*, 4: 161–76.

Fama, E.F. and Jensen, M.C. (1983), Separation of ownership and control. *Journal of Law and Economics*, 26: 301–26.

Ferguson, K. (1984), *The Feminist Case against Bureaucracy*. Philadelphia: Temple University Press.

Fine, Gary (1984), Negotiated order and organizational cultures. *Annual Review of Sociology*, 10: 239–62.

Fligstein, Neil (1985), The spread of the multidivisional form among large firms, 1919–1979. *American Sociological Review*, 50: 377–91.

(1990a), Organizational, demographic and economic determinants of the growth patterns of large firms, 1919–1979. In Craig Calhoun (ed.), *Comparative Social Research*, vol. XII: *Business Institutions*. Greenwich, Conn.: JAI Press.

(1990b), *The Transformation of Corporate Control*. Cambridge, Mass.: Harvard University Press.

(1991), The structural transformation of American industry: an institutional account of the causes of diversification in the largest firms, 1919–1979. In Walter W. Powell and Paul J. DiMaggio (eds.), *The New Institutionalism in Organizational Analysis*. Chicago: University of Chicago Press.

Ford, Jeffrey D. (1980a), The administrative component in growing and declining organizations: a longitudinal analysis. *Academy of Management Journal*, 23: 615–30.

(1980b), The occurrence of structural hysteresis in declining organizations. *Academy of Management Review*, 5: 589–98.

Ford, Robert C., Armandi, Barry R. and Heaton, Cherrill (1988), *Organization Theory: An Integrative Approach*. New York: Harper and Row.

Francis, Arthur, Turk, Jeremy, and Willman, Paul (eds.) (1983), *Power, Efficiency and Institutions: A Critical Appraisal of the 'Markets and Hierarchies' Paradigm*. London: Heinemann.

Freeman, J. and Hannan, M.T. (1975), Growth and decline processes in organizations. *American Sociological Review*, 40: 215–28.

(1989), Setting the record straight on organizational ecology: a rebuttal to Young. *American Journal of Sociology*, 95: 425–39.

Freeman, J., Carroll, G.R. and Hannan, M.T. (1983), The liability of newness: age dependence in organizational death rates. *American Sociological Review*, 48: 692–710.

Freeman, John Henry, and Kronenfeld, Jerrold E. (1973), Problems of definitional dependency: the case of administrative intensity. *Social Forces*, 52: 108–21.

Friedland, Roger, and Alford, Robert R. (1991), Bringing society back in: symbols, practices, and institutional contradictions. In Walter W. Powell and Paul J. DiMaggio (eds.), *The New Institutionalism in Organizational Analysis*. Chicago: University of Chicago Press.

Friedlander, F. and Pickle, H. (1968), Components of effectiveness in small organizations. *Administrative Science Quarterly*, 13: 289–304.

Friedman, Milton (1953), The methodology of positive economics. In M. Friedman, *Essays in Positive Economics*. Chicago: University of Chicago Press.

Frost, Peter, Moore, Larry, Louis, Meryl, Lundberg, Craig, and Martin, Joanne (1985), *Organizational Culture*. Beverly Hills, Calif.: Sage.

Galaskiewicz, Joseph (1991), Making corporate actors accountable: institution-building in Minneapolis–St Paul. In Walter W. Powell and Paul J. DiMaggio (eds.), *The New Institutionalism in Organizational Analysis*. Chicago: University of Chicago Press.

Galbraith, Jay R. (1973), *Designing Complex Organizations*. Reading, Mass.: Addison-Wesley.

Galbraith, Jay R. and Kazanjian, Robert K. (1988), Strategy, technology and emerging organizational forms. In Jerald Hage (ed.), *Futures of Organizations: Innovating to Adapt Strategy and Human Resources to Rapid Technological Change*. Lexington, Mass.: Lexington Books.

Garfinkel, Harold (1967), *Studies in Ethnomethodology*. Englewood Cliffs, N.J.: Prentice-Hall.

Garvey, Gerald T. and Gaston, N. (1991), Delegation, the role of managerial discretion as a bonding device, and the enforcement of implicit contracts. *Advances in Econometrics*, 9: 87–119.

Garvey, Gerald T. and Swan, Peter L. (1992), Managerial objectives, capital structure, and the provision of worker incentives. *Journal of Labor Economics*, 10: 357–79.

Gerwin, Donald (1979), Relationships between structure and technology at the organizational and job levels. *Journal of Management Studies*, 16: 70–9.

Ghoshal, Sumantra, and Nohria, Nitin (1989), Internal differentiation within multinational corporations. *Strategic Management Journal*, 10: 323–37.

Goggin, William C. (1974), How the multidivisional structure works at Dow Corning. *Harvard Business Review*, January–February, 54–65.

Goldman, P. (1973), Size and differentiation in organizations: a test of a theory. *Pacific Sociological Review*, 16: 89–105.

Goldman, Paul, and Van Houten, Donald R. (1977), Managerial strategies and the worker: a Marxist analysis of bureaucracy. In J. Kenneth Benson (ed.), *Organizational Analysis: Critique and Innovation*. Beverly Hills, Calif.: Sage.

Goldthorpe, John H., Lockwood, David, Bechhofer, Frank, and Platt, Jennifer (1968), *The Affluent Worker: Industrial Attitudes and Behaviour*. Cambridge: Cambridge University Press.

Gresov, C. (1989), Exploring fit and misfit with multiple contingencies. *Administrative Science Quarterly*, 34: 431–53.

Gresov, C., Drazin, R. and Van de Ven, A.H. (1989), Work-unit task uncertainty, design and morale. *Organization Studies*, 10: 45–62.

Grinyer, Peter H. (1982), Discussion note: divisionalization and size – a rejoinder. *Organization Studies*, 3: 339–50.

Grinyer, Peter H. and Yasai-Ardekani, Masoud (1981), Strategy, structure, size and bureaucracy. *Academy of Management Journal*, 24: 471–86.

Grinyer, Peter H., Yasai-Ardekani, Masoud, and al-Bazzaz, Shawki (1980), Strategy, structure, the environment, and financial performance in 48 United Kingdom companies. *Academy of Management Journal*, 23: 193–220.

Haas, Eugene, Hall, R.H. and Johnson, N.J. (1963), The size of the supportive component in organizations: a multi-organizational analysis. *Social Forces*, 42: 9–17.

Hackman, J.R., Oldham, G.R., Janson, R. and Purdy, K. (1975), A new strategy for job enrichment. *California Management Review*, 17: 57–71.

Hage, Jerald (1965), An axiomatic theory of organizations. *Administrative Science Quarterly*, 10: 289–320.

(1974), *Communications and Organizational Control: Cybernetics in Health and*

Welfare Settings. New York: Wiley.

(1980), *Theories of Organization: Form, Process and Transformation.* New York: Wiley.

(1988), *Futures of Organizations: Innovating to Adapt Strategy and Human Resources to Rapid Technological Change.* Lexington, Mass.: Lexington Books.

Hage, Jerald, and Aiken, Michael (1967), Program change and organizational properties: a comparative analysis. *American Journal of Sociology*, 72: 503–19.

(1969), Routine technology, social structure and organizational goals. *Administrative Science Quarterly*, 14: 366–76.

(1970), *Social Change in Complex Organizations.* New York: Random House.

Hage, Jerald, and Dewar, Robert (1973), Elite values versus organizational structure in predicting innovation. *Administrative Science Quarterly*, 18: 279–90.

Haire, M. (1959), Biological models and empirical histories of the growth of organizations. In M. Haire (ed.), *Modern Organization Theory.* New York: Wiley.

Hall, D.J. and Saias, M.D. (1980), Strategy follows structure! *Strategic Management Journal*, 1: 149–63.

Hambrick, Donald C. (1981), Environment, strategy, and power within top management teams. *Administrative Science Quarterly*, 26: 253–75.

Hamilton, R.T. and Shergill, G.S. (1992), The relationship between strategy–structure fit and financial performance in New Zealand: evidence of generality and validity with enhanced controls. *Journal of Management Studies*, 29: 95–113.

Hannan, Michael T. and Carroll, G.R. (1992), *Dynamics of Organizational Populations: Density, Legitimation, and Competition.* New York: Oxford University Press.

Hannan, Michael T. and Freeman, John (1977), The population ecology of organizations. *American Journal of Sociology*, 82: 929–64.

(1984), Structural inertia and organizational change. *American Sociological Review*, 49: 149–64.

(1989), *Organizational Ecology.* Cambridge, Mass.: Harvard University Press.

Hannan, Michael T., Barron, David N. and Carroll, Glenn R. (1991), On the interpretation of density dependence in rates of organizational mortality: a reply to Petersen and Koput. *American Sociological Review*, 56: 410–15.

Hannan, Michael T., Ranger-Moore, J. and Banaszak-Holl, J. (1990), Competition and the evolution of organizational size distributions. In J.V. Singh (ed.), *Organizational Evolution: New Directions.* Newbury Park, Calif.: Sage.

Harvey, Edward (1968), Technology and the structure of organizations. *American Sociological Review*, 33: 247–59.

Hawley, Amos (1986), *Human Ecology: A Theoretical Essay.* Chicago: University of Chicago Press.

Hawley, Amos H., Boland, W. and Boland, M. (1965), Population size and administration in institutions of higher education. *American Sociological Review*, 30: 252–5.

Herzberg, Frederick (1966), *Work and the Nature of Man.* Cleveland: World Publishing.

Hesterly, William S., Liebeskind, Julia and Zenger, Todd R. (1990), Organizational economics: an impending revolution in organization theory? *Academy of Management Review*, 15: 402–20.

Hickson, David J., Pugh, D.S. and Pheysey, Diana G. (1969), Operations technology and organization structure: an empirical reappraisal. *Administrative Science Quarterly*, 14: 378–97.

Hickson, David J., McMillan, C.J., Azumi, K. and Horvath D. (1979), Grounds for comparative organization theory: quicksands or hard core? In C.J. Lammers and D.J. Hickson (eds.), *Organizations Alike and Unlike: International and Inter-Institutional Studies in the Sociology of Organization*. London: Routledge and Kegan Paul.

Hickson, David J., Hinings, C.R., Lee, C.A., Schneck, R.E. and Pennings, J. M. (1971), A strategic contingencies' theory of intraorganizational power. *Administrative Science Quarterly*, 16: 216–29.

Hill, Charles W.L. (1985a), Oliver Williamson and the M-form firm: a critical review. *Journal of Economic Issues*, 19: 731–51.

(1985b), Internal organization and enterprise performance: some UK evidence. *Managerial and Decision Economics*, 6: 210–16.

(1988), Corporate control type, strategy, size and financial performance. *Journal of Management Studies*, 25: 403–17.

(1990), Cooperation, opportunism and the invisible hand: implications for transaction cost theory. *Academy of Management Review*, 15: 500–13.

Hill, Charles W.L. and Pickering, J.F. (1986), Divisionalization, decentralization and performance of large United Kingdom companies. *Journal of Management Studies*, 23: 26–50.

Hill, Charles W.L. and Snell, S.A. (1988), External control, corporate strategy, and firm performance in research-intensive industries. *Strategic Management Journal*, 9: 577–90.

Hill, Charles W.L., Hitt, Michael A. and Hoskisson, Robert E. (1992), Cooperative versus competitive structures in related and unrelated diversified firms. *Organization Science*, 3: 501–21.

Hinings, C.R. and Lee, Gloria (1971), Dimensions of organization structure and their context: a replication. *Sociology*, 5: 83–93.

Hinings, C.R., Ranson, S. and Bryman, A. (1976), Churches as organizations: structure and context. In D.S. Pugh and C.R. Hinings (eds.), *Organizational Structure: Extensions and Replications: The Aston Programme*. Farnborough, Hants.: Saxon House.

Hinings, C.R., Hickson, D.J., Pennings, J.M. and Schneck, R.E. (1974), Structural conditions of intraorganizational power. *Administrative Science Quarterly*, 19: 22–44.

Hirsch, Paul (1975), Organizational effectiveness and the institutional environment. *Administrative Science Quarterly*, 20: 327–44.

Hirshleifer, J. (1986), Economics from a biological point of view. In J. Barney and W.G. Ouchi (eds.), *Organizational Economics*. San Francisco: Jossey-Bass.

Hitt, Michael A. and Ireland, R. Duane (1985), Strategy, contextual factors, and performance. *Human Relations*, 38: 793–812.

Holdaway, Edward A., Newberry, John F., Hickson, David J. and Heron, R. Peter (1975), Dimensions of organizations in complex societies: the educational sector. *Administrative Science Quarterly*, 20: 37–58.

Hoskisson, R.E. and Galbraith, C.S. (1985), The effect of quantum versus incremental M-form reorganization on performance: a time-series exploration of intervention dynamics. *Journal of Management*, 11: 55–70.

Hrebiniak, Lawrence G. and Joyce, William F. (1985), Organizational adaptation: strategic choice and environmental determinism. *Administrative Science Quarterly*, 30: 336–49.

James, Thomas F. (1972), The administrative component in complex organizations. *Sociological Quarterly*, 13: 533–9.

Jaques, Elliott (1976), *A General Theory of Bureaucracy*. London: Heinemann.

Jensen, Michael C. (1983), Organization theory and methodology. *Accounting Review*, 50: 319–39.

—— (1989), Eclipse of the public corporation. *Harvard Business Review*, September–October, 61–74.

Jensen, Michael C. and Meckling, William H. (1976), Theory of the firm: managerial behavior, agency costs and ownership structure. *Journal of Financial Economics*, 3: 305–60.

—— (1979), Rights and production functions: an application to labor-managed firms and codetermination. *Journal of Business*, 52: 469–506.

—— (1983), *Democracy in Crisis*. Occasional Paper 8, The Centre for Independent Studies, St Leonard's, Sydney.

Jepperson, Ronald L. (1991), Institutions, institutional effects, and institutionalism. In Walter W. Powell and Paul J. DiMaggio (eds.), *The New Institutionalism in Organizational Analysis*. Chicago: University of Chicago Press.

Jepperson, Ronald L. and Meyer, John W. (1991), The public order and the construction of formal organizations. In Walter W. Powell and Paul J. DiMaggio (eds.), *The New Institutionalism in Organizational Analysis*. Chicago: University of Chicago Press.

Jones, Gareth R. (1987), Organization–client transactions and organizational governance structures. *Academy of Management Journal*, 30: 197–218.

Joyce, William F. (1986), Matrix organization: a social experiment. *Academy of Management Journal*, 29: 536–61.

Kagono, Tadao (1981), Structural design of headquarters–division relationships and economic performance: an analysis of Japanese firms. In Lars Otterbeck (ed.), *The Management of Headquarters–Subsidiary Relationships in Multi-National Corporations*. Aldershot, Hants.: Gower.

Kasarda, J.D. (1974), The structural implications of social system size: a three-level analysis. *American Sociological Review*, 39: 19–28.

Kaufman, Herbert (1985), *Time, Chance and Organizations: Natural Selection in a Perilous Environment*. Chatham, N.J.: Chatham House.

Kesner, Idalene F. (1987), Directors, stock ownership and organizational performance: an investigation of Fortune 500 companies. *Journal of Management*, 13: 499–508.

Khandwalla, Pradip N. (1973), Viable and effective organizational designs of firms. *Academy of Management Journal*, 16: 481–95.

—— (1974), Mass output orientation of operations technology and organizational structure. *Administrative Science Quarterly*, 19: 74–97.

—— (1977), *The Design of Organizations*. New York: Harcourt Brace Janovich.

Kimberly, John R. (1975), Environmental constraints and organizational structure: a comparative analysis of rehabilitation organizations. *Administrative Science Quarterly*, 20: 1–9.

(1976), Organizational size and the structuralist perspective: a review, critique and proposal. *Administrative Science Quarterly*, 21: 571–97.

Kingdon, D.R. (1973), *Matrix Organization*. London: Tavistock.

Klein, Benjamin, Crawford, Robert G. and Alchian, Armen A. (1978), Vertical integration, appropriable rents, and the competitive contracting process. *Journal of Law and Economics*, 21: 297–326. Reprinted in Jay B. Barney and William G. Ouchi (eds.), *Organizational Economics*. San Francisco: Jossey-Bass.

Kluckhohn, C. and Strodtbeck, F.L. (1961), *Variations in Valve Orientations*. Evanston, Ill.: Row, Peterson and Co.

Knight, Kenneth (1977), *Matrix Management*. New York: PBI–Petrocelli Books.

Kolodny, Harvey F. (1979), Evolution to a matrix organization. *Academy of Management Review*, 4: 543–53.

Koontz, Harold (1980), The management theory jungle revisited. *Academy of Management Review*, 5: 175–87.

Korn/Ferry International (1988), *Eighth Annual Survey of Boards of Directors in Australia*. Sydney: Korn/Ferry International.

Kosnik, Rita D. (1987), Greenmail: a study of board performance in corporate governance. *Administrative Science Quarterly*, 32: 163–85.

Kosnik, Rita D. and Bettenhausen, Kenneth L. (1988), The motivational impact of executive compensation systems in problems of corporate control. Paper to Business Policy and Planning Division, Academy of Management Meeting, Anaheim, Calif., August 1988.

Kraatz, Matthew S. and Zajac, Edward J. (1992), Invisible hand or iron cage? Market and institutional influence on organizational change. Paper to Organization and Management Theory Division, Academy of Management Meeting, Las Vegas, Nev., August 1992.

Kuhn, Thomas S. (1970), *The Structure of Scientific Revolutions*, 2nd edn. Chicago: University of Chicago Press.

Lawler, P.F. (1947), *Records for the Control of Growing Manufacturing Enterprises*. Cambridge, Mass.: Harvard University Press.

Lawrence, P.R. (1992), The challenge of problem-oriented research. *Journal of Management Inquiry*, 1: 139–42.

Lawrence, Paul R. and Dyer, D. (1983), *Renewing American Industry: Organizing for Efficiency and Innovation*. New York: Free Press.

Lawrence, Paul R. and Lorsch, Jay W. (1967), *Organization and Environment: Managing Differentiation and Integration*. Boston: Division of Research, Graduate School of Business Administration, Harvard University.

Lenz, R.T. (1980), Environment, strategy, organization structure and performance: patterns in one industry. *Strategic Management Journal*, 1: 209–26.

Likert, Rensis (1961), *New Patterns of Management*. New York: McGraw-Hill.

Lincoln, J.R., Hanada, M. and Olson, J. (1981), Cultural orientations and individual reactions to organizations: a study of employees of Japanese-owned firms. *Administrative Science Quarterly*, 26: 93–115.

Lindenfeld, F. (1961), Does administrative staff grow as fast as organization?

School Life, 43: 20–3.

Lioukas, S.K. and Xerokostas, D.A. (1982), Size and administrative intensity in organizational divisions. *Management Science*, 28: 854–68.

Lorsch, Jay W. and Allen, Stephen A. (1973), *Managing Diversity and Interdependence: An Organizational Study of Multidivisional Firms*. Boston: Division of Research, Graduate School of Administration, Harvard University.

Mace, M.L. (1971), *Directors: Myth and Reality*. Boston: Division of Research, Graduate School of Business Administration, Harvard University.

Mahajan, Vijay, Sharma, S. and Bettis, R.A. (1988), The adoption of the M-form organizational structure: a test of imitation hypothesis. *Management Science*, 34: 1188–201.

Mannheim, Karl (1936), *Ideology and Utopia: An Introduction to the Sociology of Knowledge*. London: Kegan Paul.

March, J.G. (1962), The business firm as a political coalition, *Journal of Politics*, 24: 662–78.

March, J.G. and Simon, H.A. (1958), *Organizations*. New York: Wiley.

Marsh, Robert M. and Mannari, Hiroshi (1976), *Modernization and the Japanese Factory*. Princeton, N.J.: Princeton University Press.

(1980), Technological implications theory: a Japanese test. *Organization Studies*, 1: 161–83.

(1981), Technology and size as determinants of the organizational structure of Japanese factories. *Administrative Science Quarterly*, 26: 33–57.

(1989), The size imperative? Longitudinal tests. *Organization Studies*, 10: 83–95.

Mayhew, Bruce H., Levinger, Roger L., Macpherson M.J. and T.F. James (1972), System size and structural differentiation in formal organizations: a baseline generator for two major theoretical propositions. *American Sociological Review*, 37: 629–33.

McClelland, D.C. (1961), *The Achieving Society*. New York: Free Press.

McCloskey, Donald N. (1983), The rhetoric of economics. *Journal of Economics Literature*, 21: 481–517.

McCraw, Thomas K. (1988), *The Essential Alfred Chandler: Essays Toward Historical Theory of Big Business*. Boston, Mass.: Harvard Business School Press.

McGregor, Douglas (1960), *The Human Side of Enterprise*. New York: McGraw-Hill.

McKelvey, Bill, and Aldrich, Howard E. (1983), Populations, natural selection and applied organizational science. *Administrative Science Quarterly*, 28: 101–28.

Meyer, John W. (1983), Conclusion: Institutionalization and the rationality of formal organizational structure. In John W. Meyer and W. Richard Scott, with the assistance of B. Rowan and T.E. Deal, *Organizational Environments: Ritual and Rationality*. Beverly Hills, Calif.: Sage.

Meyer, John W. and Rowan, Brian (1977), Institutionalized organizations: formal structure as myth and ceremony. *American Journal of Sociology*, 83: 340–63.

Meyer, John W. and Scott, W. Richard, with the assistance of B. Rowan and T.E. Deal (1983), *Organizational Environments: Ritual and Rationality*. Beverly Hills, Calif.: Sage.

Meyer, John W., Boli, John, and Thomas, George (1987a), Ontology and rationalization in the Western cultural account. In George Thomas *et al.*, *Institutional*

Structure. Newbury Park, Calif.: Sage.

Meyer, John W., Scott, W. Richard, and Terrence E. Deal (1983), Institutional and technical sources of organizational structure: explaining the structure of educational organizations. In John W. Meyer and W. Richard Scott, with the assistance of B. Rowan and T.E. Deal, *Organizational Environments: Ritual and Rationality.* Beverly Hills, Calif.: Sage.

Meyer, John W., Scott, W. Richard, and Strang, David (1987b), Centralization, fragmentation, and school district complexity. *Administrative Science Quarterly,* 32: 186–201.

Meyer, John W., Scott, W. Richard, Cole, Sally, and Intili, Jo-Ann K. (1978), Instructional dissensus and institutional consensus in schools. In Marshall W. Meyer (ed.), *Environments and Organizations.* San Francisco: Jossey-Bass.

Meyer, John W., Scott, W. Richard, Strang, David, and Creighton, Andrew L. (1988), Bureaucratization without centralization: changes in the organizational system of U.S. public education, 1940–80. In Lynne G. Zucker (ed.), *Institutional Patterns and Organizations: Culture and Environment.* Cambridge, Mass.: Ballinger.

Miles, Raymond E. and Charles C. Snow (1986), Organizations: new concepts for new forms. *California Management Review,* 28: 62–73.

Miller, George A. (1987), Meta-analysis and the culture-free hypothesis. *Organization Studies,* 8: 309–26.

Mills, C. Wright (1956), *The Power Elite.* New York: Oxford University Press.

Miner, John B. (1980), *Theories of Organizational Behavior.* Hinsdale, Ill.: Dryden Press.

Mintzberg, H. (1979), *The Structuring of Organizations: A Synthesis of the Research.* Englewood Cliffs, N.J.: Prentice-Hall.

(1983), *Power In and Around Organizations.* Englewood Cliffs, N.J: Prentice-Hall.

Mone, Mark A. and McKinley, William (1993), The uniqueness value and its consequences for organization studies. *Journal of Management Inquiry,* 2: 284–96.

Morgan, Gareth (1980), Paradigms, metaphors, and puzzle solving in organization theory. *Administrative Science Quarterly,* 25: 605–22.

Mumby, Dennis K. and Putnam, Linda L. (1992), The politics of emotion: a feminist reading of bounded rationality. *Academy of Management Review,* 17: 465–86.

Oliver, Christine (1992), The antecedents of deinstitutionalization. *Organization Studies,* 13: 563–88.

Orrù, Marco, Biggart, Nicole Woolsey, and Hamilton, Gary G. (1991), Organizational isomorphism in East Asia. In Walter W. Powell and Paul J. DiMaggio (eds.), *The New Institutionalism in Organizational Analysis.* Chicago: University of Chicago Press.

Ouchi, William G. (1978), The transmission of control through organizational hierarchy. *Administrative Science Quarterly,* 21: 248–63.

Palmer, D., Friedland, R., Jennings, P.D. and Powers, M.E. (1987), The economics and politics of structure: the multidivisional form and large U.S. corporation. *Administrative Science Quarterly,* 32: 25–48.

Parsons, Talcott (1951), *The Social System.* London: Routledge and Kegan Paul.

(1956), Suggestions for a sociological approach to the theory of organizations.

Administrative Science Quarterly, 1: 63–85.

(1961), Suggestions for a sociological approach to the theory of organizations. In Amitai Etzioni (ed.), *Complex Organizations: A Sociological Reader*. New York: Holt, Rinehart and Winston.

(1966), *Societies: Evolutionary and Comparative Perspectives*. Englewood Cliffs, N.J.: Prentice-Hall.

Pavan, Robert J. (1976), Strategy and structure: the Italian experience. *Journal of Economics and Business*, 28: 254–60.

Pearce, John A., II (1983), The relationship of internal versus external orientations to financial measures of strategic performance. *Strategic Management Journal*, 4: 297–306.

Pearce, John A., II, and Zahra, Shaker A. (1992), Board composition from a strategic contingency perspective. *Journal of Management Studies*, 29: 411–38.

Pennings, J.M. (1975), The relevance of the structural contingency model for organizational effectiveness. *Administrative Science Quarterly*, 20: 393–410.

(1987), Structural contingency theory: a multivariate test. *Organization Studies*, 8: 223–40.

Perrow, Charles (1967), A framework for the comparative analysis of organizations. *American Sociological Review*, 32: 194–208.

(1970), *Organizational Analysis: A Sociological View*. Belmont, Calif.: Wadsworth.

(1972), *Complex Organizations: A Critical Essay*. Glenview, Ill.: Scott, Foresman.

(1979), *Complex Organizations: A Critical Essay*, 2nd edn. Glenview, Ill.: Scott, Foresman.

(1985a), Comment on Langton's ecological theory of bureaucracy. *Administrative Science Quarterly*, 30: 278–83.

(1985b), Overboard with myth and symbols. *American Journal of Sociology*, 91: 151–5.

(1986), *Complex Organizations: A Critical Essay*, 3rd edn. New York: Random House.

Peters, Thomas J. (1979), Beyond the matrix organization. *Business Horizons*, 22: 15–27.

Peters, Thomas J. and Waterman, Robert H., Jr (1982), *In Search of Excellence: Lessons from America's Best-Run Companies*. New York: Harper and Row.

Petersen, Trond, and Koput, Kenneth W. (1991a), Density dependence in organizational mortality: legitimacy or unobserved heterogeneity. *American Sociological Review*, 56: 399–409.

(1991b), Unobserved heterogeneity or legitimacy in density dependence: a rejoinder to Hannan, Barron and Carroll. *American Sociological Review*, 56: 416.

Pettigrew, Andrew M. (1973), *The Politics of Organizational Decision-Making*. London: Tavistock.

(1985), *The Awakening Giant*. Oxford: Blackwell.

Pfeffer, Jeffrey (1972a), Interorganizational influence and managerial attitudes. *Academy of Management Journal*, 15: 317–30.

(1972b), Size and composition of corporate boards of directors: the organization and its environment. *Administrative Science Quarterly*, 17: 218–28.

(1974), Cooptation and the composition of electric utility boards of directors. *Pacific Sociological Review*, 17: 333–63.

(1977), Power and resource allocation in organizations. In B.M. Staw and G.R. Salancik (eds.), *New Directions in Organizational Behavior*, Chicago: St Clair Press.

(1981), *Power in Organizations*. Boston: Pitman.

(1982), *Organizations and Organization Theory*. Boston: Pitman.

(1993a), Barriers to the advance of organizational science: paradigm development as a dependent variable. *Academy of Management Review*, 18: 599–620.

(1993b), An interview with Jeffrey Pfeffer (Pamela R. Haunschild, interviewer). *OMT Newsletter* (Academy of Management, Organization and Management Theory Division), Winter.

Pfeffer, Jeffrey, and Salancik, Gerald R. (1978), *The External Control of Organizations: A Resource Dependence Perspective*. New York: Harper and Row.

Pickle, Hal, and Friedlander, F. (1967), Seven societal criteria of organizational success. *Personnel Psychology*, 20: 165–78.

Pinder, Craig C. and Moore, Larry F. (1980), The inevitability of multiple paradigms and the resultant need for middle range analysis in organization theory. In Craig C. Pinder and Larry F. Moore (eds.), *Middle Range Theory and the Study of Organizations*. Boston: Martinus Nijhoff.

Pitts, Robert A. (1974), Incentive compensation and organization design. *Personnel Journal*, 53: 338–44.

(1976), Diversification strategies and organizational policies of large diversified firms. *Journal of Economics and Business*, 28: 181–8.

(1977), Strategies and structures for diversification, *Academy of Management Journal*, 20: 197–208.

Poensgen, Otto H. (1974), Organizational structure, context and performance. Working Paper 74–49, European Institute for Advanced Studies in Management, Brussels.

Pondy, Louis, Frost, Peter, Morgan, Gareth, and Dandridge, Thomas (1981), *Organizational Symbolism*. Greenwich, Conn.: JAI Press.

Popper, K.R. (1945), *The Open Society and Its Enemies*, vol. II: *The High Tide of Prophecy: Hegel, Marx and the Aftermath*. London: Routledge and Kegan Paul.

Porter, Lyman W. (1964), *Organizational Patterns of Managerial Job Attitudes*. New York: American Foundation for Management Research.

Porter, M.E. (1985), *Competitive Advantage*. New York: Free Press.

Powell, Walter W. (1991), Expanding the scope of institutional analysis. In Walter W. Powell and Paul J. DiMaggio (eds.), *The New Institutionalism in Organizational Analysis*. Chicago: University of Chicago Press.

Powell, Walter W. and DiMaggio, Paul J. (1991), *The New Institutionalism in Organizational Analysis*. Chicago: University of Chicago Press.

Pratt, John W. and Zeckhauser, R.J. (eds.) (1985), *Principals and Agents: The Structure of Business*. Boston, Mass.: Harvard Business School Press.

Price, James L. and Mueller, C.W. (1986), *Handbook of Organizational Measurement*. Marshfield, Mass.: Pitman.

Pugh, D.S. and Hickson, D.J. (1976), *Organizational Structure in its Context: The Aston Programme I*. Farnborough, Hants.: Saxon House.

Pugh, D.S. and Hinings, C.R. (1976), *Organizational Structure: Extensions and Replications: The Aston Programme II.* Farnborough, Hants.: Saxon House.

Pugh, D.S., Hickson, D.J. and Hinings, C.R. (1969a), An empirical taxonomy of structures of work organizations. *Administrative Science Quarterly*, 14: 115–26.

Pugh, D.S., Hickson, D.J., Hinings, C.R. and Turner, C. (1968), Dimensions of organization structure. *Administrative Science Quarterly*, 13: 65–105.

(1969b), The context of organization structures. *Administrative Science Quarterly*, 14: 91–114.

Pugh, D.S., Hickson, D.J., Hinings, C.R., Macdonald, K.M., Turner, C. and Lupton, T. (1963), A conceptual scheme for organizational analysis. *Administrative Science Quarterly*, 8: 289–315.

Randolph, W. Alan, and Dess, Gregory G. (1984), The congruence perspective of organization design: a conceptual model and multivariate research approach. *Academy of Management Review*, 9: 114–27.

Rao, Hayagreeva, and Neilsen, Eric H. (1992), An ecology of agency arrangements: mortality of savings and loan associations, 1960–1987. *Administrative Science Quarterly*, 37: 448–70.

Rechner, Paula L. and Dalton, D.R. (1988), Board composition and organizational performance: a longitudinal assessment. Paper to Business Policy and Planning Division, Academy of Management Meeting, Anaheim, Calif., August 1988.

(1991), CEO duality and organizational performance: a longitudinal analysis. *Strategic Management Journal*, 12: 155–60.

Reimann, Bernard C. (1973), On the dimensions of bureaucratic structure: an empirical reappraisal. *Administrative Science Quarterly*, 18: 462–76.

(1974), Dimensions of structure in effective organizations: some empirical evidence. *Academy of Management Journal*, 17: 693–708.

(1977), Dimensions of organizational technology and structure: an exploratory study. *Human Relations*, 30: 545–66.

(1979), Parkinson revisited: a component analysis of the use of staff specialists in manufacturing organizations. *Human Relations*, 32: 625–41.

(1980), Organization structure and technology in manufacturing: system versus work flow level perspectives. *Academy of Management Journal*, 23: 61–77.

Reimann, Bernard C. and Inzerilli, Giorgio (1979), A comparative analysis of empirical research on technology and structure. *Journal of Management*, 5: 167–92.

Rieseman, D., in collaboration with Denney, R. and Glazer, N. (1950), *The Lonely Crowd.* New Haven, Conn.: Yale University Press.

Ritzer, George (1980), *Sociology: A Multiple Paradigm Science*, rev. edn. Boston: Allyn & Bacon.

Robey, D.M. (1977), Computers and management structure: some empirical findings reexamined. *Human Relations*, 30: 963–76.

Robins, James A. (1987), Organizational economics: notes on the use of transaction-cost theory in the study of organizations. *Administrative Science Quarterly*, 32: 68–86.

Rogers, Everett M. (1962), *Diffusion of Innovations.* New York: Free Press.

Routamaa, Vesa (1985), Organizational structuring: an empirical analysis of the relationships and dimensions of structures in certain Finnish companies. *Journal of Management Studies*, 22: 498–522.

Rumelt, Richard P. (1974), *Strategy, Structure and Economic Performance*. Boston: Division of Research, Graduate School of Business Administration, Harvard University.

Salaman, Graeme (1979), *Work Organisations: Resistance and Control*. London: Longman.

Salancik, G.R. (1976), The role of interdependencies in organizational responsiveness to demands from the environment: the case of women versus power. Unpublished manuscript, University of Illinois.

Schein, Edgar H. (1972), *Organizational Psychology*, 2nd edn. Englewood Cliffs, N.J.: Prentice-Hall.

Schoonhoven, Claudia Bird (1981), Problems with contingency theory: testing assumptions hidden within the language of contingency 'theory'. *Administrative Science Quarterly*, 26: 349–77.

Schoonhoven, C.B., Eisenhardt, K.M. and Lyman K. (1990), Speeding products to market: the impact of organizational and environmental conditions on waiting time to first product introduction in new firms. *Administrative Science Quarterly*, 35: 177–207.

Scott, Bruce R. (1971), *Stages of Corporate Development*. Boston: Harvard Business School.

Scott, W. Richard (1987), The adolescence of institutional theory. *Administrative Science Quarterly*, 32: 493–511.

(1992), *Organizations: Rational, Natural and Open Systems*. 3rd edn. Englewood Cliffs, N.J.: Prentice-Hall.

Scott, W. Richard, and Meyer, John W. (1988), Environmental linkages and organizational complexity: public and private school. In Thomas James and Henry M. Levin (eds.), *Comparing Public and Private Schools*, vol. I: *Institutions and Organizations*. New York: Falmer Press.

Selznick, Philip. (1949), *TVA and the Grass Roots*. Berkeley, Calif.: University of California Press.

Shenoy, S. (1981), Organization structure and context: a replication of the Aston Study in India. In D.J. Hickson and C.J. McMillan (eds.), *Organization and Nation: The Aston Programme IV* Farnborough, Hants.: Gower.

Shleifer, Andrei, and Summers, Lawrence H. (1988), Breach of trust in hostile takeovers. In Alan J. Auerbach (ed.), *Corporate Takeovers: Causes and Consequences*. Chicago: Chicago University Press.

Silverman, David (1970), *The Theory of Organizations*. London: Heinemann.

Simon, Herbert A. (1957), *Administrative Behaviour*. New York: Macmillan.

(1965), *Administrative Behaviour: A Study of Decision-Making Processes in Administrative Organization*, 2nd edn. New York: Free Press.

Singh, Jitendra (ed.) (1990), *Organizational Evolution*. Beverly Hills, Calif.: Sage.

Singh, Jitendra V., House, Robert J. and Tucker, David J. (1986), Organizational change and organizational mortality. *Administrative Science Quarterly*, 31: 587–611.

Singh, Jitendra V., Tucker, David J. and Meinhard, Agnes G. (1991), Institutional change and ecological dynamics. In Walter W. Powell and Paul J. DiMaggio (eds.), *The New Institutionalism in Organizational Analysis*. Chicago: University of Chicago Press.

Smircich, L. (1983), Organizations as shared meanings. In L.R. Pondy, P.J. Frost, G. Morgan and T.C. Dandridge (eds.), *Organizational Symbolism*. Greenwich, Conn.: JAI Press.

Smith, Adam (1937), *An Inquiry into the Nature and Causes of the Wealth of Nations*. New York: Modern Library.

Smith, M.R. (1978), Profits and administrative intensity: a longitudinal analysis. *Sociology*, 12: 509–21.

Sorokin, P.A. (1956), *Fads and Foibles in Modern Sociology and Related Sciences*. Chicago: Henry Regnery.

Starbuck, William H. (1965), Organization growth and development. In J.G. March (ed.), *Handbook of Organizations*. Chicago: Rand McNally.

(1981), A trip to view the elephants and rattlesnakes in the Garden of Aston, in 'The Aston Program Perspective'. In A. Van de Ven and W. Joyce, *Perspectives on Organization Design and Behavior*, New York: Wiley.

Steer, Peter, and Cable, John (1978), Internal organization and profit: an empirical analysis of large U.K. companies. *The Journal of Industrial Economics*, 27: 13–30.

Stieglitz, H. (1962), Optimizing span of control. *Management Record*, Sept., 25–9.

Stigler, George J. (1951), The division of labor is limited by the extent of the market. *Journal of Political Economy*, 59: 192–3.

Stigler, George J. and Friedland, Claire (1983), The literature of economics: the case of Berle and Means. *Journal of Law and Economics*, 26: 237–68.

Stinchcombe, Arthur L. (1965), Social structure and organizations. In James G. March (ed.), *Handbook of Organizations*. Chicago: Rand McNally.

Stopford, J.M. and Wells, L.T., Jr (1972), *Managing the Multinational Enterprise*. New York: Basic Books.

Sullivan, Mary Kay (1988), Outsider versus insider boards revisited: a new look at performance and board composition. Paper to Business Policy and Planning Division, Academy of Management Meeting, Anaheim, Calif., August 1988.

Sutton, R.I. (1991), Maintaining norms about expressed emotion: the case of bill collectors. *Administrative Science Quarterly*, 36: 245–68.

Sutton, Robert I. and D'Aunno, Thomas (1989), Decreasing organizational size: untangling the effects of money and people. *Academy of Management Review*, 14: 194–212.

Sutton, R.I. and Rafaeli, A. (1988), Untangling the relationship between displayed emotions and organizational sales: the case of convenience stores. *Academy of Management Journal*, 31: 461–87.

Suzuki, Y. (1980), The strategy and structure of top 100 Japanese industrial enterprises 1950–1970. *Strategic Management Journal*, 1: 265–91.

Swaminathan, A. and Wiedenmayer, G. (1991), Does the pattern of density dependence in organizational mortality rates vary across levels of analysis? Evidence from the German brewing industry. *Social Science Research*, 20: 45–73.

Swedberg, R. (1990), *Economics and Sociology Redefining their Boundaries: Conversations with Economists and Sociologists*. Princeton, N.J.: Princeton University Press.

Teece, David J. (1980), The diffusion of an administrative innovation. *Management*

Science, 26: 464–70.

(1981), Internal organization and economic performance: an empirical analysis of the profitability of principal firms. *Journal of Industrial Economics*, 30: 173–99.

Terrien, Frederick W. and Mills, D. (1955), The effect of changing size upon the internal structure of an organization. *American Sociological Review*, 20: 11–14.

Thompson, James D. (1967), *Organizations in Action*. New York: McGraw-Hill.

Thompson, R.S. (1981), Internal organization and profit: a note. *Journal of Industrial Economics*, 30: 201–11.

Tolbert, Pamela S. and Zucker, Lynne G. (1983), Institutional sources of change in the formal structure of organizations: the diffusion of civil service reform, 1880–1935. *Administrative Science Quarterly*, 28: 22–39.

Tricker, R.I. (1984), *Corporate Governance: Practices, Procedures and Powers in British Companies and their Boards of Directors*. Aldershot, Hants.: Gower.

Tucker, D.J., Singh, J.V. and Meinhard A.G. (1990), Organizational form, populations dynamics, and institutional change: the funding patterns of voluntary organizations. *Academy of Management Journal*, 33: 151–78.

Tushman, M. (1978), Technical communication in R&D laboratories: the impact of project work characteristic. *Academy of Management Journal*, 21: 624–45.

Urwick, Lyndall F. (1956), The span of control – some facts about the fables. *Advanced Management*, 21: 5–15.

Utterback, J.M. and Abernathy, W.J. (1975), A dynamic model of process and product innovation. *Omega*, 6: 639–56.

Van de Ven, Andrew H. and Drazin, Robert (1985), The concept of fit in contingency theory. In B.M. Staw and L.L. Cummings (eds.), *Research in Organizational Behaviour*, vol. VII. Greenwich, Conn.: JAI Press.

Van de Ven, Andrew and Ferry, Diane L. (1980), *Measuring and Assessing Organizations*. New York: Wiley.

Van de Ven, Andrew H., Delbecq, A.L. and Koenig, R., Jr (1976), Determinants of coordination modes within organizations. *American Sociological Review*, 41: 322–38.

Vance, S.C. (1978), Corporate governance: assessing corporate performance by boardroom attributes. *Journal of Business Research*, 6: 203–20.

Weber, Max (1968), *Economy and Society: An Outline of Interpretive Sociology*, ed. Guenther Roth and Claus Wittich. New York: Bedminster Press.

Weick, Karl E. (1969), *The Social Psychology of Organizing*. Reading, Mass.: Addison-Wesley.

Whetten, David A. (1980), Sources, responses, and effects of organizational decline. In John R. Kimberly and Robert H. Miles (eds.), *The Organizational Life Cycle: Issues in the Creation, Transformation and Decline of Organizations*. San Francisco: Jossey-Bass.

Whisler, Thomas L., Meyer, Harald, Baum, Bernard H. and Sorensen, Peter F., Jr (1967), Centralization of organizational control: an empirical study of its meaning and measurement. *Journal of Business*, 40: 10–26.

Williamson, Oliver E. (1964), *The Economics of Discretionary Behavior: Managerial Objectives in a Theory of the Firm*. Englewood Cliffs, N.J.: Prentice-Hall.

(1970), *Corporate Control and Business Behavior: An Inquiry into the Effects of Organization Form on Enterprise Behavior*. Englewood Cliffs, N.J.:

Prentice-Hall.

(1971), Managerial Discretion, Organization Form, and the Multidivision Hypothesis. In Robin Marris and Adrian Woods (eds.), *The Corporate Economy: Growth, Competition and Innovative Potential.* Cambridge, Mass.: Harvard University Press.

(1975), *Markets and Hierarchies: Analysis and Antitrust Implications.* New York: Free Press.

(1981), The modern corporation: origins, evolution and attributes. *Journal of Economic Literature,* 18: 1537–68.

(1983), Organizational form, residual claimants, and corporate control. *Journal of Law and Economics,* 26: 351–66.

(1985), *The Economic Institutions of Capitalism: Firms, Markets, Relational Contracting.* New York: Free Press.

(1988), Corporate finance and corporate governance. *Journal of Finance,* 43: 567–91.

(1991), Comparative economic organization: the analysis of discrete structural alternatives. *Administrative Science Quarterly,* 36: 269–96.

Woodward, Joan (1958), *Management and Technology.* London: HMSO.

(1965), *Industrial Organization: Theory and Practice.* London: Oxford University Press.

Young, Ruth C. (1988), Is population ecology a useful paradigm for the study of organizations? *American Journal of Sociology,* 94: 1–24.

Zajac, Edward J. (1988), Interlocking directorates as an interorganizational strategy : a test of critical assumptions. *Academy of Management Journal,* 31: 428–38.

Zald, M.N. (1970), Political economy: a framework for comparative analysis. In M.N. Zald (ed.), *Power in Organizations.* Nashville, Tenn.: Vanderbilt University Press.

Zammuto, R.F. and Connolly, T. (1984), Coping with disciplinary fragmentation. *Organizational Behavior and Teaching Review,* 9: 30–7.

Zedeck, S. and Blood, M.R. (1974), *Foundations of Behavioral Science Research in Organizations.* Monterey, Calif.: Brooks/Cole.

Zey-Ferrell, Mary, and Aiken, Michael (1981), *Complex Organizations: Critical Perspectives.* Glenview, Ill.: Scott, Foresman.

Zucker, Lynne G. (1977), The role of institutionalization in cultural persistence. *American Sociological Review,* 42: 726–43. Reprinted in Walter W. Powell and Paul DiMaggio (eds.) (1991), *The New Institutionalism in Organizational Analysis.* Chicago: University of Chicago Press.

(1987), Institutional theories of organization. *American Review of Sociology,* 13: 443–64.

(ed.) (1988), *Institutional Patterns and Organizations.* Cambridge, Mass.: Ballinger.

Zwerman, William L. (1970), *New Perspectives on Organization Theory: An Empirical Reconsideration of the Marxian and Classical Analyses.* Westport, Conn.: Greenwood.

Author index

Subject index